Period details

Wallpapers used on the endpapers
and on pages 1 , 3 , 4 & 5 are from
The Temple Newsam Collection
from Zoffany.

JUDITH AND MARTIN MILLER

PERIOD DETAILS

CROWN TRADE PAPERBACKS, NEW YORK

PERIOD DETAILS
A SOURCEBOOK FOR HOUSE RESTORATION
JUDITH AND MARTIN MILLER

American Editor **Fayal Greene**
Chief Contributor **Margaret Crowther**
Kitchens chapter **Robin Murrell**
Project Manager and Senior Executive Art Editor
Jacqui Small
Executive Editor **Robert Saxton**
Assistant Art Editor **Prue Bucknall**
Production **Philip Collyer**

This book contains instructions for restoring interior architectural details. Reasonable care should be given to following the instructions, especially regarding the use of potentially harmful materials and tools.

LIBRARY OF CONGRESS CATALOGING-IN-PUBLICATION DATA

Miller, Judith H.
  Period details.
  Bibliography: p.
  Includes index. 1.
  Buildings - Details. 2. Architecture - Details.
3. Dwellings - Remodeling. I. Miller, Martin. II. Title.
TH2025.M55 1987
ISBN 0-517-88013-X

10 9 8 7 6 5 4 3 2 1

First American Paperback Edition

Cover photograph by Fritz von der Schulenburg

Code letters in picture captions refer to the photographic sources listed on page 191.

CONTENTS

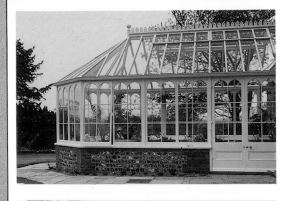

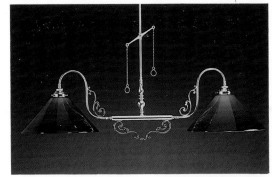

The only way you can decorate for today is to know what the past was like. It's like growing up – if you don't learn from experience, you don't ever find out, and you fall into a pattern of mistakes. Although architects and designers are required to learn about the past in school, they don't necessarily put that knowledge into practice. Therefore, you need constantly to educate your eye as I do, by looking at paintings, at furniture and at buildings. Visit museums, read books and magazines, and all your life gather ideas. I don't mean only in memory – take notes, tear out pictures from magazines, keep clippings of details that look right to you. My favorite clients are the ones who come and show me something, saying, "This is what I like". You can do a lot with almost anything, if you have a clear idea of what you want to achieve.

Having rejected the past for part of this century, people are beginning to find that buildings that once looked hideous now seem appealing. We see old buildings as old friends. Obviously, our houses here in America are not as old as those in Europe, but we have some very fine buildings that reproduce similar styles of architecture. On one subject I'm a stickler. If people want to add on to old houses, be they Greek Revival from 1830 or Neo-Georgian from 1929, the addition should have a sense of what the house is all about, not just be stuck on as an afterthought. There's nothing nicer than the sort of Cape Cod house that just rambles on but has a consistent character. It's been added to over the years, but each addition has respected the details of the original. And we've always borrowed from English style. It has meant to many people in this country, including members of my own family, a sense of belonging to a civilized tradition. Perhaps it's because English houses often have come together over seven or eight generations, whereas the average American moves seven or eight times during his lifetime.

Often a client, current or prospective, comes to me to ask for help on an old house which needs restoration, or a new one which is pleasant enough, but lacks character. Rather than talk about the house itself at first, I try to explain what I believe to be the basic principles that make a house attractive and welcoming.

What we aim for in a restoration is the feeling of a house that's been lived in over the years and loved and cared for. It's important to begin with a well-constructed, beautifully-detailed house. You can always add the fine furniture to go in it as you go along through life. Doors and windows must be in the right place, and of the right proportion. These, along with correct details such as cornice moldings and chair rails, are absolutely essential. It's important to respect the true character of the workmanship of years ago. Too much perfection looks unreal and cold, whereas handcarved wood has a few cracks in it, and handcast plaster inevitably shows a few little mistakes. That's what makes a house feel real and right.

What's fortunate today is that there are young people with a wonderful respect for the past, who are making and reproducing wooden moldings and plaster details using traditional techniques. This was not true some years ago, but now I'm amazed at what's possible. You can, with an idea of how things have been done by the best builders over history, make something new that looks as though it's been there all along. An attractive house does not have to be large or grand, but it does need an overall sense of design, and it's the finishing touches that make the picture great.

MARIO BUATTA

When we think of the British domestic architecture of the past, we think first and foremost of grand country houses and town mansions – buildings that are rightly famous thanks to their distinguished history or association with a particular architect such as Inigo Jones or Robert Adam. In America, where the first European settlers arrived during the 17th century, original folk dwellings such as shingled New England saltboxes or Kentucky log cabins come to mind as reminders of the hardships faced by the early colonists. Whatever the origin or scale of these historic houses, however, they are all related by the fact that they were built not as conscious works of art but as homes, encompassing the thousand daily routines of family life.

Whether large or small, period houses owe something to the taste of their age. In this the great English architects and patrons were the trend-setters, even for Americans, until the last century. Fashions filtered down the social scale while becoming geographically more widespread.

Classical ornamentation and Neo Gothic detailing – to take just two examples – enjoyed their various waves of popularity not only in the homes of the fashionably rich but also in thousands of proud but unpretentious dwellings built for the prosperous middle classes on both sides of the Atlantic. The middling professional man, building a home for his family, wished to convey something of his standing in the community by aping what was smart in aristocratic circles. A display of wealth was a good advertisement for his business. But at the same time a careful economy would be observed:

display was all very well, in moderation. These feelings, or something like them, have been prevalent for centuries. Despite financial restraints there remains today a great reserve of fine period homes, well constructed, simply and appropriately ornamented, in which it was – and still is – a pleasure to live.

From 1550 to the end of the 19th century, style was more likely to begin with a fashion than with a new solution to a practical problem. The staying power of a fashion, however, generally depended upon how compatible it was with practical requirements. This is why classical features based on the architecture of the ancient Greeks and Romans continued to appear over such a long period: they could be adapted to many different building types. With decorative details that can be applied to anything from a palace to a potting shed, classical design remains a constant. However, there are wide variations within the constant. Classicism has meant many different things to different generations, departing far from the original intentions of Greeks or Romans.

Because of the continuing popularity of details such as classical columns, they are not a reliable proof of a house's exact age. In the absence of documentary evidence, dating a house depends on careful detective work, assessing such clues as materials, layout, general architecture and specific stylistic details. Some English houses incorporate a date-stone. The older American houses often have a date inscribed on a door-frame or chimney. However, these indications must all be viewed with suspicion. The inscription may denote a date of repair or refurbishment, or even commemorate a marriage. Occasionally, a date-stone has been imported from another building altogether.

Architectural style is more reliable as a dating guide, but you should always bear in mind that the pace of change varied in different regions. Generally, fashions started in the towns and spread out slowly to the countryside. However, the grander rural homes usually flaunted the latest fashions some time before smaller country houses caught up with the trends. The picture is complicated further by regional variations. If the dating of an old house proves difficult, your local history society will usually help.

Many period homes have evolved by a process of gradual "improvement" and accretion. Modern extensions are generally thought to be unfortunate unless they are built in a style that makes some concessions to history. However, an early house that has been modified over the centuries so that it manifests a wide range of historic styles, different but compatible, may be regarded as no less "authentic" than a house that remains as it was originally conceived. This is largely a matter of personal taste.

Some people prefer the charm of the piecemeal. Others like their homes to he homogeneous. Some people even find something to be said in favor of "facadism" – preserving or restoring the facade while leaving the remainder of the building out of period.

Period features providing concrete evidence of a house's origins will sometimes be found during the course of refurbishment – perhaps a blocked-off door or distinctively shaped window opening that comes to light after you have removed plaster from a wall. In such cases, you might consider halting the work in progress and changing your plans to incorporate the newly discovered feature.

Decoration, furnishings and interior layout cannot easily be separated in period homes. Each aspect of an interior emerge in association with all other aspects of the house – all of which need to be taken into account when refurbishing in period style. For example, it is not enough to ensure that you have the furniture of the appropriate period. Plasterwork, door frames, chimneypieces and doors are equally important as indexes of style, and the taste of a period can be obliterated from a room simply by a mistake in the choice of one or more of these elements. On the other hand, certain compromises are inevitable.

Few people would want to sacrifice every modern convenience for the sake of total historic authenticity. However passionately you feel about your period home, there is no reason to go back to unhealthy sanitation, inconvenient cooking facilities, primitive bathrooms or icy-cold drafts. Fortunately, up-to-date equipment is often available either in traditional styles or in low-key modern styles that will not clash with a historic interior. This need for sensible compromise is

1 This modest but very fine example of early 19thC architecture is in north London. In its symmetry, and its ornamental detailing on the fanlight and lower windows, it exhibits the characteristic features of the era.

page 7: An example of true conservation in Roslyn, Long Island, New York, this house built in 1836 has been painstakingly restored with absolute attention to detail both outside and inside.

2 Detail is all-important in period homes: the fireback is no less interesting or significant than the front door. This particular example is a modern reproduction of a 16thC original.

2

highlighted most clearly in the case of working buildings that have been converted for living in. Barns, schoolhouses, chapels, churches, windmills and railroad buildings that have been adapted as homes have all required radical alteration, with decisions taken at every turn as to what to change and what to leave intact. In the end these decisions must be made using a combination of historical knowledge, taste and common sense.

Materials used in building a house offer further clues to its age. Until the 17th century most houses in Britain were made of wood. It was the holocaust of the Great Fire of London in 1666, more than any other influence, that encouraged the use of non-flammable materials. However, wood remained cheap, easily accessible, and economic to work. Carpenters could build more quickly than stone masons, and in wooded areas without suitable building stone, wood was in any case the obvious choice. In America, where wood has remained plentiful, it has been the material of choice for most houses; they have been timber-framed and wood-sided from early pioneer times until the present day.

The timber-frame house developed from that functionally simple structure, the barn. The principle was to provide a framework that through its members carries the weight of the roof to the ground. The walls of these houses are infill only: they bear no direct load. At its simplest, the system consists of two wooden upright members forming together a gable frame, which is linked by a horizontal ridge beam to another, similar frame. Together the frames support the skin of roof and wall. This type of house, in some regions known as the "cruck" house, existed in Britain by 1300; from it, all later sophistications of the timber house descend.

By the middle of the 14th century the disposition of

rooms and people in the English house was well established. The center of the structure, the heart of community life, was the two-story hall. Here all ate together, whether it was the lord of the manor and his servants or the yeoman farmer and his farmhands. The staff quarters lay to one side of the hall, and on the other side a single room at each level gave privacy to the master and mistress. The first-floor parlor was the sitting room for the master of the house; above it was the solar, a private bedroom for the family. The open fireplace in the center of the hall, its smoke rising to a hole in the hall roof, was a symbol of the communal, cheek-by-jowl way of living. Interestingly, the open fire persisted in ordinary dwelling places long after the technology of chimneys and fireplaces had been introduced. Loyalty to the open fire as a gathering point in life preserved it in Britain into the 15th century, serving to illustrate an important aspect of the way in which houses developed over the centuries. Technological advances, at least initially, are not always potent enough to overcome the emotional and psychological needs answered by an earlier arrangement. Thus, in an age of central heating, the fireplace – even if it throws out no heat – serves an important function as a focal point and symbol of family warmth. And indeed, the pleasure of living in a period home surrounded by period details is similarly based on evocations of traditionalism, community and historical continuity.

The structural evolution of the house from shelter to home was reflected in the parallel evolution of interior furnishings and fittings. Floors that had previously been laid with mud or rushes were now paved with stone, tiles or brick. The comfort of a wealthy 15th-century English home was further improved by replacing the central hearth by a wall fireplace which provided an effective means of warming the rooms.

Purely decorative elements became more elaborate at this time. In the houses of the great, from the 14th century on, tapestries were used as wallcoverings – usually over just the upper parts of walls. The lower half would sometimes be wainscoted with overlapping vertical timbers, a style which developed into the characteristic linenfold paneling of the Tudor period – ribbed woodwork giving the impression of pleated cloth. Owners of more modest dwellings contented themselves with painted linen hangings. Alternatively, plaster or wooden interior walls might be decorated with painted designs. These decorations were the forerunners of modern wallpaper.

Stone, of course, had been used for castles, palaces and cathedrals in Britain throughout the 14th and 15th centuries. It resisted fire, as well as assault. However, it was expensive to work, even in areas where stone was plentiful. Some stone dwellings date from the 13th century, but only in the late 15th century did stone come into general use, largely as an expression of national prosperity at that period. The overall planning of a stone house was not very different from that of a frame house – except when the building served a defensive role. However, stone offered greater scope for design. Projecting structures known as "oriels" are sometimes found nestling in the angle between the main hall and a private wing. Later the term "oriel" came to be applied to a projecting window, which developed with the passage of time into the bay window. Glass remained a luxury until the 16th century.

In this early period, houses tended to grow haphazardly, rather than following a fixed and conscious design. But with the turn of the 16th century we find new ideas and design forces penetrating Britain from France and Italy. This was the first wave of influence from the great European Renaissance,

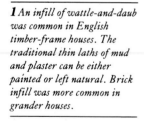

1 An infill of wattle-and-daub was common in English timber-frame houses. The traditional thin laths of mud and plaster can be either painted or left natural. Brick infill was more common in grander houses.

1

2

3

4

2 The Van Nostrand Starkins house in Roslyn, Long Island, shows the functional quality of building of the late 17thC.

3 A 19thC reconstruction porch added to a 15thC house. The timber framing is in this case purely ornamental.

4 This 15thC English weaver's house is a good example of timber framing. It is not surprising that many such houses have undergone *alteration over the years. Here, the introduction of oriel windows, copied from stone houses, has augmented the basic dwelling.* CG

5-7 *Timber-framed construction in England was a popular method of building well into the 17thC, and brick with timber infill was again used in the 19th and 20thC. These pictures of a 17thC house belie the fact that much of the building was done this century.*

8, 9 *These garden features from the same house sustain the nostalgic mood outdoors.*

10 *Smallhythe Place in Kent, southern England, is an early 16thC half-timbered house, with the typical overhanging (jettied) upper story.*

1

2

which had its origins in Italy. During the early 15th century, centered on Florence, there was a tremendous revival of interest in the art, literature and design of the ancient Romans, and this had an important effect on the work of Italian architects – initially just in public architecture but later in the grander sorts of houses. Classical columns, pilasters (shallow columns applied to wall surfaces) and rounded arches were incorporated in buildings notable for their symmetry and harmonious proportion. The columns, and the distinctive decorative entablatures which they supported, were categorized according to the ancient system of classical "Orders", depending on the precise decorative arrangement. Columns could be solid-looking Doric, fluted Ionic or delicate Corinthian, with its acanthus-leaf capital. The Composite capital combined Ionic volutes (scrolls) with Corinthian acanthus leaves.

Tudor England, in its anti-papal isolation, was initially not well-placed to be influenced by Renaissance architecture. By the early 16th century a few aristocratic houses had acquired Italianate flourishes, but in a superficial manner only, without radically affecting native English styles. However, the impact of Renaissance architecture was precipitated by the appearance in 1563 of the first English architectural treatise, John Shute's *The First and Chief Groundes of Architecture*, inspired by an architectural study tour of Italy. Before long, the classical Orders

1, 2, 3 The influence of classical architecture from the 16thC onwards cannot be overemphasized. These examples of the proud use of classical features are a magnificent classical porch of a 17thC house in southern England (1) and a Port Washington (New York) house of 1735.

which Shute describes were being used as decoration, and as badges of high fashion, on the facades of grand and elaborate English country houses such as Longleat in Wiltshire (1546-80) and Burghley House in Northamptonshire (1560-87).

The significance of this revivial of classical style for the future of architecture in Britain and America cannot be overestimated. Every column, architrave and frieze on even very simple houses of the 18th or 19th centuries has come to be there, indirectly, as a result of the Renaissance passion to recover the glory of Rome in its heyday.

By the mid-16th century many fashionable small manor houses in England were being built entirely of brick, rather than of stone or of timber with a brick infill. The wonder of the age was Hampton Court Palace, an enormous establishment just outside London. It was expensively built in brick and enriched with terracotta ornament and towering chimneys, setting a fashion which persisted through the century. Even in relatively modest English houses of the period a complex skyline of spiraling chimneypots may be found, loudly proclaiming the owner's taste and discernment. Tudor brickwork, together with a complex silhouette of stacks and gables and a garden full of topiary, were to become a powerful archetype, an "ideal home", copied in the earlier 20th century not only in new country houses but also in the more unlikely setting of suburbia on both sides of the Atlantic.

The first decades of the 17th century saw a more thorough-going classicism emerge. This was the achievement of one man, Inigo Jones (1573-1652), who was the first architect to bring to England the pure forms of classical architecture.

Jones was entirely at home in the world of classical allusions, and unlike most of his fellow designers actually went to Italy. There he encountered the work

3

4

of Andrea Palladio. The greatest Italian architect of the 16th century, Palladio had revived and revised the architectural theory of the Roman writer Vitruvius, whose *Five Books of Architecture* describe various building types which Palladio adapted – notably the villa. The Roman villa was a spreading country house with attendant farm buildings. Palladio turned it into a classical pavilion – compact, elegant and well-suited to life in the country estates of the Veneto, the area around Venice where Palladio chiefly worked. It was these buildings which Inigo Jones saw and copied on his return to England – with the help of Palladio's own publication, *Four Books of Architecture*.

In London, the Queen's House, Greenwich (1616-18; 1629-35), East London, built as a small-scale retreat for James I's Queen, Anne of Denmark, is the single pre-eminent domestic building which we know for certain that Jones designed. Incorporating many innovative features derived from Italy, this is the first classical English villa, ancestor of many other villas, large and small, designed for daily life. The ground floor is rusticated – finished with cut stone resembling monumental blocks. Each window is marked by a dropped keystone, which lends weight and individuality to the composition. The upper story is contrastingly lighter, its smooth wall surface broken by windows beneath which there are blind balustrades – that is, balustrades applied to the wall. These prepare the eye for the central loggia taken from Palladio's designs. The floorplan is simple, effective and adapted to the purposes of the house. The whole is a modern building in many ways: perhaps the first English house in which a 20th-century spectator can sense the contact between his own world and that of the original occupants.

Many 18th- and 19th-century houses are arranged around a square – an aspect of city planning that originated in the 17th century. In this too Inigo Jones

4 *Despite the infiltration of classical influence, many English houses retained a particularly English style. There is nothing Italianate about this stone manor house built in 1640 and substantially enlarged in the mid 19thC.* S&P

5 *Melton Constable Hall in eastern England, designed by Sir Christopher Wren and built between 1644 and 1670, shows an English interpretation of classical styles, with its great central pediment echoed by the pedimented doorway, and its hipped roof. The house is reminiscent of the work of Sir Roger Pratt, a follower of Inigo Jones.* S&P

6 *This house near London illustrates the continuing appeal of classicism in the late 19thC, when pilasters, balconies and classical swags were added.*

7 *The delight in the classical facade was to last in England well into the 18thC. Chilston Park, Kent, was built in the 16thC with a central three-story porch-turret and a central courtyard. In 1728 the owners refaced the house in refined classical taste.*

6

5

7

This idea too was derived from Italian practice – in 16th-century Italy the ground floor of a house or palace was heavily defended against the street, with small dark windows. Covent Garden points forward to modern city design.

Even after the concept of the integrated square had been introduced to England, most houses continued to be individually built in brick, following designs closer to those prevalent in Holland than those in Italy. There was a considerable enthusiasm in England for the Dutch style of building – the red brick steep-gabled style favored by the burghers of Amsterdam and Antwerp. Culturally, England and Holland had much in common in the 17th century. Both were Protestant mercantile countries, opposed to the Catholic might of Spain and the Holy Roman Empire. They welcomed refugees from Catholic countries while persecuting Protestant dissenters, many of whom emigrated to newly-discovered America as a result. The Dutch style traveled with them to colonial America either in its adopted English form or as the native style of settlers from Holland. The English/Dutch style prevailed in the South and may still be seen in Williamsburg, Virginia. True Dutch houses were built along the Hudson River and on Long Island in New York State, which was for a short time a Dutch colony.

The archetypal English house at the close of the 17th century is built of brick dressed with stone – that is, stone was used for the door frame and other architectural details. The style of detailing was imitated in all-wooden houses of the period in America, notably the Norris-Jumel Mansion in New York City. The windows were quite tall and narrow,

was involved. The first fully worked out and planned piazza in Britain is that of Covent Garden, for which Jones designed the church, St Paul's. This square reveals a new approach to urban living. It follows the principles of Italian city design by allowing light and air to reach individual houses. Designed to look like a series of grand palaces set around the central space, it in fact provided behind its great facade a number of houses of more modest scale. The tall windows on the first floor indicated the main living level – the *piano nobile*, or parlor floor, raised above the noise and dirt of the street and inaccessible to thieves or enemies.

4 Regional variations should always be taken into account by anyone restoring a period house. This English street of the Georgian age is characterized by flintwork, some of which hides earlier timber-framed dwellings.

5, 6 These beautifully restored houses in Roslyn, Long Island, New York, were built in the mid-1830s but owe much to the previous century. The interest in vernacular architecture is an interesting trend in conservation today.

1 In small English country towns such as Mayfield, Sussex, houses and cottages from the 15th to the 19thC present a delightfully varied picture. Many early houses have been refaced – particularly with weatherboarding in the mid-18thC.

2 This English 1680s red brick house is actually timber-framed. This is unusual at this date: the explanation is that the owner was a timber merchant.

3 Another timber-framed house – a 17thC example, hung with tiles.

with a lean elegant line encouraged by the innovation of the sash window. The roof was high-pitched – perhaps with a wooden balustrade replacing the stone balustade of grander homes. Of course, this pattern was not followed rigidly. More sophisticated houses might have a richly carved broken pediment and coat of arms above the door, with stonework and other fine details on the facade adding a sense of density and brilliance to the house. Elegant gate posts and railings might also play their part, strengthening the effect of gracious formality. Such houses, belonging to doctors, lawyers, men of property and gentlemen, were to be found in both city and country.

In a townhouse of this period, however grand or simple the facade, the general disposition of rooms and the style of life within them would tend to conform to a certain pattern. The standard format for the single-fronted row house was developed in the early 18th century and held sway in modified form until the early 20th, in both England and America. It featured a front door and hallway at one side and two rooms, one behind the other, at the other side. This kind of house, which ranged over three or four floors with a basement, became known as the "universal plan". Variations on the theme ranged from the simple to the relatively grand.

In double-fronted houses the prevalent plan was based on a square divided into four rooms, arranged two deep in pairs on either side of a central hall or reception area. Front and back rooms were linked by connecting doors. The hall led directly to the staircase, which would often be flanked by columns or pilasters to emphasize its importance. Stairs became increasingly gracious, although it was only in the grandest homes that wrought-iron balusters in swirling patterns replaced the wooden posts of earlier times. Highly polished wooden handrails were sometimes curved at the ends into elegantly scrolled volutes instead of ending abruptly with a plain solid newel post.

The Queen Anne style was a late simplification of Georgian elements. The most distinctive aspects of a typical Queen Anne house of around 1720 were its happy and agreeable proportions and its suitability for daily life. Windows and doors would be placed in harmonious balance. The staircase, broad and shallow, would have a fine balustrade. The parlor might be lined with good paneling, but there would be nothing ostentatious in its decoration.

The rest of the 18th century was to be dominated by a new wave of classicism, called Palladianism, which swept through both English and American architecture. Chief among the prime movers in this new rule of taste was the young and very rich Lord Burlington. Inspired by a book by the designer Colen

5

6

Campbell, *Vitruvius Britannicus*, Burlington traveled to Italy and there absorbed the same lessons that Inigo Jones had learned a hundred years before – but with subtly different effect. He took with him William Kent, a brilliant designer who was to be his main ally in introducing Palladian taste to England. Their idea was to resuscitate the classicism begun by Inigo Jones, but following a new set of rules by which all builders and architects should be guided. Burlington's plan was ambitious: the transformation of the face of English architecture. This dream was very nearly realized, for in one form or another the format adopted by Campbell, Burlington and Kent was to influence the building of all grand houses, and many modest ones, for sixty years.

Among the most interesting Palladian buildings in England are the villas built by Campbell and Burlington in imitation of Palladio's Villa Rotonda at Vicenza, with its central domed space and portico on each of the four facades. The original is a folly, essentially a banqueting house, and suitable only for a warm climate. Campbell's Mereworth Castle followed this model closely, adapting the plan as much as possible, but with only limited success, to the needs of

1

1 It is sometimes believed that all building in England in the early 18thC was influenced by the Palladian style, but this is far from the truth. This is a fairly typical early 18thC red brick house of the kind found in villages and towns all over southern England.

2 This classical English doorway exhibits an open-bed entablature with associated pilasters. Such features were influenced by the designs of Kent, Burlington and Campbell and other 18thC innovators, which filtered down from grand houses to more modest homes.

a small country house. Burlington's own exercise on the same theme, the Chiswick Villa, was designed as an addition to the family house on his estate west of London, and there was thus no need for the plan to take account of daily life: the building is purely for show. It was not until forty years later, in 1768, that a house based on the Villa Rotonda was successfully designed for comfort and daily living – Thomas Jefferson's Monticello in Virginia.

One of the great virtues of Palladian design was the simple and pleasing relation of room to room in the overall plan, and this had a major impact, even in relatively modest houses: planning becomes particularly important when working in a limited space. Individual elements of Palladianism were also taken over. For example, the Palladian portico, although perhaps serving a more practical purpose in the hot south than in northern zones, was widely

2

copied as an imposing style of entranceway. Another characteristic feature is the "Palladian window" – an arched central opening flanked by two rectangles, with columns in between. This detail has had lasting popularity: it is incorporated even today in the more stylish American ski condominiums.

The development of classical proportions in the 18th century shows a marked tendency towards increasing slenderness and attenuation. Height and refinement were the keynotes, sometimes expressed by giant Orders of columns rising through all floors. Even the window bars became more and more slim as the century progressed. Such changes reflect a new spirit of faithfulness to ancient Roman architecture, ushering in the age of Neo-classicism.

From the middle of the 18th century on, several architectural styles were popular simultaneously. Neo-classical (or Classical Revival) buildings were being built in England and America until the middle of the 19th century. They incorporate details from other styles, such as Georgian fanlights over entrance doors. At the end of the 18th century, America began to produce her own school of architects including William Jay, Benjamin H. Latrobe and Thomas Jefferson, who were completely familiar with both historical precedents and European fashion.

While scholarly architects were designing in the Palladian manner, a very different strain in building styles was emerging – first in England but later also in America. This was the taste for Gothick (the final κ is

3

7

8

4

5

9

used on the 18th-century style to differentiate it from the medieval architecture which inspired it and from the Victorian Gothic Revival which would succeed it). The vogue for pointed Gothick arches and other mock-medieval features, in both small houses and whimsical garden buildings, grew through the 1750s and 60s, becoming widespread by the end of the century. There is a playfulness in the way these features were adapted in form and color which makes the surviving examples of Gothick style perennially delightful.

For many people the characteristic style of the later 18th century is "the Adam style" – especially in room decoration. The design ideas introduced by Robert and James Adam in the late 1750s and through the 60s and 70s were new and sophisticated variations on the traditional classical motifs. The secret of the Adam style was the cumulative effect of many finely wrought

6

3 This somewhat later house, in the Queen Anne style, shows fine proportions and symmetry with a good classical portico. The combination of glorious brickwork with stone corners and other details help to give the building its impact.

4, 5 Simple Georgian cottages such as these tell us as much about the 18thC as do the grand manor houses and stately homes. Restoration of such buildings will benefit from thorough research into their origins. CG

6 This shallow internal arch in a reconstructed 1760 house in New York shows subdued classical influence, especially in its keystone. This is a fine example of Colonial architecture.

7, 8 The Palladian pediment is sometimes seen in combination with a small circular window and often with dentils – small square or rectangular blocks evenly spaced in ornamental series.

9 A detailed view of stone dentils on a brick townhouse of the 18thC.

elements. The genius behind the style was the way in which so much variety was subordinated to a greater plan. Furniture, carpets, curtains, door handles – all fitted in harmoniously with the grand plan. This was the definitive statement of Roman opulence toward which English architecture had been tending for fifty years. The Adam brothers, like most successful English designers of the period, published pattern books detailing all of their designs, from window frames and moldings to chairs, mirrors and curtains. These books were immensely popular both in England and in America. Their influence was felt in all regions of the newly-established United States, generally as reproduced in wood by local carpenters of greater or lesser skill. Adam detailing was so ubiquitous that many architectural historians now refer to what has traditionally been called the Federal style as "American Adam". The style remained dominant in interior

1-4 These interiors (in Royal Crescent, Bath, England designed by the Wood family) show a delicacy and liveliness indebted to the designs of Robert Adam, whose work became influential from the middle of the 18thC. Adam treated classical motifs with an unprecedented lightness and simplicity, and subordinated every detail – including the bell-pushes – to an overall conception. RC, SC

design even while new influences were changing exteriors of houses.

The Adam brothers and their followers in England increasingly designed classical interiors enclosed within a Gothick shell. The overall exterior profile of the house could be pleasingly irregular, in accord with the fashionable Picturesque taste. Such exotic exercises need not, however, be Gothick or castellated: they could equally well be Italian in style, and in the latter years of the 18th century and in the early 19th century this was a frequent choice.

Just as important for houses of moderate scale was the revival of interest in ancient Greek architecture,

5, 6, 7 The crescent – a curving row of homes – was an architectural form devised by John Wood the Younger at Bath in 1761-65. Note the giant columns which unify the facade.

5

6

7

8

9

8, 9 These two fireplaces from a Georgian house in Bristol show the late 18thC fondness for exquisite decorative details. Such fireplaces were always intended to be painted white to add to the overall effect of airy grace.

which was extremely fashionable in the 1780s and 90s. Here the stylistic similarities between aristocratic and middle-class housing become closer. The Greek Revival style was extremely popular in America through the 1860s, dominating both high-style and vernacular design in the North as well as the South, and as far West as Texas and Indiana. The great colonnaded plantation houses of the Deep South belong to this tradition.

English and American 18thC townhouses are characterized by unity, balance and elegance, not only when viewed as a whole but also in individual details such as doors, windows and ironwork.

Externally, the Georgian house, whether large or small, had a plain dignity and elegance, owed in part to the balance between a handsome door and generously proportioned sash windows, symmetrically arranged. The ornamental door, whether on a house of brick or of wooden construction, is the universal hallmark of Georgian style in America. The sense of proportion and order, immediately recognizable on the facade, was also reflected within. In the grander homes, the plain, dignified exteriors encompassed interiors that were highly ornamented, full of exquisite detailing, yet controlled by good proportions. A living room was treated as an architectural composition in its own right, with classically inspired features echoing each other to create an integrated effect. For example, a molded architrave over the door might complement a pediment above a fireplace. Doric pilasters in a doorcase might be echoed in pilasters in the wall paneling, which in turn might reflect the ceiling pattern. Ornamentation could include swags, scrolls, fruit and flower festoons, gryphons and arabesques, or urns and vases. In modest Georgian houses the ornament was less emphatic, but without losing the sense of elegance. Indeed, most houses are not architecturally articulated inside – except for the baseboard, chair rail and door frame.

Among the experiments unleashed in Britain by the Picturesque movement, with its fondness for other times and other places, was the mock country cottage, complete with thatched roof. The Regency idea of a cottage was highly fanciful, bearing little relation to the realities of rural life. However, this cosy ideal, the *cottage ornée* ("ornamental cottage"), initiates on a modest scale a whole century of romantically revived styles of housing.

One of these, which remained popular right through the Victorian era in America, was the Gothic Revival. Oriels and pointed arches again became the rage, sprouting all over houses, mock-baronial castles and, most notoriously, university buildings. This time, there was nothing light-hearted about the medieval allusions. Victorian architects took their chivalry seriously.

Most urban Victorians in England lived in very simple row houses. From the "universal plan" of the 18th century developers created a row house with two living rooms, kitchen and scullery, four bedrooms, bathroom and attic. The detail varies but the plan does not. The facade has a two-story bay, its mullions tricked out with a debased form of Gothic decoration – for example, formalized flowers. The keystone of the arch of the porch often had a grotesque head for ornament. Above the front door, a single window marked the small bedroom. Whatever the shortcomings of this ubiquitous housing type, it certainly adapts well to modern family living.

Variations on this standard type of Victorian row house were rare in English building. It is therefore rewarding to turn to parallel developments in 19th-century America. For example, in San Francisco in the 1880s there was a rich diversity of experiments on the basic single-fronted format. These houses were usually detached but set close together on narrow urban lots. The surprise is in the carpentry. For the standardized ornament repetitively applied in the London type, California style substitutes the inventiveness of the individual carpenter. The painted clapboard and exuberant elaborations of the basic "stick style" decoration indicate how individual a simple building may become. Row houses of a less lavishly-detailed style were built in wood and brownstone in Eastern cities like Philadelphia, Baltimore and Brooklyn. Some of these incorporated original decorative ideas, but many shared the monotony of their London counterparts.

In the late Victorian period, the row house gradually became less fashionable. The stylish thing in England was to have a detached "villa" in the newly-expanded suburbs – or, alternatively, a semi-detached house. The scale of life that could be lived in either type of small house was relatively modest.

1-5 *These grand English townhouses capture the mood of the early 19th Clearly Victorian period. Highly influential at this time were Sir John Nash's Regent's Park Terraces in London and contemporary developments at Bath. Stucco was favored on facades, while balconies and canopies added touches of individuality.*

6, 7 *This New York house built in 1864 has one of the earliest mansard roofs in America. Note the decoratively exuberant brackets and cornices.*

8

9

10

11

12

13

8-12 The Victorian row house gave plenty of scope for design variations. The diversity of styles drew on centuries of local, national and international traditions. Such eclecticism adds greatly to the visual interest of our towns and cities.

13 These San Francisco houses of around 1880 are typical in their diversity of decoration. The well-maintained paintwork is an all-important aspect of their period charm.

Live-in servants would of necessity be kept to a minimum, although there would be some servant accommodation in the attic. The privacy of individual lots, with gardens front and back, reflects a new desire in England for privacy from one's neighbor – a trend that has remained prevalent into the 20th century. Americans generally had preferred single-family housing from the beginning, and accepted two-family dwellings only out of economic necessity.

The first apartment buildings were developed during the late Victorian period. They were more popular in American cities, particularly New York with its severely limited space on Manhattan, than in England. Architecturally, they adopted the currently fashionable stylistic details, often imitating the configuration of an Italian palazzo or medieval monastery on a giant scale. Inside, the apartments were arranged as much as possible like houses, with details of cornices, moldings, doors and windows appropriate to the architectural style of the building.

These were purely urban developments. Meanwhile, the vernacular tradition on farms and in isolated villages had continued for centuries largely unchanged. The important factors in vernacular building have always been practical innovations. For the average farm worker the sash window had more appeal than the Greek Revival portico simply because it was more useful.

Suddenly, in the late Victorian age, aspects of this sensible, vernacular tradition were reclaimed for fashion by architects and critics. For example, in a rural farmhouse, windows might be placed where they are needed to light the rooms rather than to present a regular pattern from outside. By taking elements from the vernacular, some architects were able to create a pseudo-vernacular house, irregular for practical reasons rather than simply because irregularity was all the rage.

From the 1870s onwards, the Arts and Crafts Movement led a reaction away from the mediocrity of mass-produced Victorian design. The guru of the movement in England was William Morris, who argued for dignified simplicity and honesty of materials. Morris's ideas were shared by the major Arts and Crafts architects Philip Webb and Richard Norman Shaw. Both were inspired in part by the age in which English architecture had produced the most habitable house: the 17th century. The new style they created is known as "Queen Anne" – a reference to the 1720s style upon which it drew. The historic elements – for example, the combination of warm red brick and white woodwork – were transfused by a freshness and originality in the detailing. Windows might be elongated to admit more light, in the process creating a sense of airy delicacy. This was architecture well suited

to reduction to the scale of a suburb. It did not rely on size for effect.

The Arts and Crafts movement was highly influential in the United States. It had many regional variations. Stick style, applied to houses in all parts of the country, married Gothic decoration to wooden buildings. American "Queen Anne" houses gloried in echoes of Tudor half-timbering. Their porches and gables were decorated with carved wooden "gingerbread", while exterior walls were hung with fish-scale slates or shingles in imitation of English tile-work. Decorative terracotta panels inexpensively recalled the carved stonework of some European prototypes. Towers and brick chimneys made the silhoutte as lively as the surface decoration.

The "shingle" style was a more restrained and intellectual architectural fashion. It combined elements of "Queen Anne" with the Romanesque Revival style, which was most commonly used for stone public buildings. Shingle-style houses were bulky in form, but related to the vernacular past by being surfaced with the humblest of materials, split wooden shingles. Architects like Stanford White designed magnificent large houses in this style, but it could not easily be adapted to smaller dwellings.

Vernacular elements were incorporated in the houses of two of the most innovative and influential architects of the early 20th century in America. Frank Lloyd Wright's Prairie houses in the Chicago area combine local natural materials with a new sort of horizontally-oriented design derived from the lines of

the flat Midwestern landscape. The Greene brothers, in southern California, brought a consciousness of Oriental influences appropriate to the Pacific basin to a quintessentially American architecture of superb workmanship. These architects, however, represent the first stirrings of future Modernism rather than a continuation of the stylistic details of the past.

The characteristic swirling forms of Art Nouveau, which first appeared in France after 1890, made a contribution to furniture, tiles and light fixtures, and to a lesser extent to decorative windows and wooden paneling. However, the style had only a minor impact on American design.

Equally admired today is the Art Deco style of the

1, 2 The interior of Leighton House, London, may seem eccentric, but it encapsulates all the self-confidence of the late 19thC, as well as reflecting the taste for travel and collecting. The 15thC tiles are Persian. The whole feel of this room is quite unEnglish. Such opulent strangeness seldom fails to delight visitors. LH

3, 4, 5 In the late Victorian/ early 20thC era, houses that may seem rather anonymous to the unaccustomed eye reveal interesting decorative flourishes. Any historic style might be borrowed, from classical pillars and porticos (5) to brick gables of the English Renaissance and mock-Tudor oriel windows (3). Tragically, such buildings are often given unsympathetic modern extensions (4).

6

7

8

6, 7, 8 This house dating from 1890 is in a Neo-Renaissance style. The hipped tile roof and projecting bays with gabled pediments are typical of large English houses of this period. Some such houses were designed to be light and airy inside, as here; others have a deliberately dark and cloistered feel. The marble fireplaces and other interior details would fit easily into a house of about 100 years earlier. S&P

1920s and 30s, whose plain lines (sometimes combined with geometric ornament) accorded well with mass-production techniques and the need for economy. Art Deco-inspired homes sprouted sporadically in suburbia, in England and notably in Los Angeles, alongside traditional-looking houses. In England, false half-timbering evoked the Golden Age of Elizabeth I, while in America Colonial Revival houses reminded their occupants of pioneer values.

International-style modernism was never widely accepted as a domestic style by either English or American home-owners. Perhaps the obstacle to its acceptance was simply that it was associated with factories and office buildings, or perhaps its wide expanses of glass and unadorned surfaces seemed cold and strange. As in the 19th century, dwellers in modern cities and suburbs wanted their homes to be comfortable, familiar and stylistically evocative of admired periods of history.

The front door is usually the most eye-catching feature of the house, and altering or replacing it without due forethought is all too often disastrous. Interior doors also need to be looked at carefully in relation to the style of their surroundings. Cheap modern doors in a baldly utilitarian style will look totally out of place if the rest of the interior has well-judged period details. A solid plank door, however well-made, will be intrusive in an elegant townhouse. And an 18th-century-style door, despite its good proportions (or because of them), will look ill at ease in a rustic setting.

Other common pitfalls include using knobs and knockers of the wrong type (such as wrought-iron on painted paneled doors) and the inserting of glass panes of the wrong type in the wrong place. When storm doors are necessary, they should harmonize with the style of the original door. Wrong choices can spoil not only the door but the house itself.

1 An original wrought-iron spur knocker for a six-panel front door. BH

2 This original 1680s door was enlarged in the 18thC. The hinges are old replacements which fit exactly the marks found on the door. This attention to detail makes all the difference when authentic restoration is the aim. VNS

3 A reproduction of a mid-16thC Gothic arched door and frame. This is an elaborate example for the period, with deep chamfered framing and small panels. SI

4 A classical Italianate front door and porch on a London row house of 1868-74. It is important to research suitable colors for different periods. Here the white-painted stucco and two shades of green on the door are authentic, but the steps are no longer whitewashed every day by a maid! LSH

5 The brass door hardware of the late-Victorian era was highly refined in comparison with 16thC wrought-iron examples. The contrast is graphically illustrated in the four examples below. Both wrought-iron pieces are modern reproductions. LSH,SI

MOUNTY SAMBOURNE
NOT AT HOME

6 A genuine early-mid 16thC door with linenfold panels. These doors can be tracked down, but not easily. Frequently they do not fit the space intended. It would be a tragedy to cut down such a piece, so you should always take dimensions into account before buying. AH

7 The six-panel door came into vogue at the end of the 17thC. This is a late 19thC example.

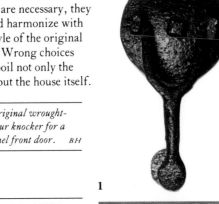

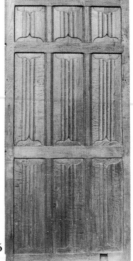

8

8 *A massive oak door of the type standard in England from the 15thC until it was overtaken by the framed door with inset panels in the 17thC. It's worth remembering that oak was not always dark. When these houses were built, the oak was a glorious honey color. Reproduction oak doors are "aged" to suit modern tastes. Imagine a 15thC house with bleached floor boards, honey-colored beams, doors and baseboards.*

9 *An oak plank door hung on sturdy iron hinges of the strap and pin type. Note the enormous strap or iron arm which stretches across two-thirds of the door – this drops into a pin set into the door post. The leaded side lights bordering the door and matching the windows are typical of the 15th and 16thC.*

10 *An interior view of the same door, showing the original fittings.*

THE OAK STUDDED DOOR

In 16th-century England doors were built to last. Amply wide, they were almost invariably of oak. The simplest were rows of planks, laid vertically, edge to edge, joined and strengthened by oak pegs or iron nails driven through to similar planks (the ledges), usually four in number, set across the back. For simpler houses this type of door, known as the board-and-batten door, continued to be made, in softwood versions, well into the 20th century in Europe and America.

Variations on the theme include doors with narrower boards, or tongued and grooved, or with molding on the face, or joined like overlapping clapboard; also doors whose ledges are let into the thickness of the wood. Broader planks might be grooved to make them look narrower. Double-thickness doors had edge-to-edge

9

10

planks across their width at the back. On external doors the vertical joins were usually protected from the weather by thin strips of oak.

In early English timber-framed buildings, inside and outside doors were mostly square-headed, but when set in stone they were often low-arched, like the windows of the period. Square-headed doors might be set against an arched head under the lintel or molded to give the appearance of an arch.

Linenfold molding was developed and refined in England during the Tudor period and applied to doors as well as paneling in the great houses. It later became a hallmark of the Neo-Tudor style.

1

2

3

1 Iron butterfly hinges like these have frequently been replaced.

2 Handmade ironwork lends a more authentic "feel" to a reproduction.

3 A plain oak door (right) consisting of vertical planks with oak pegs or iron nails driven into horizontal ledges on the back. On external doors the smooth "right" side faced outward, while on internal doors it faced into the room.

4 A 17thC Spanish or Portuguese door with fielded panels.

5 An early paneled door. Rather crude paneled doors were produced in the 16thC but the style really came into its own in the 17thC.

6 An original door with double bead molding.

4

5

6

7

7 *These basic three-plank doors were used from the early 17thC well into the 18th.* BH

8 *This three-plank door in the same New York house is divided and has slightly more intricate wrought-ironwork hinges and locks. Note the differing shape and size of the handmade hinges — uniformity was not called for: function was more important than form.* BH

9 *Double entrance doors to a late 19thC house with leaded side lights have as their inspiration the plank doors of the 15thC and 16thC.*

10 *The exterior of this restored New York house of 1680 shows the original placement of the doors. The tall upstairs door is for loading as the staircase was too narrow.* VNS

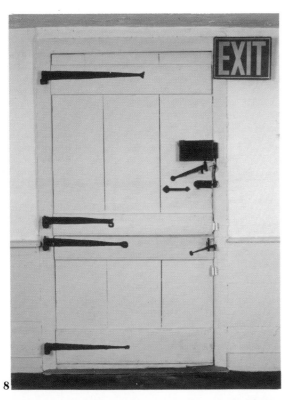

8

9

10

1 *The porch and plank door of an English house dating from the 16thC. The much later stained-glass panels harmonize and, perhaps because of the rather amateurish cutting of the "windows", lend their own charm to the house.*

2, 3 *These oak plank doors were introduced into a 17thC house in the early years of the 20thC. The importance of using properly aged wood, traditional methods and wrought-iron work cannot be overemphasized.*

4 *This wrought-iron boot scraper is an early 20thC copy of a 17thC design.*

DOOR FRAMES

The early, simple method of hanging a door was to attach it to timber posts that formed part of the structure of the building. But later, doors came to be hung on doorposts set against the wall. The join between the post and the face of the wall was concealed by an architrave, which made a surround or frame for the door. During the later 17th century, such frames were given increasingly decorative treatment in the grander houses. They were ornamented with classically inspired swags and medallions and headed with bold pediments. Inside the house, pediments were often broken: that is, they terminated in an open curve instead of a completed triangle, thus creating a lighter effect. Some pediments incorporated panels designed to contain pictures.

The treatment of door frames reflected that of mantelpieces (or chimneypieces as they were sometimes called in Britain). Similarly, the style of molding or carving on the doors themselves was echoed in the panel work on the walls.

5 An 18thC door typically enhanced by decorative architraves and door frames. The addition of paneling elegantly solved the problem of unusually thick walls.

6,7,8 These early 19thC architraves show the classic Greek Revival style in both ornate and simple forms. OMH

9 By the late 19thC stepped molding was the most popular form of architrave: sometimes simple and narrow other times elaborate and deep.

10 This chestnut and walnut door with fielded panels is in a New York house dating from 1875. The details of the door and architrave are echoed by the chair rail and paneling.

6

7

8

5

9

10

PANELED DOORS

Doors constructed as two panels set within a frame began to appear in the great English houses late in the 16th century, and soon became the norm, taking over from the solid plank door. Until late in the 17th century paneled doors were elaborately molded and carved, painted and gilded. By the early 18th century, paneled doors were becoming common in America.

At the beginning of the 17th century the two-panel form remained the most common, with the heavy panels fielded – that is, raised in profile. Panels were given applied molding in geometric patterns, and the broad door frames were treated to match. By mid-century, as classical proportions began to govern the design, six, eight or ten panels were inset; and by 1700 the six-paneled door was settling in for its long period of popularity. This was the favorite front door of the entire Georgian period and of the classical style in America. Interior doors had six, four or sometimes only two panels. The paneled door ceased to belong only in the houses of the wealthiest, and was repeated in less expensive wood, often with remarkable craftsmanship, for over a hundred years across the social scale.

In the smallest 18th-century townhouses, where a six-panel front door would be out of proportion, four panels were more usual. Both inside and out, the hand-sawn, increasingly slim panels were set into a rabbet into the frame, with applied molding around their edge. This molding was absent in humbler houses and, for example, on the backs of cupboard doors.

At the beginning of the 18th century, door panels were raised or fielded. However, on external doors, the lower two panels were often flush with the frame. This helped rainwater to run off – as did the outward-curving rails at the bottom of the door. By the end of the century, sunk panels are more frequent.

1 This light oak reproduction linenfold door blends perfectly with an early house. The simplicity of the wrought-iron hinges and door latch maintains the period character.

2 These 17thC oak double doors were introduced into a 15thC house in Kent in the 1950s. It is important to remember that all is not always what it seems. Early houses have often had many adaptations through the centuries.

3 An interesting mid-17thC divided door showing the influence of both English and Dutch regional architecture on a New York house built in 1661.   BH

4 By the middle of the 17thC, oak paneled doors had six, eight or ten panels. These doors were frequently used as replacements for the earlier plank doors, particularly internally.

5 *Eight-paneled solid mahogany doors were much favored by the first half of the 18thC and often replaced earlier examples.* CP

6 *This double or split door is made to resemble a paneled one by a simple frame around a board-and-batten body. The plank edges are beaded, a typical form of primitive ornamentation.* VNS

7 *From the late 17thC on, the six-panel door became the most popular form, particularly for front doors, and this was to be the most fashionable for the next hundred years.*

8 *This early 19thC four-paneled door in its original door frame remained standard in both Britain and America throughout the 19thC. The white paint work is totally authentic.*

9 *Today you will often find pine doors stripped of generations of paint – a simple treatment which works successfully in many cases. However, the original owners would probably be horrified to see so humble a wood being given such importance.*

6

8

5

7

9

1 *A classic six-panel door from the late 1760s. The paint on this door simulates the slightly streaked effect produced by the thinner paints used in the 18thC.* RL.

2 *These sturdy iron hinges work as well today as they did in the late 18thC.* MJ

3 *The rectangular fanlight over this six-panel internal door with simple door frame and architrave reflects the understated proportion of late 18thC and early 19thC design. Such features tended to be used in secondary positions or in lesser houses.* MJ

4 *The same door has plain but sturdy brass door hardware with a well-concealed lock on the underside.* MJ

6

5 *The front porch and doorway of a classic Greek Revival house built in New York State c.1835.*

6 *Behind a later louver door is a mahogany one of 1835 with its original brass hardware. These doors cope well with most weather conditions, except for strong sunlight, and need virtually no maintenance.*

5

1

2

3

4

5

6

1 *The porch, double doors and fanlight were most important in changing the facade, in 1728, of an earlier house. In the 18thC, householders had no qualms about bringing an old-fashioned house right up to date — with pleasing harmonious results.* CP

2,3,4,5 *By the end of the 18thC the front door of the house had developed into a solid multi-paneled door, and the variations were endless. The 18thC builders were particularly keen on the semi-circular fanlights which predominate in city rows. These were originally divided by wooden bars and tended to be of simple design, but as the century progressed classical influences and the use of cast iron allowed intricate designs.*

7

8

9

10

11

12

6,7,8 *Both late 18thC and early 19thC houses gave greater prominence to the front door, by use of pillars, brick arches or white-painted stone.*

9,10 *In the 19thC front doors continued to mirror the changing faces of architecture. The square fanlight had appeared in the 18thC.*

11 *This wonderful example of a Victorian Gothic Revival door and fanlight is in a square in North London.*

12 *An attractive early 20thC door has replacement etched glass in its panels, side windows and rectangular light above.* LDC

The color of front doors

One of the most important decisions to be made is what color to paint the front door. Opinions vary considerably. Experts, museums and societies often disagree. Therefore, all that can be suggested is what the authors have found works in practice. On 18thC houses:- white, black, dark green, dark blue, burgundy. On Victorian houses:- brighter colors are acceptable, as is a two-toned effect. If the house is in a row consider the whole ensemble, avoiding jarring colors. Brickwork should also be considered. For example, red doors can often compete with the brick color if the shades are mismatched. You should remember that the color of the front door is something we inflict on the outside world more than on ourselves: great care should therefore be taken.

FANLIGHTS

From about 1700 (1750 in America) the glass fanlight over the front door was developed as a way of letting light into the hall and passageway. With glazing bars first of wood, and later of lead or wrought iron, the fanlight window offered scope for endless pattern variations. The influence of the Adam brothers encouraged increasing use of cast iron for delicate patterning. By the end of the century fanlights were being mass-produced in a wide range of increasingly informal designs. Loops and spider webs took over from fans and scallops, and elaborate heart and honeysuckle motifs were popular in the early 1800s.

No one nowadays would want to remove one of these lovely features. However, many were unfeelingly ripped out earlier in the present century. Fortunately, it is possible to find craft workers who will provide new fanlights following designs contemporary with the house.

1

3

4

2

1 This classical 18thC six-paneled front door has an equally classical fanlight. Such features should, of course, be restored and retained. They are functional, adding to the light in the hallway, and delightful, adding to the overall splendor of the facade.

2 The proportion and feel of this hallway owe much to the American Empire style in this New York house built in 1765 and refurbished, after the owners' visit to France, in 1826. The fanlight and side panels, which are original to the house, are copies of early Colonial glass.　MJ

3 This house is a reconstruction of the best colonial architecture from Maine to Charleston, South Carolina. It was built in 1929-30 by the architect Richard Henry Dana as a replica of a 1760 house. Some elements are original, salvaged from old houses being demolished, many more are copies – but perfect and sensitively made. This entrance door of stone is in the formal pedimented Greek Revival style.　HH

4 The divided front door (sometimes called a Dutch door) from the inside. The sophisticated paneling reflects that of the chair rail in the hall. By the mid-18thC in this quality of house far more attention was being paid to detail; ornamentation was taking over from pure functional design.　HH

5

6

7

8

9

5 *This fanlight from an 1830s house in New York shows all the exuberance of the period. The front door was an important statement of wealth and position. Such a fanlight and associated decoration were intended to portray an owner of great gentility. Restoration of such a detail requires a skilled craftsman, and even repainting should be done with great care.* OMH

6,7,8,9 *These typical 18thC fanlights were still popular in the 19thC. The intricacy of design was at its height in the mid-18thC and tended, in modest homes, to become less delicate as the century progressed. Standard shapes, such as circles, loops and spiderwebs, were mass-produced and used in rows in cities and towns in both Britain and America.*

10,11 *Many Victorian houses had simple square fanlights, which should be retained, especially when they mirror other houses of the same design.*

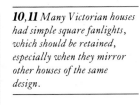

10

11

HOODS

When not placed within an entrance porch or under a projecting upper story, outside doors in English houses were initially set beneath a molded projecting lintel which helped to keep off the rain. Alternatively, stone houses had drip moldings across the tops of doors. In the 1650s decoratively carved wooden hoods began to appear at the top of the door frame to afford protection from the weather and add a superb ornamental flourish to the flat front of the house. Supported visually by carved brackets (though often with further concealed support), these hoods are still frequently found, as an unaltered feature, in houses dating from this time onward. Until the 1720s, English examples were often carved in a florid Baroque manner. However, the vigor of the curving acanthus leaves, cherubs and lions' heads, fruits and flowers, was curbed by the influence of stricter Palladian classicism, and hoods went out of fashion.

The brackets and hoods were made of well-seasoned softwood, which was quite deeply carved. Successive applications of white paint has often blurred the details, in which case the old paint should be carefully stripped or burned off and fresh white paint applied. In shape, hoods of the later period might be arching, coved or modeled to suggest shells. The smaller townhouses had simple, flat, molded projections which nevertheless had elaborate scrolled brackets. In the 19th-century English row house, hoods provided a needed touch of individuality. However, hooded entries were uncommon in America.

1

1 This interesting thatched house on an estate in London has an equally eccentric porch. Porches frequently mirrored the style of the house and the Victorians, in particular, liked to add interest to a plain facade.

2,3 Columns were frequently employed to give a classical feel to the entrance. These are common features in the 18thC but were also used by the Victorians as a classical revival.

4 In this example the functional use of the porch – to give shelter from inclement weather – finds a natural expression.

2

3

4

5 *A successful modern porch added to a 16thC English farmhouse using old timbers and a classic regional design.*

6 *The influence of chinoiserie is to be found in the design of porches and furniture at the end of the 18thC and beginning of the 19thC. The pagoda-style top is typical of the English Regency.*

7,8 *Porches were often thought inappropriate, and by the late 18thC the style had reverted to the hood.*

9 *This late Victorian row is an example of hoods used solely as decorative features. That such detail was added to quite plain doors shows the Victorians' concern to beautify.*

18TH-CENTURY DOOR FRAMES

From the mid-1700s, a classical door frame was
preferred, with columns or pilasters on each side of the
door and a horizontal entablature over the top, with or
without a triangular or segmental (curved) pediment.
This type of frame, christened the tabernacle frame,
was much loved by the Adam brothers. Both inside and
out the tabernacle frame persisted throughout the rest
of the century, with console brackets later replacing the
columns. Above interior doors, broken pediments were
often used. In Colonial America these styles were
known as Georgian Federal, becoming more elaborate
in Adam and Greek revival houses until the 1860s.

Towards the end of the 19th century, pediments had
fallen out of favor. Inside the home, the areas above the
doors now had stucco panels to match the stucco on
exteriors.

1

*1 This door and frame of the
early 19thC exhibit all the
style of the Egyptian Revival
popular at the time. The
sphinxes and tall pillars are
actually the entrance to the
house. The front door is in a
small external hallway.*

*2 This spectacular door and
frame epitomize the classical
influences of the later part of
the 18thC. Such doors were
usually painted white. As with
internal cornices, the
decoration at the head of the
columns can be greatly
improved by careful cleaning
and repainting.*

2

3 *This wonderful broken pediment above classical columns develops a style popular in architecture and furniture from the mid-18thC on. The beautifully proportioned front door reflects the period's love of symmetry.*

4,5 *On less grand houses, entablatures were often much simpler but still had the effect of increasing the elaboration of the door. This was also the case in later 18thC houses. If your entablature is in a bad state of repair or has been removed, a qualified carpenter can copy a similar design.*

6,7 *In the late 18thC the classical columns could be either freestanding or incorporated into the door frame. These columns developed into a mainly decorative feature rather than a structural one. White painted stucco was a common treatment for a door frame. Pilasters were also common, as in picture 7.*

CHANGES IN STYLE

Greek Revival, Gothic Revival and Italianate influences began to be felt in England in the early 19th century; in America some 25 years later. These styles demand less stylistic conformity. Decorative details varied immensely according to individual taste.

A feature of the period was the door with two vertical panels side by side, sometimes narrowing toward the top like Doric columns. Sometimes a door would be ornamented with a rectangular frieze and a central circular motif or a reeded lower half. In England the frame was more and more played down. Front doors became less significant decoratively, the focus shifting to the fanlight. Treatments ranged from the classic radiating bars to loops and swirls and spiderwebs. In humbler houses, right until the early 20th century, plainer rectangular fanlights were to be seen in abundance. In America, elaborate doorways were still the rule.

In very grand houses, the doors might have been made of mahogany, but generally they were made in softwoods, carefully painted to imitate the graining of nobler woods. For front doors that were not wood-grained, white was the preferred color, but black was sometimes chosen, and dark green or brown was also considered suitable.

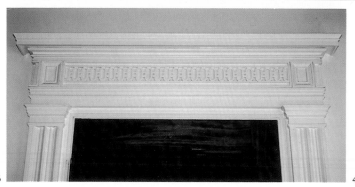

1 A Federal-style entrance built in 1832 with coffered stone sides and columns. Note that the outer fanlight is heavier than the inner one and the doors echo but do not duplicate each other. This is one of only two surviving examples of the hundreds of similar houses built in New York in the first half of the 19thC. OMH

2 The outer door and fan seen through the inner doorway. The regular paneling owes more to the Greek Revival than to the Federal style. OMH

3 The parlor door frame. On more unusual door frames like this, you may have to make molds to copy the detail. OMH

4 The classic division of a 19thC American house – sliding doors in a double Greek Revival doorway between twin parlors. OMH

5,6,7 *Three examples of Greek Revival door frames from a New York Neoclassical stone mansion built between 1837 and 1846. The first with understated elegance; the second and third, with their wonderful carving, demonstrating the true opulence of the period.* BP

8 *A six-panel door in the upstairs reception room has a simple classical frame.* BP

9 *Another Greek Revival door frame from the same house, similar to the one in picture 6, but with a different motif.* BP

10 *The frame of these large mahogany sliding doors is molded as Corinthian columns.* BP

5

6

7

8

9

10

THE LATER 19TH CENTURY

The narrow Georgian Federal row house demanded a narrow entranceway, and a front door proportioned accordingly. However, when a detached townhouse was built, its wider entrance hall allowed a more generous entrance area, which permitted the introduction of side windows beside a wider front door, often set within a porch. This set the style for Victorian houses.

By the time of the building boom in the middle of the 19th century, mechanization had taken over from hand labor. Hand-sawn door panels had been around five-eighths of an inch thick. The later machine-sawn panels were thicker, making the doors sturdier (and also more fireproof). The rules of 18th-century proportion had required the height of a door to be twice (or a little more than twice) its width. Now, although they were still paneled, doors were more various in their ratio of dimensions.

In English houses basements, where they existed, were not so deep as before. The raised ground-floor story replaced the Georgian *piano nobile* (parlor floor), and the front door set into it was reached by a longer flight of steps.

The Gothic style that was favored for public architecture also affected domestic buildings profoundly. In doors and window frames, colored brick or carved stone were used – or a stone substitute of molded papier mâché or powdered wood, frequently painted. Woodwork was grained artificially to look like oak. This style was extremely popular in America.

With the spread of simpler row houses, the door position was variable. The rhythm of door/window, door/window down the street gave way to window/ door, door/window, window/door. To provide privacy, a wooden partition might be added between the two neighboring doors. Apartment buildings were being built to look like row houses, with double doors, one for downstairs and one for upstairs.

By the end of the century many houses had paved paths leading to the stone steps and front door sheltered

1 *This original doorway to the west wing of a 1735 Wisconsin house has simple pilasters and sidelights.* SWH

2 *By 1845, when the east wing porch was added, the taste was for something a little more ornate. The classical Doric columns and the porte-cochère are typical Victorian details.* SWH

3 *Etched glass panels like these are a feature of houses throughout the Victorian period. Fortunately, there are craftsmen who can reproduce the traditional designs.* LSH

4 *These narrower front doors were common in English row houses. The square fanlight is typical of the early 19thC.*

5 Heavily ornamented brass door hardware vies for attention with the decorative paint treatment. Note the vase motif on the finger plates echoing that on the panel (although in different style).   *LSH*

6 Another view of the same door showing more of the painted panels. This English house is a unique example of its type. The owner was the chief political cartoonist of Punch magazine and the interior has been kept the same since his death in 1910.   *LSH*

7 This heavily molded architrave repeats the design of the single door panel. The whole is given greater importance by the classical pediment and somber, marble-like effect of black gloss paint.

8 A wide internal door and frame of the late 19thC with a series of formalized carved decorations emphasizing the proportions. 18thC proportion required doors to have a height of a little over twice their width. By 1870, however, many were higher or, as here, wider.   *LH*

9 The motto incised over this dining room door salutes the guests and wishes them "good luck". The gilded scroll design repeats that around the door frame.   *LH*

within a porch (often with a curved or pointed arch) supported on thin columns. Sometimes now quite brightly painted, doors were four-paneled, with a rectangular light (high window) above. Stained glass became more and more popular, the familiar narrow blue or red framing panels with white stars at their corners later giving way to a more Arts and Crafts treatment, with subtle colors in leaded lights or the curvilinear Art Nouveau patterns.

It is perfectly possible to have leaded or etched panes restored and reinserted in a front door, or to have a new panel made in the original style. However, such a panel does offer easy entry to burglars and should be backed with toughened burglar-proof clear plastic screwed well into the door.

1 A heavy, patterned velvet curtain trimmed with a deep fringe and thick cord drapes a painted door. Before restoring a Victorian house to this degree of authenticity, it is as well to consider whether you could live in such a claustrophobic atmosphere. It is possible to be true to the character of a house and still live in the 20thC.   LSH

2 Another glorious example of Victorian self-confidence! The painted upper panels of the door pick up the motif of the walls, the lower panels are ornamented with coats of arms and the brass hardware is highly elaborate. The door is swamped, and the whole area given new proportions and greater importance by the heavily trimmed curtains and a matching massive valance filling the space between cornice and picture rail.   LSH

1

2

3 *This American house built in 1875 has its original chestnut doors with period etched-glass panels which open to reveal a pierced iron grille.*

4 *This late 19thC back door has as its central feature a stained-glass panel which mirrors the designs used throughout the house.* LSH

5,6,7 *It is possible to buy restored doors or new doors made in the style of the late 19thC or early 20th C.* LDC

8 *As the 19thC came to a close, Art Nouveau patterns became more and more popular for stained glass, as for other forms of decoration.*

DOOR HARDWARE

Until about 1700, latches, hinges and door handles were usually of wrought iron, and although simple in their conception they could be beautifuly ornamented. The simplest hinges, used on batten doors, are those of the strap and pin type, with a long strap attached to the door dropping on to a sturdy pin fixed to the door post.

The H hinge was also frequently used on batten doors. This has two "legs" which interlock by means of a bar across the middle: one leg is screwed to the door and the other to the post. The legs were given fancy, double S-shaped sides, the terminals of which were often embellished with curlicued cockspurs in true Gothic mannner.

Early external doors had no handles, being closed only at night and barred with wood on the inside. The simplest latches then became common: the iron latch, catch and guide were operated by a large wrought-iron ring on the plain side of the door. This type of hardware or simple versions of it remains in keeping with cottage doors.

Brass rim locks were introduced in the late 1660s. The knob and working parts were set into a metal box mounted on the door, and the latch closed into a metal catch mounted on the door frame. These devices were much more finely ornamented and were installed on fine paneled doors. Elegant little brass handles were introduced instead of knobs for internal doors, and if there is a key hole it should be accompanied by elaborate escutcheons. Finger panels protected the door from finger marks and provided further scope for decoration. The basic design stayed in fashion, in porcelain, pressed metal and finally bakelite (an early plastic), until the 1940s.

1

2

4

5

6

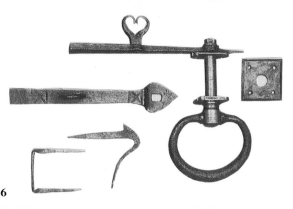

3

7

1 *A side door of a mid 18thC New York house showing the iron hardware.*

2 *Thorough research into old types of hardware found in the house gave the actual designs for these replacements. The doors are put together with clenched nails – soft wrought-iron nails that are almost impossible to loosen. Contrary to popular belief, board-and-batten doors were always nailed.* VNS

3 *It is essential to use wrought-iron hinges to give an authentic feel to early doors.* SI

4 *By the 17thC, internal door latches had become more decorative and more ingenious than formerly, and made use of brass as well as iron.*

5 *A strap-and-pin hinge on a lightweight plank door.*

6 *These authentic reproductions are readily available.* SI

7 *The original iron hinge on an internal stripped and polished pine door.* HH

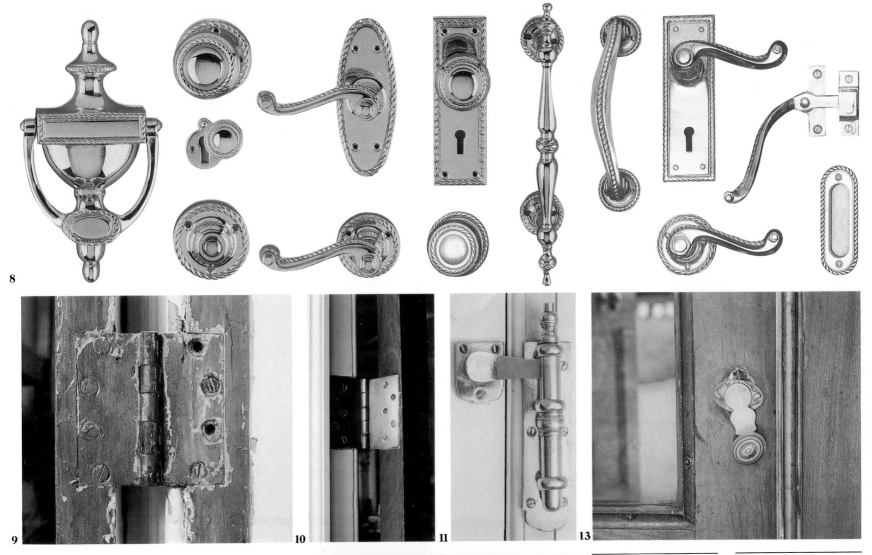

8

9 **10** **11** **13**

12

By the beginning of the 18th century door knockers were widely used on front doors. These were made of iron and lent themselves to all sorts of designs, usually based on animal heads. To complement these knockers, plain, bold doorknobs, also of iron, were set at waist height. Later brass knobs and knockers were more showy, but remained modest compared with 19th-century equivalents.

Brass was much less used before the 19th century than we seem to think now. Cast iron was by far the favorite material for door hardware in the early 19th century. Ostentatious use of brass became commonplace later in the 19th century, when bells with pulls replaced knockers, until the introduction of porcelain pushes for electric bells.

Art Nouveau lent itself particularly well to door hardware. Its sinuous patterns can be found on large finger plates and bold mail-slots.

8 It is possible to find excellent reproduction brass hardware. These examples are perfect for doors from the early 19thC on. BE

9 This large solid early 19thC iron hinge supports triple doors. It should be noted that such hinges are brittle and can snap if attacked with a chisel or hammer. They were frequently covered with the stain used for the wood and were meant to blend with their surroundings rather than dominate.

10 Substantial brass hinges like this were used on both solid and glazed mahogany doors. CP

11 This beautifully-made late 19thC brass door catch is both functional and attractive. LSH

12 The original door lock and key of an early 19thC house. These should always be repaired and restored if possible.

13 Brass had become the main material for hardware in most houses of stature by the beginning of the 19thC. CP

1 *A late 19thC example of useful information conveyed by means of a revolving brass plaque.* LSH

2,3 *Two examples of brass door hardware of the late 18thC.* RC

4 *This plain brass reproduction door hardware is perfectly suitable for doors of the late 18th and 19thC.* BE

5 *This wonderful late 19thC brass mailbox is original, although reproductions abound.*

6 *The choice of reproduction door hardware to suit a late 18th/early 19thC door is vast. The more ornate tends to suit a later house.* BE

7 *As well as brass door hardware, the Victorians used porcelain. These modern examples are available in many paint finishes.* BE

8, 9, 10, 11, 12, 13, 14 *Original brass Victorian door furniture is well worth seeking out as it has the added patina of wear, although there are good reproductions copied from old designs. All these examples are originals.*

15 *A lock imported from England to New York in the 1830s; the knob is 1890s.*

16 *You can see how successive generations have renewed the door hardware here from the marks on the wood. The house was built in 1765 but this polished wooden door knob was made in the 1890s.* MJ

17 *This 19thC brass and glass door knob has a matching keyhole and escutcheon.*

18,19 *This original polished brass door hardware gives an elegant look to late 18th/early 19thC mahogany doors.*

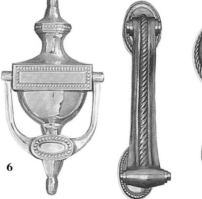

6

1

4

2

3

5

7

8

9

10

11

12

13

14

15

16

17

18

19

Britain had its own glass industry from the 13th century but it was very rare for windows to be glazed until Tudor times. Even then it was only the nobility and wealthy new classes who could afford to use glass.

Windows were "wind-holes" or "wind-eyes" – necessary to let smoke out and let light and air in. They were unglazed and tiny – a tradition which continued in smaller houses and in remoter areas well into the 16th century and beyond. Very early American houses, and simple log or mud pioneer dwellings, had unglazed windows.

In stone buildings, vertical stone posts, or mullions, helped to support the lintel of the window opening. They also served to deter intruders; and timber mullions were fitted in timber-framed houses for the same purpose, although they were not structurally necessary.

1 Vertical mullions were fitted into the windows of timber-framed houses as well as in stone ones, even though they were not structurally necessary. Setting the square mullions diagonally into the frame admitted more light than square-set posts.

2 The delicate glazing bars between the solid timber mullions would have been added at a much later date.

3,4 The gable of a 16thC timber-framed house which has square leaded quarries. These are not original but 19thC replacements which harmonize with the building.

5 Diamond-shaped quarries are quite correct for a 15th or 16thC house. Never replace such windows with double-glazed imitation leaded lights, which gives a most unsuitable flat look.

3

1

2

4

Mullions, whether stone or wood, were usually square in section and set diagonally into the frame, splay fashion, admitting more light than square-set posts. Splayed reveals might be provided around the openings, both outside and in, to let in more light.

Before the introduction of glass, other materials were used – for example, oiled or waxed paper or linen cloth stretched across a lattice frame. Better still was parchment, also on a lattice frame and often decorated with figurative patterns or coats of arms before being brushed with oil. The frames (known as *fenestrals*), made of wicker or fine strips of oak, were still used in remoter places well into the 17th

5

century, and later still in the poorest houses, where sheepskin or sacking would take the place of parchment. Their criss-cross pattern was echoed in the lead strips (*cames*) which held in place the small diamonds (*quarries*) of glass in the first glazed windows.

MULLIONS AND TRANSOMS

The simple mullions of smaller Tudor houses were used decoratively in grander ones. Taller windows were made, their lights divided horizontally by transoms. Windows were elegantly proportioned, usually with the dividing line of the transoms positioned half-way up the window plus the width of the transom.

In timber houses the transoms and mullions were carved as if they were stone, and wood lent itself to a blossoming of ornamental work. The tallest windows would be topped with tracery, usually set within the shallow late medieval depressed arch or the Tudor arch. Such windows often had glazing in their upper parts and shutters and fenestrals opening below.

THE CASEMENT WINDOW

Early glass was blown. The end of the bubble was cut off and the cylindrical bubble itself was flattened before being cut out into "quarries", which were fitted into a lattice work of lead cames. At first quarries were diamond- or lozenge-shaped, but roundels of stained glass bearing coats of arms were made by European craftsmen for English houses. There was soon a multitude of quarry shapes, all of which were small, due to the limitations of the lead cames. While grand new houses were being built with what must have looked like walls of glass, smaller houses were having casements fitted into their existing window openings. Stone jambs and mullions were hung with iron casements, while timber-framed houses had casements of wood. The whole casement, rather than the pieces of glass within it, was known as the "window pane".

By the 17th century, glass was quite readily available, even in the most remote or poor American settlements. In Britain, the glass industry moved to

6 *A substantial late 19thC family house has a huge bay in the drawing room with five windows of four panes each divided by heavily carved mullions and transoms. This was the late Victorians idea of a Tudor "cottage"!*

7 *This six-paned arched window is a later addition to a timber-framed house in the south of England.*

8 *Casement windows became popular in the 16thC. By the 17thC, glass was readily available and larger rectangular quarries began to be seen. The bull's eye was a feature of spun glass. Often this section was remelted, although it might be used in the windows of poorer homes. When its use is as regular as here one would assume it to be a later placement.*

6

7

8

Cleaning old windows
To clean old glass, gently scrub with a soft brush and warm water, which will remove grime and moss. Make sure that any lintels or drip moldings around the windows are in good condition, as rainwater can damage antique glass. If chemical deposits have built up on a lattice window, cleaning is a job for the specialist, who will need to remove all the quarries (panes). Before doing so he will take a rubbing of the lattice work to use as a model when the glass is replaced. If you need new leading for lattice work, be sure to use milled lead.

3,4 These 19thC windows in a 17thC house blend well with the early surroundings. Old stained glass was used for the decorative roundels, probably taken from an old church. Our predecessors frequently reused old features and materials.

5 In this 19thC extension to the same house, leaded lights and oak frames were used to blend the extension perfectly with the 17thC core. From the facade it is difficult to distinguish the modern wing.

Lancashire and Newcastle, where sand was plentiful and coal could be used. Larger rectangular quarries of various proportions began to appear, and in the latter part of the century casement windows consisting of wooden mullions and transoms set in a wooden frame, able to hold larger pieces of glass.

Spun (or "Crown") glass, blown and spun out into a flat disk, was introduced during this period. The best parts of the disk were used in the wooden frames which were replacing the recently installed leaded lights. Those parts of the disks not suitable for use in the first replacement windows were usually remelted. However, these "bull's eyes" might be used in the casement windows of the poorer homes – although they were certainly never used in houses of quality.

Despite the fact that windows continued to be subject to renovation over the years, much 17th- and 18th-century spun glass has survived. It is glossy, often marked by tiny air bubbles and recognizable by the fine curving lines of the spinning and its slightly curved surface. As a clue to the age of the house, early glass deserves respect and care when old houses are being restored. Spun glass is still made by specialists and old glass is available second-hand.

1 This window in a 16thC English house has diamond-shaped quarries. As well as the usual lead cames there are lead bracing bars and decorative catches, both fairly typical on a house of this age.

2 A decorative window catch in the same house. In areas such as this (south-east England) where many houses have leaded lights, it is relatively easy to find a glazier to undertake restoration work.

6

7

9

10

12

13

8

11

6 *This stained and painted 19thC glass is in the medieval mood. Notice the return to lead cames and square quarries.* LSH

7 *More 19thC glass – delicate tracery makes a background for a central monogram in jewel colors; the whole window is bordered with a design of formalized flowers.* LSH

8 *A small 19thC stained-glass window.*

9 *This early stained-glass window is a 17thC addition to a 15thC house. Glass like this was reproduced in the late 19thC as part of the Arts and Crafts Movement.*

10 *A beautiful Arts and Crafts roundel, with lilies.* W&W

11 *Another example of the medieval theme in 19thC decorative glass.* SC

12 *The designs on the brass catches pick up the motifs from nature on the windows.* LSH

13 *An inset painted glass panel of Ariel from the side window of a Victorian bay. It shows the influence of the Arts and Crafts Movement in England.* LSH

1 This west wing of a house in Port Washington was built in 1735. The windows are of the sash type and on this bay are dominated by a massive stone chimney. SWH

2 By the time this house was renovated early in the 18thC, sashes were the order of the day. In existing houses casements were often removed and new sash windows installed; the proportions of later casements – 2½ to 1 – made conversions easy. CP

3,4 An 18thC sash window of elegant proportion dominates a small room. With the introduction of pine window frames in the 18th century, painted woodwork became normal. White lead paint was universally used and so it is quite legitimate to use white paint in houses of this period. The authentic catch design completes the effect. CP

Sash Windows

Toward the end of the 17th century, sash windows were introduced and began to displace casement windows. The English may have heard about them from the Dutch, but the French regarded them as characteristically English; whatever their origin, they were certainly a feature of British and North American dwellings until well into the 20th century. Well suited to classically inspired architecture, the sash was to appear in every main street and town development throughout the Georgian period.

In the simplest and earliest sashes the panes were propped in position on pegs while open or held in place by a pivoted iron quadrant which fitted into notches in the beading strip. The upper pane would often be fixed, in the Dutch manner. The earliest weighted sash windows had solid wood frames flush with the wall, with grooves for the weights. Soon these constructions were replaced by boxed frames in which the pulleys were set and the weights hung – a system which was hardly to change over a period of two hundred years.

The weighted sash was not universal. In some areas of Britain casement windows were superseded by sideways-sliding sashes. These too were built into the 20th century. Despite their name, "Yorkshire windows", they are in fact found in many English counties. The sliding sash was suitable for smaller windows and could be used in smaller houses and upper stories where the rooms were low.

The 18th Century

Until the early 18th century in England, the most popular wood for windows frames was oak or other locally available hardwood. Glazing bars were very broad (roughly two inches (5 cm) across and never painted. Although oak continued to be the principal

wood for important work, occasionally imported mahogany was substituted. By the 1720s cheaper Baltic fir had been introduced.

The softwoods fir and pine acquired immense popularity. As neither of these woods weathers as well as oak, exposed woodwork required a protective coat of paint. White lead paint, primed with red lead, was universally used until the Victorian period. These softwoods were also common on the East coast of America, where painted windows were the norm from an early date.

From 1709, window frames in London had to retreat to a minimum of four inches (10 cm) behind the outer surface of the wall to reduce risk of fire. This created a reveal in the exterior brickwork which was usually plastered and painted white. Elsewhere, houses

still had their window frames flush with the wall or only slightly set in. London houses after 1709 have flat gauged brick arches above the reveals instead of a timber lintel, although white pine lintels were still to be found inside. The new recessed windows were usually furnished with shutters inside the house. These folded back above the window board into splayed or recessed reveals and were fastened with pivoted iron locking bars. Although glazing bars were becoming thinner and thinner in towns, they remained relatively thick in country regions. In grand houses wide oak bars would be carved inside to match the carved moldings of the paneled shutters.

By 1820 most glazing bars had been reduced in width to half an inch (1 cm) or less, and twelve-pane windows (known as six-over-six windows in America)

had become standard. In another wave of window replacement, earlier sashes were removed and twelve-pane windows fitted. The rule of classicism, made fashionable by the Palladians early in the 18th century, was applied to buildings of all sizes in Britain and North America.

VARIATIONS

During the 18th century the decorative treatment of window frames varied widely. Plain windows were commonly embellished with misunderstood classical details taken from the many "copy books" which served as textbooks to the British and American building trades at this time.

The Venetian or Palladian window, with three

sections, the side ones narrower than the round-arched central one, had been used by Inigo Jones early in the 17th century. A century later, when classical architectural features were commonplace, this style of window was in evidence even in quite modest houses. In various proportions and with different decorative details, the Palladian window enhanced many a facade at (usually) second-floor level for two thirds of the century. More simply, rectangular windows were divided into three with fixed side lights and a central sash which could be opened.

The bay or bow typical of mid and late 18th-century row houses in many towns became very popular. The word "oriel", once applied indiscriminately to any projecting window, now denoted a window supported by brackets and projecting from an upper floor, as

1 *Six-over-six sash windows are characteristic of virtually any house of the period in the East Coast of America. The gargoyle carvings in this example appear over the front windows only.* VC

2 *A dining room window of the 1830s. By 1850 most woodwork was painted white.* OMH

3 *This imposing bay of a house dating from 1875 is flanked by pilasters and defined by the cornicing and ceiling details. The bay is composed of five sash windows, each with just two panes The ready availability by this time of large sheets of plate glass made it possible to dispense with glazing bars.*

distinct from the built-in angled bay or curved bow which often extended almost the entire height of the external wall. Bays were practical, especially in towns, letting in more light and cunningly extending the front room without increasing the width of the house. In the 1770s, elliptical and canted bays became popular, forestalling the neighbors' complaints about buildings advancing into the street.

At the same time, in British town houses, the *piano nobile* or parlor floor, providing rooms of greater height at second-floor level, was being developed. Architects began to focus their creativity on this story, by adding entablatures above the windows and pilaster strips which ran between them vertically to the cornice, and by increasing the height of the windows themselves. Some grand American houses, particularly in the South, emulated this fashion.

By the end of the 18th century, even modest builder-designed row houses in Britain had a *piano nobile* of increased height, sometimes with small projected balconies, and often with windows decreasing in proportion.

Windows of this period were more likely to have square than arched heads and tended to be set closer to the face of the wall. Attic rooms were lit by dormer windows which could be square-, round- or segmental-headed. Crowned with their own little roofs, they projected from the roof in varying degrees from the house roof and were concealed behind the parapet if one existed.

4 *A finely detailed brass opener from the sashes shown in picture 3.*

5 *A built-in seat is a pleasant feature of this 18thC window.* CP

9

9 This detail of stripped-back glazing bars shows the late 18thC miter. When replacing such bars it is essential to duplicate this design. Many mass-produced examples have flattened bars.

6

7

8

The 19th Century

Plate glass was first introduced in 1773, cast and ground to remove flaws. However, it was not widely used until after the 1830s when polished sheet glass became commercially available on both sides of the Atlantic. Already Gothic influences had begun to make their mark on classical facades. The new age was prepared to sacrifice proportion altogether in pursuit of maximum light and air. Glazing bars could be dispensed with now that large sheets of glass were available.

In the mid-1800s, many older multi-paned windows were replaced with six- and soon four-paned windows. In English houses that were reglazed at this time, windows on upper floors were often left undisturbed and many can now be found with four-paned sashes at ground-floor level, Georgian twelve-paned sashes above, and even Stuart casements at the top floor. In America, however, the entire house was often reglazed.

The 20th Century

By the turn of the century, in England and America, houses were being built with big sash windows, each consisting of one huge pane. Shutters, which could be closed to keep out the light were now more or less abandoned, but in England were replaced by exterior blinds. Despite a growing demand for old-fashioned cosiness, the plate glass sash survived, developing into the modern "picture window". A frequent compromise is the sash in which the lower part is one sheet of glass, with smaller panes in the upper part.

There was also a medievalist strain – dating back to William Morris in the second half of the 19th century – which manifested itself in the reintroduction of casements and leaded lights. Mock lattices of applied lead strips appeared in the 1930s and are now common features in "pseudo Tudor" houses in England, despite the horror with which they were once viewed and their glaring inappropriateness in older buildings. Equally popular are the metal-framed, smaller-paned windows of the mid-20th century, which today have a period look of their own.

6, 7 Two examples of shutters from English Regency villas, one showing the original brown varnish, the other painted white. It is a matter of personal taste whether to paint or revarnish; however there is no doubt that shutters should be restored and used. They are a form of double glazing and provide security.

8 This view shows the shutters in picture 7 open and folded back. Even with curtains these are useful additions. The windows, in an early 19thC house, have the interesting addition of small side panes.

SHUTTERS

Window openings could be shuttered to give substantial protection from intruders and the elements. In Britain and early America, shutters were almost always hung on the inside, which is why the European-style external shutters unwisely added nowadays look so out of keeping in houses following British styles. Shutters were made strongly of wooden boards, sometimes hinged and folding and sometimes sliding horizontally or vertically, and fastened with wooden bars or iron fastenings. Those which opened horizontally were often housed in the reveals of the inside walls. Outside shutters began to be used in America around the turn of the 19th century.

1 *The late 19thC fascination with Oriental styles shows here – red and gold wallpaper, rich green curtains trimmed with gold, shining brass curtain pole. The painting of the woodwork, including the shutters, adds to the somber grandeur.*

Although the window area is large it has the same heavy "feel" as the rest of the room. The tall concertina shutters were a common security feature. Each shutter is made up of four tall narrow sections; these fold into a small wall niche. LH

2 *The artist who had this London house built in 1877 traveled extensively and was fascinated by Eastern art, and the decoration of this room reflects this taste. The bay is almost a half circle with floor-to-ceiling sash windows taking up most of it. The circular form is defined by the ceiling decoration and emphasized by the unusual curved brass curtain pole. The shutters work on a brass pulley system and are housed in reveals in the wall.* LH

3,4 *The paneling below this window in an 18thC room matches that on the two pairs of shutters. The back of the shutter is typically plain while the front had intricate molding.*

5 *The unusual cutout over the bed in this room in an American house was probably intended to hold fabric. It dates from 1720, when the room was added to an earlier house, and still has its original studs and shingle lath.* VNS

6 *Two pairs of bi-fold shutters are still in good working order in this 18thC house in New York. The radiator "box" is paneled to match.* VC

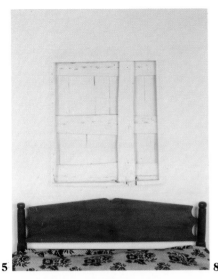

5

6

7

8

9

10

11

12

7 *This small 18thC window in a New York house has a pair of triple-fold shutters. In this upstairs room the normal six-by-six panels have been adapted to three panes over six.* MJ

8 *Houses evolve over the centuries and thus may show a variety of window styles. Early 19thC shutters blend well with 17thC features on this New York house.* BH

9 *Triple-fold shutters in this dining room of a New York mansion built in 1765 are paneled only on the section which is seen when they are housed in the reveal. The color of the woodwork is correct for the Federal Period and exactly the same paint formula was used; hence the streaked effect. The wallpaper is a reproduction of one of the era.* MJ

10 *The narrow proportions of this 1860s floor-to-ceiling sash window in a New York house are changed dramatically when the adjustable shutters are open – the width is doubled.* WW

11 *This house was built in 1929-30 – a replica of a mid-18thC one; the aim of the architect was to represent the best of Colonial architecture between Maine and Charleston, South Carolina. For instance, this Palladian window in the ballroom was copied from a New England mansion.* HH

12 *The New York mansion featured in picture 9 also shows the influence of later tastes. The hall was designed in American Empire style c.1800 and you will notice that the tall narrow windows with their plain bi-fold shutters are a foil for the rather flamboyant decoration.* MJ

1,2 It is important to have the correct accessories. The silvered glass and pewter tieback and the Empire style brass knob are both suitable for the windows and curtain treatments in this 1830's house. BP

3 These parlor windows have Victorian curtains and rods from 1867; the mirror too is Victorian. To gain the full effect it is important to study the whole "look": curtains in particular can give an 18thC or Victorian feel. OMH

4 The "Volunteer" chintz by Tissunique Ltd hanging in the Brown Study at Castletown House, Celbridge, County Kildare. It is an exact reproduction of an 18thC Irish chintz showing the review of the Irish Volunteers, Phoenix Park, Dublin, in 1782. T

1

2

3

4

5

5 *A fairly elaborate example of the Greek Revival style, this window has a carved pediment over the top and Corinthian columns on either side. The draperies are a copy of originals of 1826.* BP

6 *This is an excellent example of curtaining a Victorian bay. The machine-made lace inner curtains are absolutely in period.* LSH

7, 8, 9 *It is important to drape period windows in an appropriate style. Many firms produce copies of historic designs which blend well with a period room. These are some oustanding examples.*

O & L, O & L, O & L, C & F

Sash windows

The lower rail of sash windows may have rotted if rainwater has been trapped around it. It can be professionally repaired by "scarfing" in new wood after the rotten wood has been cut out. The new wood should be well primed before you repaint the frame.

It is a fairly simple job to replace a broken sash cord yourself. However, if the glass is heavy, two people working together will cope better. Upstairs windows should not be tackled by the inexperienced.

1 *Remove the guard beads.* **2** *With the lower sash raised, cut through the unbroken cords at the pulleys.* **3** *Remove the lower window.* **4** *Take off the parting beads.* **5** *Push up the upper window and cut through the unbroken cords.* **6** *Remove the upper window.* **7** *Take out the cover of the weight boxes in the boxed frame (at bottom of sides). (To make this easier, remove old paint with chemical paint stripper.)* **8** *Note how the old cords are tied to the weights. Replace them with new cords cut to the same length: thread the cords through the pulleys and allow to drop down the hollow inside of the frame. Tie to the weights at the bottom. Fix the other ends of the cords to the grooves in the sides of the sash, by nailing.* **9** *Replace the weight box covers and reassemble the window by following instructions 1-6 in reverse order.*

The basement or first floor can be one of the most vulnerable parts of the house. Although most materials used for floors are hardwearing, they may still have suffered from damp and rot. Many have been concreted, or adulterated by stick-on tiles which destroy the atmosphere and authenticity of the room. Irrespective of the type of floor or the cause of its deterioration, careful consideration should be given to replacement. A simple regime of maintenance should then make your floor last for centuries more.

TIMBER FLOORS

These were first used for upper rooms as lofty houses were divided by the insertion of a ceiling. Sometimes they even served as ceiling, floor and ceiling beams in one; alternate boards were extra thick, giving them the strength of beams, and the thinner boards in between rested in angular grooves cut along the length of the thicker ones. The underside of the floor was whitewashed to make a light ceiling downstairs.

Although oak is by English tradition the finest building timber, elm has often been preferred for floorboards since their earliest use, and with good reason. Old elm floors, in cottages as well as larger houses, have developed a beautiful color and sheen and have a hardness and grain which even oak cannot match.

Early boards were of course sawn by hand, and this was done with a carefree disregard for standardization. As a result the generous boards of older floors, all at least a foot (30cm) wide, are often of different widths and depths, with the supporting ceiling beams packed out as necessary to make the boards lie evenly.

As early as the 17th century, imported firs (referred to in England as *deal* when imported in ready-cut planks) came into use as a cheap and ready

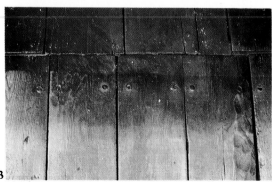

1 *These yew floorboards are new replacements in a late 18thC house. It is well worth considering bleached boards when replacing a floor, particularly in a basement or kitchen area.* RC

2 *A floor with 16thC wooden floorboards. These were covered with oil cloth in the later 19thC and hence do not have the deep color of wood floors polished in the Victorian taste.*

3 *17thC boards with wooden pegs are more regular and even than those of a century earlier. It is a pity to cover period boards but leaving them exposed causes problems in itself: the floors are frequently uneven, and stiletto heels inflict permanent damage.*

4 *There is some hesitancy about leaving boards bleached when combining them with period mahogany furniture. However, this 18thC house in Bath, south-west England, shows this can produce pleasing results.* RC

5 *The deep, glorious color of these oak boards is totally unoriginal. An American visitor to England in 1772 commented that the floors were "washed and rubbed almost daily" and "have a whitish appearance". This pallor did not appeal to the Victorians, who polished the boards.*

6 *It is possible to buy salvaged floorboards. This early 19thC French oak flooring has good color and patination.* LAS

alternative to solid oak or elm. Red fir was reckoned to be almost equal in quality to oak and less subject to woodworm than white fir. Good hardwood boards have often survived intact. In America, softwoods such as pine or fir were used from the earliest times, as well as native woods such as chestnut and cypress

In Stuart England the nobility had their floors inlaid with woods in different colors, a treatment known as parquetage. By the early 18th century, wooden block floors were being introduced into all the best houses of the gentry, but at the same time boards had become the norm for most floors.

Floorboards which had not usually been fixed, and like casements and locks, could be removed if the house was vacated, were now fixed to the ceiling beams and the boards themselves began to be narrower. Perhaps partly because of the increasing development of a basement level, first floors, which had rarely been boarded at the beginning of the 17th century, were now also made of wood.

7

8 Parquetage had been used in the grandest houses from the Stuart period; it lost popularity but was reintroduced in the 19thC. The Victorian use of parquet flooring gave an interesting new look to wooden floors; it often replaced the plain oak boards and was covered in places by Persian carpets.

9 To polish wooden floors, use a dry polish and polisher – a cloth impregnated with kerosene and malt vinegar gets rid of dust while leaving the boards shiny.

10 In this late 19thC American house, the boards are totally regular due to mass production. If the color of the boards offends or the dust becomes unbearable they can be sealed. Try a test area first – seals seep into the boards and too often give a very yellow color.

11 For the purist these Victorian pine floorboards give an authentic look to a 19thC floor. LAS

8

10

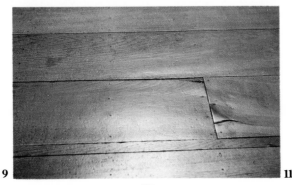

9

11

DECORATION AND COVERINGS

Until the 17th century, wooden floors were strewn with rushes for warmth and to keep down the dust. Sometimes instead of boards, lathes or rushes were laid to make the floor itself and smoothly coated with lime or gypsum plaster. Mats of rush or straw became more usual in the 16th century either on their own or as underlay for rare imported carpets. In the 17th century carpets began to be introduced more widely, especially in London; but they were generally used as hangings or table covers and it was not until at least a hundred years later that they would become at all common for floors. Prosperous settlers brought them to America.

Throughout the 18th century, floor coverings other than rush, straw or grass mats were still unusual, but paler, knotted deal boards were painted to darken them and hide their imperfections. Later in the century, although the fashionable new houses were often carpeted, even when their floors were of good quality pine or oak, other fashions were developing. Floor coloring and patterning and the use of patterned, oiled floor cloths were much more common than carpets going into the 19th century.

To make plaster floors suitable for elegant houses pigments were added to plaster of Paris, and different parts of England had long had local ways of coloring and patterning solid floors. Painted floors were an extension of this tradition and became very popular. With the application of stenciled patterns as well as plain colored floors, the simple technique developed in North America into a fine craft which is enjoying a revival today.

In America, as in England, patterned cloths were used to hide the imperfections of a floor. When placed under the table they made cleaning easier, and their geometric patterns in strong colors provided a decorative alternative to woven mats before cheap domestically-manufactured carpets became available.

THE 19TH CENTURY

More carpets were to be found in the 19th century, but floor painting survived in plain-painted and glazed floors, and in the borders around the carpet, which were often painted in the same color as the rest of the room's woodwork. Oil cloths were also still used, on their own or to provide a frame to a central carpet; these were floral-patterned, with designs more and more like Turkish carpets, or any other covetable carpet pattern. They developed a *trompe l'oeil* quality for, like the linoleum flooring and modern vinyls of which they were ancestors, they were patterned to look like natural materials – stone, marble or wood, knots and all.

By the middle of the 19th century carpets were common in the main rooms of even small houses, and linoleum replaced oil cloths at the end of the century. Floor boards, still about an inch (2.5cm) thick, were only about four inches wide (10cm) in better houses, though up to nine inches (23cm) wide in poorer quality dwellings. Tongued and grooved boards, which had been introduced in the 1820s, were increasingly machine-prepared and hence of even width. The timber used was well seasoned and will not usually have shrunk.

1 *Floor cloths were a practical 19thC solution to floor covering, especially in entrance halls. Either domestically made or commercially manufactured, they were usually of canvas covered with many layers of paint and varnish, and were the forerunners of modern linoleum. This example, with a marbled pattern and a border adapted from a design in timber, is an exact copy, painted onto linoleum, of a design that might have been used originally in this New York mansion of 1840.* BP

2 *This floor covering from this mid-19thC house in Lancaster, Pennsylvania, is laid throughout first-floor front and rear halls. It is stencilled in a geometric pattern to imitate tiles. The backing is made of cork, the surface is oil cloth. This was a popular method of floor covering in both America and Britain at this time* JBF

3,4 *This late 19thC linoleum border interestingly mimics the key pattern chair rail.* LSH

5 *This bleached beech tongue-and-groove flooring is a good modern solution to the challenge of replacing a period floor.*

6, 7, 8 *In parallel with the current interest in polished floorboards, stenciled floors are now very popular, and can be found in many colors and designs.* LG

9 *This staircase is carpeted in "Higford", a design based on an early 19thC pattern and seen here in its original coloring, in an American house.* C & F

6

7

8

9

PROBLEMS AND SOLUTIONS

Timber had become standard for first floors during the 19th century, though it was not until 1860 that such floors were required by law to have an air space beneath them. From 1900, air bricks were also provided in order to keep the air circulating, but neglect together with dislike of drafts have meant that this ventilation has often been stopped and the timber floors may well now be rotten as a result. To prevent deterioration of floor boards at ground level it is important to restore good ventilation by clearing away any earth lying against the outside walls and reopening any blocked air bricks. A few American houses in the South are built in this way, and may have the same problems.

Termites can totally destroy a period floor. They are usually found in softwoods, but certain of the forty different species of the insect common in North America are attracted by the rich cellulose of good timber. They thrive on the inner fibers of the wood. Armies of them may penetrate a floorboard and devour its inner fibers until it is hollow, without leaving a trace of their course on the outer surface. This makes detection, and therefore counterattack, very difficult. Houses in areas known to be prone to termite infestation should be professionally inspected at least twice a year. There are various chemicals on the market with which to attack these destructive pests, once they have been discovered.

Dry rot, detected by its damp smell, as well as signs (such as wood distortion) of the damage it has caused, is a different problem, which often affects poorly ventilated first floors. It must be carefully checked for and dealt with immediately when found. The fungus can spread rapidly through sound timber, plaster and even brickwork causing untreatable decay in any conditions once it has a hold. It is essential to remove and burn every bit of rot-affected timber when renovating an older house.

SOLID FLOORS

From the earliest times and into the 20th century solid floors were widely made of baked, dampened and beaten earth, patched with clay. Superior beaten earth floors could be made by mixing clay with ox blood, which dried to make a hard, smooth and gleaming surface, not unlike the quarry tiles which later replaced them.

During the 17th and early 18th centuries in Britain, the earth floors of prosperous farmers' houses were replaced with brick or kiln-burnt paviors (shaped like bricks but only about an inch and a half (4cm) thick) or square quarry tiles just like those still being manufactured today (measuring roughly nine by nine inches (23×23cm)). These are unglazed, but technically non-porous and therefore practical.

If suitable stone was available locally, huge flags would be laid instead of tiles. The various English marbles: Purbeck, Sussex, Kent and Derbyshire, were

1 A stone floor emulating a type made of Portland stone and marble popular from the 17thC. CP

1

2 Basic stone flags have been a popular floor covering from the 17thC to the 20thC in more modest houses or servants' areas. They are serviceable but care should be taken not to leave the floor wet as salt deposits can damage the surface. These particular huge blue stone slabs can be found in many Bristol houses of the late 18thC.

3 Light colored stone flags are typical of many floors from the 17thC on. They varied according to the availability of local stone and were used extensively in the service areas of larger houses.

4 Warm-colored tiles make a solid floor less utilitarian. They look more inviting still when covered by rugs. FE

2

3

4

used only when the finest materials could be afforded. Many of the freestones were not suitable for flooring; but Bristol houses had blue stone slab floors, and other areas had a suitable local stone for flagging. More fashionable houses reserved both flagging and tiling for pantries or other service rooms. In Devon and South Wales "pitched" floors were made from small pieces of stone cut with wedged backs and laid like street cobble-stones. These were arranged in patterns curiously like those of woven straw mats – a craft which survived into the 19th century. Local slate was successfully used for solid floors in parts of Wales and Cornwall, and this extremely waterproof material was transported to other parts of Britain in the 19th century. American floors were made of slate, local flagstone or brick.

Portland stone was used in big houses from the 17th century, often laid in diamond pattern rather than on the square, and with a small square of black marble at the intersection of the cut-off corners of every four meeting slabs. It was not until late in the 19th century that marble and other polished stones became available to the ordinary householder. Tessellated floors of white and black marble and colored stone then became quite common, especially in entrance halls. From 1900 all sorts of stone, slate and ceramic tiles were used within the house to complement the tiled paths and porches which led in from outside. Marble floors were equally popular in America, where outside paths were generally made of stone slabs or bricks.

CLEANING AND POLISHING

All these floors can be cleaned by scrubbing with water to which a little detergent has been added. When old polish has built up excessively, a cup or more of detergent should be mixed in a pail of water, and the floor should be kept wet with this for half an hour before being scrubbed and rinsed.

Special cleaners for tile, stone and marble are available but, unless badly stained, these floors can easily be kept clean with a mild detergent and water. Marble should be dried with a chamois or soft towel, and stains in it can sometimes be lightened with bleach, although they may reappear in time.

These materials are all relatively maintenance-free, and it is simply a matter of taste whether or not they are polished. Special sealers and polishers are sold for all kinds of hard floors, but generally they look best simply kept clean.

Liquid wax polish, well-buffed, brings life to dulled marble and polished stone but it should be used very sparingly if the floor is not to become dangerously slippery.

1

3

4

2

5

1 *Reproductions of square quarry tiles. Many realistic copies of tiles dating from the 17thC in different parts of Britain and North America are now manufactured.* FE

2 *These original square quarry tiles have been relaid in a refurbished kitchen.* PC

3 *Brick paviors replaced the beaten earth floors in rural areas from the 17thC. These were popular until the late 19thC and are often used as replacements in country kitchens today.*

4,5 *It is possible to buy original tiles to be relaid. The tiles shown here are taken from period houses and châteaux in France prior to their being demolished. These have the advantage of a certain charm due to their age although they would not be strictly correct outside France. However, it should always be borne in mind that throughout history, particularly from the 18thC, the rich have imported period details from Europe to houses in Britain and North America* PC

6

6,7 *This mosaic floor was designed by George Aitchison, architect of Leighton House. It was executed by Italian craftsmen around 1879-80 and although it was probably of local English marble, the floor has proved a problem to restore.*

8 *Mosaic floors of white and black marble and colored stones became very common in entrance halls in the late 19thC.*

9 *Geometric tiles were popular in entrance halls in the late 19thC. These were probably made by Maw of Coalbrookdale. The "welcome" mat is also in period.*

10 *The mid-19thC "encaustic" tiles in the Minton residence in Torquay, Devon, are identical to those supplied by the Minton company to the Capitol, Washington D.C.*

11 *The tiles in the a hall of the Minton residence are a form of early Victorian mosaic pavement. These tiles became increasingly popular during the 19thC especially in hallways and terraces. They added color and interest while primarily being functional.* c

9

10

7

8

11

Bare walls are like giant canvases, and the impulse to decorate them is almost as old as civilization itself. But the origin of most methods of treating internal walls was functional — to make houses less damp and drafty.

The thick stone walls of medieval houses absorbed some water from outside and were hard and cold, encouraging condensation on the inside in winter. To reduce this, and to cut down drafts in the large open halls, the rich hung imported tapestries on walls and across doors. Later, woollen or canvas hangings in imitation of tapestry became increasingly common in houses of all sizes, and these were among the ancestors of modern wallpapers. Paneling was also used to line walls and act as screens. By Tudor times, this was often exquisitely carved in grand houses; in more humble ones it was developed into the built-in furniture that we find so useful in small houses today. By the 17th and 18th centuries simple oak or softwood paneling was common in the houses of the

gentry, and wood was further employed to add the classical detailing so much in vogue at the time.

Plastering walls began in Britain as a method of reducing heat loss or fire risk and strengthening wattle-and-daub walls. Yet color washes of yellow ochres, blues and umbers can be found in plaster layers of early Anglo-Saxon origin. From this basic decorative start there developed the art of stucco and the parget work (see page 82) of Eastern England, culminating in the decorative swags of the Adam brothers in the 18th century.

Narrative scenes, patterns or simple color washes enriched nearly all these wall coverings. The range of pigments and techniques has of course widened greatly and continues to change in line with fashion. Machine-printed rolls of paper brought quick, inexpensive decoration to every householder in the 19th century, and it is probably behind layers of this that you will find the clue to the original scheme for your house.

1 Many companies now produce excellent wallpapers which use designs and colors to blend with a period house. Both 18th and 19thC designs are available. These hand-printed designs use traditional subjects in new ways. MA

2 This wonderful wallscape in a row house of the 1870s has, as a central feature, a bookshelf built into an unused doorway. Note too the use of olive green paint for baseboards, chair rail and architrave. LSH

3 A faithful copy of a mid-18thC ballroom, reconstructed by careful study. HH

4 Decorative ceramic tiles were features of many 19thC or early 20thC houses. Original examples have become expensive, but designers are now producing attractive examples such as this based on old patterns. MR

5 Plaster archways in this 18thC house mirror the design of the cornice. The fake marbling is also in period. RC

6

PANELING

In the 13th century Henry III imported wood from Norway to line the rooms at Windsor Castle, in central England. These boards, unpaneled and unframed, were the first wainscots. They were painted, as were the plain plastered walls of the palaces. They were decorated with paintings of biblical stories, or stenciled (literally "starred") with gold, and whitewashed walls were "pointed" or patterned with a framework containing flowers. By Tudor times the fashion for paneling had spread in areas where timber was available. Oak paneling was used for screens, to line walls and as internal partitions to make more, and smaller, rooms within the large open walls. In these partitions, the narrow paneling boards were attached to vertical studs, which were either split in half and fastened on each side of the boards or grooved to hold them. It was simpler to make narrow grooves, and accordingly the panels themselves were narrowed along their edges, creating the effect of raised surfaces. The middle of such panels would be molded with a rib as if to imitate stonework. The panels would usually also be set into a timber sill at the base and a frieze or molded beam at the top, which gave the effect that was to develop into what is now known as linenfold.

The creation of linenfold, or "wavy woodwork" as it was called, had developed into a fine art by the early 16th century. Rectangular panels had fluted ribs placed close together, with realistic open folds at the tops, which were punched and carved to look like a needlework border. Sometimes the flowing ribs were opened out into honeycomb patterns or twined and interwoven and adorned with carved fruit and flower motifs.

By the middle of the 16th century, a crude Renaissance classicism was taking over, as medallion heads and urns replaced linenfold. Sometimes, geometric patterns with an inner square or rectangle surrounded by "L" shapes of molding echoed those on the two-paneled doors. In the best examples different woods were used instead of painting for pattern, and by the end of the century arcading was sometimes used to

7

8

9

6, 7 These panels of wainscot have had an adventurous history. Carved in the mid-16thC for a chapel in southeast England, they eventually found their way into a late 19thC staircase made to fill the courtyard of a 17thC house. CP

8 A Victorian reproduction of linenfold paneling in the same area of this house is an illustration of how elements from different periods can work together in harmony. CP

9 Detail of a carved pilaster which is part of a careful restoration of a 16thC house in southwest England. SI

separate the various panels, especially on the upper parts of the walls.

Applied pilasters began to appear on paneling in the grand houses of the 17th century. They were like those of the door frames, and were used for a similar reason – to provide an architrave which elegantly concealed the joint between the stiles and the panels set into them. This device became prevalent in the big houses; like other classical borrowings it was often applied in a cheerfully unscholarly way, but sometimes the effect was very pleasing, with divisions in the length of the columns matching the divisions in the paneling itself. Applied pilasters – and columns – continued to be used in grand houses as classical architecture became a stricter discipline in the 18th century. As paneling went out of fashion, pilaster strips and columns were applied to punctuate the wall surface or emphasize the window positions and give a flowing look to long rooms, as well as to divide the shelves in libraries.

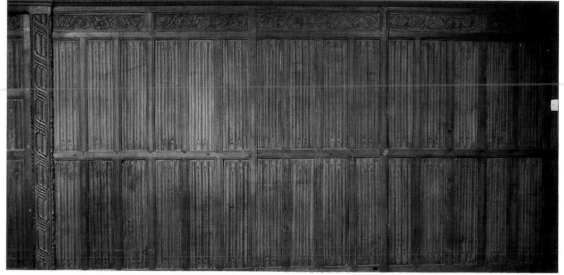

2

3

4

1

1, 2, 3, 4 Before decorative interior wall finishes became widely popular, it was not unusual for the boards that made up the fabric of the house to form the interior surface as well. VNS

5 Salvaged Tudor linenfold paneling with decorative pilasters and frieze has here been installed to create an authentic 16thC interior. C of SI.

5

6

8

10

7

9

6, 7, 8 *Simple paneling with recess-framed squares or rectangles was popular in the 16th and 17thC and is a particularly appropriate choice when restoring a country manor house. Such paneling is still made today using 17thC methods.* AS

9 *This room in a 17thC manor in the south of England had been robbed of all of its original features over the centuries, but recently it was completely restored — fireplace, paneling and ornate overmantel are all new but faithful 17thC reproductions.* SI

10 *This paneling was put into a 17thC New York house about a hundred years after it was built, demonstrating how succeeding generations have always "improved" on their old houses. From the mid-17thC it was the fashion to paint not only softwood paneling, but also oak. So, if you have painted paneling in your house, do not feel you necessarily have to strip it.* BH

1, 2 *The original paneling of this room of 1720 has been repainted in the style of the period, with marbled panels and authentic colors. At that period, paint for wood had a slightly glossy finish — oils, waxes or milk were included in the recipe to achieve this effect.* SI

3 *Water-based paint with a streaked effect gives the correct period flavor to this 18thC room.* RC

4 *A mid-18thC paneled room, rescued complete from a house that was being demolished and reinstated in another house of the period.* C of SI.

5 *An interior of the same period that has undergone the same happy fate. This time the paneling is waxed pine. The room has a dentil cornice and door frame and a mantelpiece carved with masks flanked by drapery swags.* C of SI.

6

7

8

9

10

6 *Simple but elegant painted paneling is featured in a house built in the Bronx in the second half of the 18thC. The coloring is authentic.* VC

7 *An elegantly carved pediment over this door is set off by fairly plain paneling and cornice. The room is a copy of a 1760s interior. The pine paneling, unpainted in the original, has mellowed to a marvelous honey.*

8 *A late 19thC answer to the problem of concealing the heating system. This cast-iron grille conceals a hot air duct. It neatly fills one whole panel, its formal decoration complementing the chestnut and walnut.*

9, 10 *Paneled rooms of the 18thC often featured ornate carving in the form of swags, fruit, leaves and classical motifs. These are by a follower of William Kent.* C of SL

EARLY BUILT-IN FURNITURE

Wooden partitions and straightforward boarded or rectangular-paneled wainscoting were used increasingly in modest British houses from the beginning of the Tudor period. From such features, the first built-in furniture developed. Lack of space meant that living rooms had to double as bedrooms. In the 16th century, many two-roomed dwellings consisted of two bed-sitting rooms, with the beds neatly boxed into an alcove and hidden by a curtain during the day – a tradition strong in Scotland.

During the 17th century this development was refined, with beds hidden completely behind wainscot-like paneling by sliding doors across the opening. Similarly, a built-in bench might run along the paneling, with the paneling itself acting as a settle back, perhaps decorated with a painted pattern, perhaps folding down to form a bed. Examples of this built-in furniture survive throughout England, in Brittany and in parts of America first settled by the Dutch.

In rural buildings, where change was slow, the wooden partition dividing the rooms from the hallway often contained seating or cupboards on the room side. Beside the fire, a built-in spice cupboard was worked in similar style, and sometimes a much larger cupboard was to be found in the same position. These handsome features, rather than filtering down from higher up the social scale, developed out of necessity and are rare examples of features which then ascended the social ladder. From early in the 18th century, the alcoves produced on either side of the fire by the chimney breast were put to use as cupboards in the new townhouses, in England and in North America, with paneled and well-proportioned doors and frames — the modern instinct to build cupboards or shelves in this position has a long history. Fireside alcoves were also adapted into niches, sometimes with covered tops of modeled plasterwork, in imitation of styles in grander houses.

1

1 Building furniture – particularly closets – into a period house can all too easily spoil the period feel. It can be done, but the style must be chosen carefully. This wall of cupboards, drawers and glazed display cabinets, for example, would work well in a well-proportioned 18th or early 19thC bedroom. S

2 A Neo-classical room with finely molded cornice and walls painted in one of the light shades favored by the brothers Adam. GH

3 A cleverly faked and antiqued library in an 18thC building. The cornice (an elaborate reproduction) and also the bookcases were painted in two shades of green, which gives the wood a look of age. CP

2

3

4 *This paneled hall and staircase are a 19thC addition to an earlier house. This is a good example of the Victorians' habit of imposing their own taste on a building with little regard for its original character. However, it is here done with such confidence that somehow it works!* CP

5, **6** *A restored turn-of-the-century room with mahogany paneling and doors and Art Nouveau-style marquetry panels. Fortunately, there are still craftsmen able to carry out this type of work.* RDL

7, **8** *Built-in furniture is by no means a recent invention. This built-in chest-of-drawers (**7**) and sideboard (**8**) in an 18thC English house look quite surprisingly modern.* GH

Plaster

The plasterer's art developed along with the use of timber. Stucco or molded plasterwork was much used in Palladian and Neo-classical houses of the 18th century, but it had first been used some 200 years earlier in Henry VIII's palace of Nonesuch in southern England. It appeared in friezework and panels in many of the great 16th-century houses, modeled into stylized scenes, with countryside, forests, beasts and huntsmen, or scenes from mythology, and often painted.

Modeled stucco was a European, especially Italian tradition, but in the late 16th and early 17th centuries a native style developed in England. This was known as parget work. It was executed in the plaster mix of lime, sand, animal hair and dung with which the walls were usually lined. Parget work is particularly associated with eastern England, though by no means confined to that area, and is found on both internal and external walls for friezes, overmantels and gable ends. The craft died out at the end of the 19th century as it became difficult to obtain plaster of the right quality.

This plaster was so strong that much parget work has survived. Its formal patterns are still familiar to us today, with their herringbone, basket weave, combed

2 *This 18thC room had several "layers" of restoration. It was refurbished during the later 19thC, and recently the two doors were added. When creating new doorways, make sure that they balance with the existing architecture. Here the proportions of the doors are correct and their symmetrical positioning within the arch is in harmony with the room.* CP

3 *A niche in a Neo-classical interior may be painted a darker shade of the wall colour to give it more definition and set off objects placed against it. The choice of a marble pillar and bust is correct for the period.* BP

4 *Around the turn of the century there was something of a classical revival in both architectural detail and wall colouring. Creams, pinks and pale greens and grays are good choices for such interiors.*

1 *The wallpaper border in this American house shows clearly the way in which Empire decoration has been overlaid on earlier, Federal period architecture.* MJ

waves and charming and naive figures.

Hand-modeled plasterwork was originally applied to ceilings, cornices and friezes. It was the Palladian architects who, abandoning the use of paneling, introduced wall plasterwork and plaster wall panels based on French patterns. Examples of such plaster modeling, with scenes from mythology set within panels of plaster architrave, with pediments and swags, can be seen in the houses built in Bath, western England from 1727.

Later in the century the Adam brothers used plaster ornament widely for inside walls. Despite its classical appearance, their graceful decorative work was something of an innovation. They used a mixture containing gypsum or fiber and glue, the exact composition of which is not known. Instead of being modeled *in situ*, it was pressed when hot into metal molds. The Adams painted their groundwork in light tints of pink, green or blue, and sometimes the ornament itself was painted. The mass-produced moldings of the 19th century were merely a development of this approach.

Elegant American houses of this period followed the English style. Their beautiful plasterwork was produced locally or by English workmen brought over for the purpose.

5

6

7

8

5, 6 A good alternative to painting the walls to resemble marble, woodgrain and so on is to use one of the many paint-effect wallpapers currently on the market. Here such papers have been successfully used in a grand 18thC interior. The plaster columns followed the classical tradition of the early 19thC.　　CP

7, 8 The Victorians were great travelers and collectors. Lord Leighton, who lived in this grand English house, traveled extensively in the Middle East and his wanderings greatly influenced the decoration. The columns in this case are marble. The screen was brought back from Damascus, and the room is hung with brocaded silk creating an opulent Arabian mood.　　LH

PAINT AND PAPER

The most frequently used hand-mixed paints, for over six hundred years, were simple whitewash; color washes with pigments added to the whitewash to give ochre yellow or red, blues and greens; or limewash, which had slaked lime as a main constituent and seems to have had disinfectant qualities. A more glossy finish came from paints which contained a proportion of oils, waxes, or even milk; these were the ancestors of today's paints. They were used for wainscots and indoor woodwork from the mid-17th century, and we now know that all but the finest timbers were painted – our taste for stripped pine would have seemed very odd to our ancestors.

With the increasing variety of paint pigments available during the late 1600s, it became fashionable to completely hide the timber used for paneling by covering it with cloth, paper, or even leather. At the same time silks and papers were used to decorate plastered walls in expensive interiors, backed with linen and mounted on wooden frames that were nailed to the walls. Small pieces of patterned paper, publishers' rejects, had also been made available since the 15th century in an enterprising waste-not, want-not spirit and were glued by artistic householders to the insides of cupboards and chests.

As printing developed, printed wallpapers were produced to replace more expensive cloth hangings.

But even wallpaper was quite a luxury. It was made by hand from shredded cloth, and as part of the manufacturing process involved draining it in flat sieves, it was available only in quite small pieces, based on the dimensions of the sieves. Nevertheless, it was common enough to be taxed from 1694.

Elizabethan wallpapers were patterned and colored with stenciling or hand-painted designs, often to match the plasterwork of the time. Tiny flowers on bright backgrounds were popular in the 16th and 17th centuries, and well into the 18th century in America. By the end of the period brocades were imitated, and flocked papers replaced real hangings.

Increased Eastern trade late in the 17th century meant that luxurious papers could be imported from China. These came in large pieces decorated with scenes of flowers, birds, villages, mountains and clouds and were popular in the stylish Palladian houses of the 1700s. Towards the end of the 18th century, plasterwork was again imitated with delicate Neo-classical prints, while Georgian townhouses had another treatment for walls in which water-based paint backgrounds were "distressed" or "scumbled" with oil paints to produce the effect of marbling or graining.

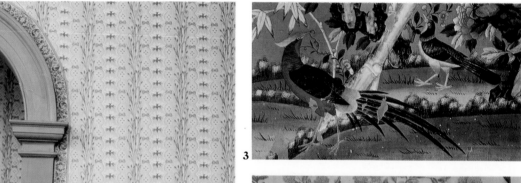

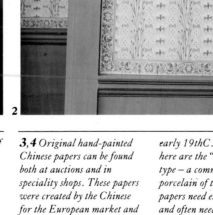

1,2 These are two examples of 20thC reconstructions of 18thC wallpaper taken from fragments discovered on the walls. These paper borders were a fairly common device in American houses redecorated in the Empire taste. MJ

3,4 Original hand-painted Chinese papers can be found both at auctions and in speciality shops. These papers were created by the Chinese for the European market and were used in English stately homes during the 18th and early 19thC. Those shown here are the "bird and flower" type – a common design on the porcelain of the period. Such papers need expert hanging and often need some restoration once they are installed. TC

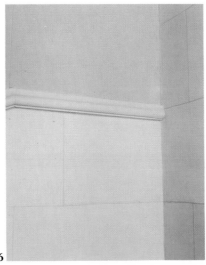

5

6

7

8

9

Simultaneously, cheaper "domino" prints with little geometric designs, of the type often found again today, were produced. Their use was generally restricted to the sitting room and the best bedroom; elsewhere, whitewash or tinted whitewash was still the rule, with stenciling providing any pattern. Stenciling was extremely popular in America from the late 1700s and survived well into the 19th century.

Printing methods improved, and early in the 19th century a method of producing continuous rolls was patented with the result that wallpapers became much more common. Nevertheless plain tinted whitewash continued well into the 20th century in Britain and was given a further lease on life by the restrictions caused by the Second World War.

While other manufacturers were producing cheap substitutes for stone and wood, and casting molded plaster by the yard, Victorian wallpaper makers developed imitation paneling and molding in embossed papers which soon completely replaced wall plasterwork. By the end of the 1800s every house had this embossed paper up to the chair rail and machine-printed patterned paper above. Very similar, but much lighter and more pliable embossed papers are available now to give the original look to Victorian houses, although the rich patterns and somber colors of some of

10

11

the printed papers may not be to everyone's decorative taste.

Since the practice of stripping off old wallpaper is a recent one, the layers of old papers can usually still be found in unrestored Victorian and later houses and this will give a clear idea of how the house was decorated. You are most likely to find machine-printed papers, which almost completely ousted hand-blocked prints by the middle of the 19th century. Woodblock printing was kept alive by designers such as William Morris, but their use was restricted to those discerning people who could afford to pay for hand-craftsmanship. These deliberately two-dimensional prints have remained in production for over a hundred years, and are still available. Ironically perhaps, they are more often found in Victorian houses now than when they were first produced.

1 *The decoration in this 18thC mansion, built in the Palladian style, is mainly in the French Empire manner.*

The walls in the bedroom were papered and then finished with a paper border. The color is authentic to the 18thC. MJ

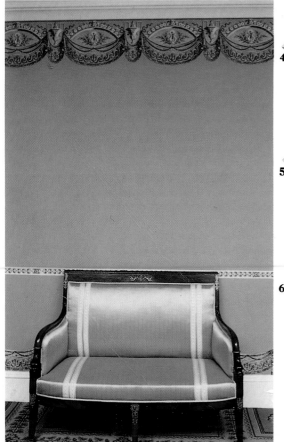

1

2-13 *A range of modern wallpapers based on original designs of the late 18th-early 19thC. The paper shown in picture 12 is derived from motifs chosen by Lady Hertford for the Chinese Room at Temple Newsam, northern England, in the early 19thC. Number 13, though surprisingly modern-looking, is an exact copy of an 18thC paper.*
Z, Z, Z, C&F, Z, Z, Z, C&F, HW, C&F, Z, C&F

17 *This paper is based on one illustrated in a pattern book of c.1840.* HW

18 *Wallpapers with a Chinese inspiration have been popular since the 18thC. This copy is another from the Temple Newsam collection.* Z

19 , 20 *These two copies of early 18thC papers would suit a house from that period through to the early 20thC.* Z

21 *A handprinted frieze by Louis W. Bowen Inc., N.Y., suitable as a replacement for a cornice.* TC

22 *A design by A.W.N. Pugin (1811-1852), rediscovered in 1975. This paper would fit well into Gothic Revival and Arts and Crafts interiors.* Wa

14 *A fine example of an original wallpaper from Robespierre's apartment in the rue St Honoré, Paris, dating from 1793.* T

15 *This wallpaper is an accurate reproduction of a fragment found in a house in Bloomsbury Square, London, dating from c.1810.* HW

16 *A pomegranate design taken from a mid-18thC wallpaper found at Temple Newsam.* Z

1 *The Victorians had no hesitation about mixing pattern and surface decoration in their interiors. This late 19thC artist's house exemplifies how well such mixes can work. The whole interior is beautifully integrated.* LSH

2 *This wallpaper in the same house was made in Japan by an English firm, Rothman and Co. It is embossed and gilded to look like leather and was so expensive that it was used very sparingly: there is none behind the pictures or the Florentine mirrors!* LSH

3 *The dark color under the chair rail and the darker baseboard all add to the enclosed feel of this Victorian interior.* LSH

4,5 *These embossed papers are based on Art Nouveau and Edwardian originals.* C

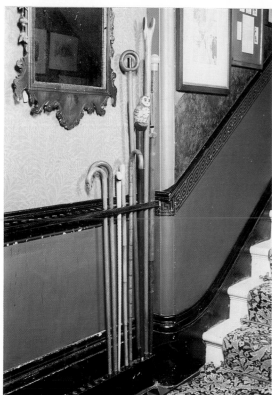

6

7

8

9

10

6 Murals, frieze pantings and trompe l'oeil *can be effectively introduced into most period houses. The decorative style of* trompe l'oeil *works best in 18th and 19thC houses.*   CB

7 *Figure painting was of special interest in the 18thC. It works well in period houses, but you should select the artist carefully. Ask to see photos of previous work before coming to a decision.*   TP

8, **9** *The range of possibilities for* trompe l'oeil *is extensive. Vistas, windows and furniture are popular themes.*   TP

10 *Stenciling is an effective wall decoration and can be used in most period houses so long as the general feel of the room is taken into account. It has always been popular in America and has recently come into vogue in Britain.*

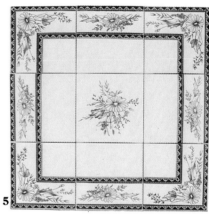

1 *These wonderful 15th and 16thC Persian tiles were brought back by a Victorian collector and now decorate a late 19thC London house.* LH

2,3 *These allegorical tiles are based on a traditional 17thC design and made by the traditional method. This gives them the slight imperfections which blend with period settings.* PC

4 *Hand-painted tiles like these Spanish examples can be used as a panel or a border.* PC

5 *Blue and white is such a classic tile coloration that modern designs still retain a period feel.* BCS

6 *Hand-painted tiles made by traditional methods may be more expensive but successfully recreate the Dutch Delft originals. These tiles were designed by ceramic artist Doug Wilson.* PC

8

7,8 *Tiles can also create a* trompe l'oeil *effect and can give the impression of a niche in a wall. Geometric patterns and flowers are classic motifs here used in an innovative and interesting way.* SR

9 *By the end of the 19thC tiles were produced in strong colors. This modern tile has a similar inspiration and could be used successfully in 19thC as well as 20thC homes.* MR

10 *Vases of flowers with simple borders have been used on tiles since the 18thC. These hand-painted tiles in strong colors provide excellent panels.* SR

11 *This blue and white panel successfully uses themes popular on tiles from the 18thC. As many original panels have been damaged, such hand-painted modern tiles are a useful alternative.* SR

12 *Tiles can also be used on exteriors and these highly glazed ochre, brown and deep blue tiles form an interesting archway to a late 19thClearly 20thC facade.* S of D

13 *As original 18thC Delft tiles become more expensive and difficult to find, replacements using sketchy designs can be found from manufacturers specializing in modern reproductions.* FE

9

10

11

12

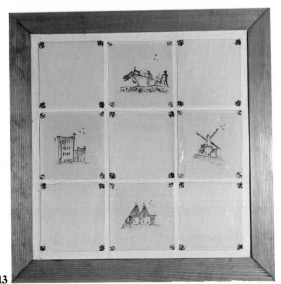

13

1 *Prints interestingly placed on a staircase wall will lead the eye upward. The plain walls in this example of a late 19thC hallway are brought to life by the prints in maple frames, some original and some reproduction.*

2,3,4 *These exuberant examples of Victorian wallscapes show great confidence in mixing dark colors, wallpapers, prints, mirrors and Chinese porcelain. The owner of this house was a noted cartoonist and obviously had a special interest in drawings, paintings, prints and photographs. But the general effect can be recreated by similar handling of masses of mostly monochromatic pictures. Used singly on such busy backgrounds the pictures would have been lost; but grouping them to almost cover the walls gives them unity and importance. In picture 3 it is interesting to note the combination of oil paintings, Japanese prints, silhouettes, mirrors and medallions.   LSH*

5 *Simply framed photographs (mainly of the house's owner) cover a bathroom wall. Again the whole effect is gained by the sheer quantity of pictures decorating most of the wall area.   LSH*

1

2

3

4

5

1

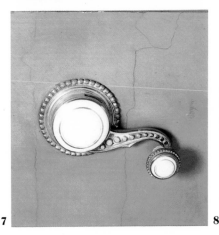

2

3

4

5

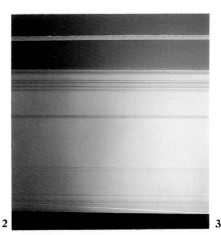

6

7

8

9

CHAIR RAILS

Chair rails (which in Britain are known as dado rails) complemented baseboards. Again they are a reminder of earlier wall treatments, being placed at the height of the middle rail in paneling. Visually pleasing but also practical, chair rails protected the wall where chairs were most likely to scrape.

Often the chair rail was inversely related in outline to the baseboard; the greatest projection was at the upper part of the rail, whereas on baseboards it was nearest the floor. In the later 19th century, chair rails are found less frequently, except in entrance halls and on stairways, and moldings became simpler.

When walls are being replastered to tackle damp, it is well worth keeping a record of the exact position and profile of the original baseboards and chair rails, as even in the simplest houses these were often sensitively proportioned and deserve to be carefully replaced. Where the baseboards and rails are in plaster and you cannot match the moldings in wood, make new ones from a mold taken from the originals: they will then blend in perfectly.

1 In the very grandest rooms in 18thC houses, walls might be covered in fine fabrics such as silk damask. Here the joints have been covered in gilded beading which serves also to define the lines of the room. There are many companies today specializing in putting fabric on walls and advising on appropriate types to use. Braid would be an apt substitute for the beading. Note the deep molding on this chair rail which reflects the deep baseboard below. RC

2 An 18thC house can have walls simply painted in a suitable color. Here, blue walls are set off by paneling and moldings in white. The chair rail is part of the paneling – a common feature at this time. RC

3 From the 17thC small geometric wallpaper designs were being used in the houses of the gentry. This paper in the bedroom of a restored 18thC house is a copy of one of the period manufactured in northern England. Wallpaper designs in country regions lagged dramatically behind those in capital cities. Laura Ashley's early mini-prints were based on fragments of wallpaper found in a 19thC cottage in Wales. As these would have been up to a hundred years out-of-date by London standards, her designs fit well into 18thC as well as 19thC interiors. The paper is given a more authentic look in this well-researched Georgian house by the plain color from chair rail to baseboard. RC

4 This late 18thC room has paper of a much later period, but the design successfully picks up the detail from the paneling, giving the room the correct feel. The chair rail here is quite elaborate with the central motif picked out in gilding. GH

5 If you cannot afford to line the walls of your 18thC drawing room with fabric, a paper which simulates a fine fabric (such as moire) is a helpful possibility. CP

6 Strong colors can work in well-proportioned period rooms – provided that they are based on authentic colors of the period. The secret is to use them with conviction. CP

7,8,9 These three examples show the interesting variety in bell pulls. The Georgians often used sashes or decorative brass pulls. The Victorians also used these but added china pulls decorated with gilding or painted with flowers. An interesting feature of picture 8 is the revival of the classical key pattern frieze under the chair rail. Most homeowners today do not need bells to summon up legions of servants. However, if you are lucky enough to find pulls intact in your house, leave them in as a novel period feature. LSH

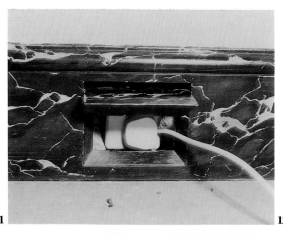

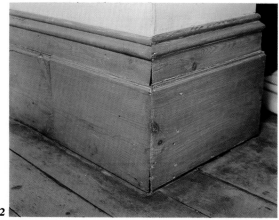

10

11

12

13

14

15

Paneling: THE NAMING OF PARTS

By the mid-17th century a pattern based on classical proportioning had been developed for the wainscot. A base, or *sill*, had a panel above it known as the *lying panel*. This was attached at the top into the *middle rail*, *chair rail* or *dado rail*. The second level of paneling, known as the *large panel*, was attached at the bottom to the middle rail and at the top to the *frieze rail*, above which ran a further panel, the *frieze panel*. In higher rooms the frieze panel would be surmounted by an upper rail and cornice, and extra rails would be placed above the base and above and below the middle rail. The diagram, which shows the typical arrangement for higher rooms, would make a suitable model from which to plan reconstruction work for wainscoting in 18th- or 19th-century houses.

Diagram labels (top to bottom): Cornice / Upper rail / Frieze panel / Frieze rail / Stiles / Large panel / Middle rail / Chair rail or dado / Lower frieze rail / Lying panel / Lower rail / Base from which skirting board derived

10, *11* These marbled baseboards in an 18thC house in Bath in southwest England have been skillfully adapted to conceal the electric receptacles essential to 20thC life.   RC

12, *13*, *14* Stripping woodwork of its painted surface is very much a modern fashion, but one which often works well in a period house. Painted woodwork is correct for most Victorian interiors, but bare wood is fine for an 18thC or early 20thC context, and is certainly easy to live with.

15 Somber colors are typical of the Victorian period, although black woodwork like this can be a little too much to live with!   I.H

BASEBOARDS

The baseboard (or skirting board) was a consequence of the 18th-century preference, in grand houses, for plastered walls rather than paneling. Marble floors had a marble baseboard which protected the wall when the floor was being cleaned. However, 18th-century baseboards were usually made of wood. Plaster was frequently found in 19th-century houses.

A reminder of the sill of old paneling, these deep skirtings were molded and often intricately carved – in keeping with the architraves around windows and doors and with the shutters of the room. Palladian houses have rich but restrained and subtly varied carving: the "egg-and-dart" type of molding was especially popular. Deep but simply molded baseboards are characteristic of Victorian and early 20th-century houses, becoming shallower and more austere as the 20th century wore on.

When houses were chiefly of one high open space the only ceiling was the inside of the roof. In England, timber-framed houses were usually thatched and the underside of the thatch, increasingly blackened by soot, was all that could be seen from the room below. In early America, the underside of hand-split shingles was similarly visible.

The introduction of an upper floor naturally created a ceiling in the lower room. At first the term "ceiling", or "sealing", referred to the paneling which lined or sealed the walls of a room.

However, when the underside of upper floors came to be treated in the same way, the word came to acquire its current usage.

As with so many architectural elements, the earliest methods of treating the undersides of floors survived in vernacular buildings long after they had been superseded elsewhere. This was especially true of the very spare early American houses. Thatch roofs were often sealed on both sides with lime plaster, partly to reduce fire risk and partly to make them longer-lasting and even warmer. Sometimes upper floors were simply plastered rushes laid between the narrowly spaced ceiling beams. Wooden floorboards laid over the beams were often sealed on the underside with plaster too, for

1 Many original beamed ceilings were painted, and any traces of this should be preserved. Complete restorations should follow appropriate period colors. In this example red, cream, blue and gilding give the room a mellow "aged" feel.

insulation and cleanliness, leaving the beams exposed. Ceilings like this continued to be made in country houses for hundreds of years and still look right today.

The bare undersides of floorboards made a simpler ceiling still. However, if the original wide floorboards have been replaced with narrower boards of less quality, the visual impact may be inferior, and it will be preferable to apply a coat of plaster between the ceiling beams for sound or heat insulation between lower and upper floors. When this was done in the 17th century, the space between the boards and the plaster was filled with straw. The modern version of this is to use lengths of fiber-glass insulation between floorboards and plaster-board panels on the ceiling below.

As vernacular building skills began dying out early in the 20th century, there was a curious fashion for painting ceiling beams black to give an "olde worlde" country look. However, this has no foundation in history. Fine timber in better-quality houses was usually left untreated, but for centuries in British cottages and farmhouses the beams and floorboards have been whitewashed, or painted, to match the walls, or patterned with flowers and leaves. With patience you can remove 20th-century black or colored paint and restore the ceiling woodwork by sanding and treating with paint stripper. Often the dark staining has penetrated the wood, so that planing may be necessary. An alternative is to put white or off-white paint directly over the black to give an acceptable and hard-wearing period effect. Whitewash, which needs to be reapplied more frequently, may be used by the purist restorer.

2 Tudor beams were often painted. Such decoration should be preserved if possible. Restoration should only be undertaken by an expert, as colors have to be carefully matched.

3 Friezes are one of the great joys of the interiors in the English Tudor period. The carving often reached great heights of grotesque ornamentation.

TUDOR ORNAMENT

Timber beams and joists were at first merely functional, but the Tudors saw decorative possibilities in them, giving them champfered corners and moldings similar to those on stone ribs. Very simplified versions appear in early American buildings. Many handsome Tudor ceilings have survived, with oak beams chiselled and gouged into smoothly flowing ribs, like those in the linenfold paneling of the same period. The undersides of beams could be carved with Gothic ornament, and gaps between them further divided by moldings.

The Tudors also became prolific plasterers. Like the wooden ceilings, the plaster ones were at first divided into compartments by molded ribs with plaster bosses or pendants at their intersections, just as in stone vaulting. Gradually, ribs became flatter and developed into the characteristic strapwork, with lozenges and geometric shapes, scrolls and Tudor roses.

Early in the Tudor period wooden friezes were carved and molded to match the heavy beams. Plaster ceilings also were soon accompanied by a modeled plaster frieze. Although coving was sometimes used at the conjunction of wall and ceiling, deep plaster friezes were more often applied at the tops of walls. They had an even greater wealth of decoration than the ceilings

5

7

4

6

8

themselves. There was no real precedent for the frieze, and its ornament developed freely. Dolphins and mermaids were much liked; secular and biblical narratives were told in high relief; scrolls, lozenges, acorns and flowers complemented identical motifs on the ceilings; and landscapes based on Flemish engravings unfolded around the top of the walls. Sometimes the ornament featured personifications of the Virtues or the senses. Such flourishes, naturally restricted to the grander houses, came to an end as purist classical influences were felt, although they were to enjoy a revival some hundred years later.

In lesser houses plastered ceilings also became more ornamental, though less spectacularly so. They spread over the beams themselves, with ornamented panels on the flat infilling and moldings on the beams.

Unplastered ceilings were frequently lined between the beams with tongued-and-grooved boarding, again divided into compartments by strips of molding and sporting carved wooden bosses – when, that is, the owners could afford such embellishment. Plain timber boards were often used for farmhouse and cottage ceilings in succeeding centuries, usually whitewashed or painted and sometimes extending over the beams to form a flat ceiling.

4 Some deterioration has to be expected in beams that have survived 300 years. Parts of beams can be replaced, and this may well be essential with structural beams. If possible, however, you should cut back to good wood and splice into the gaps sections of sound wood. Over-restoration can be counter-productive. CP

5 The 18thC addition to this house saw little improvement in insulation. The ceiling is just the inside of the roof shingles.

6 It has recently been accepted that the natural honey color of oak is in itself a delight and the practice of painting or staining it black is totally unnecessary. If beams have been painted, sanding is the most effective solution. Protect your furnishings adequately against the dust.

7 This 17thC New York State house has a perfect example of a beamed ceiling of the time. The beams were hewn from white oak close to the house and the ceiling is merely the underside of the floorboards above.

8 Taking a ceiling down to expose the beams underneath reveals beams scarred with lathe marks. You can remove these by sanding, although this gives the beams a very new look. Waxing with a clear furniture wax will often create a pleasing effect.

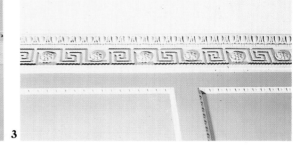

1

2

3

1 Note the fine cotton damask used in the first-floor drawing room of this late 18thC house. This was usually the most richly decorated room, as it was used principally for entertaining. The cornice and frieze are original. RC

2 This pierced cornice is typical of the late 18thC. Such cornices should be vacuumed at least once a year. If the molding is finely carved, clean with a small brush. RC

CLASSICISM

In his work for the English Court in the 1620s and 30s Inigo Jones introduced smoothly plastered and often coved and painted ceilings decorated with moldings and gilded ornament in a much more authentic classical tradition. After 1630 and as a result largely of Jones's influence, plaster dolphins, badges and pendants took over from compact fruit and flowers, ribbons and wreaths, musical instruments and suspended cherubs in many great houses. Perhaps by this time British plasterwork had lost some of its verve but it remained highly decorative in Palladian houses in Britain into the 18th century and in North America up to the 1750s. By the early 19th century, the divided ceilings of the Palladians with their heavily ornamented compartments and elaborate friezes and cornices were thought to be ponderous and ugly. The Adam brothers ridiculed them almost as much as they ridiculed the mid-century vogue for French Rococo ornament.

In Georgian houses right across the scale of wealth, a simpler but still elegant style of plasterwork was in

4

3,4 Two examples of cornices which show the refined classical taste so prevalent in the late 18th and early 19thC. RC

5,6 Classical swags on the frieze were a popular late 18th and early 19thC design. The first example here is a modern reproduction. The second, with a Greek key pattern cornice, is original.

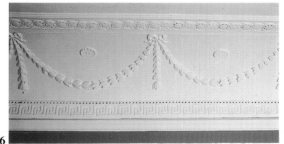

5

6

7

8

15

9

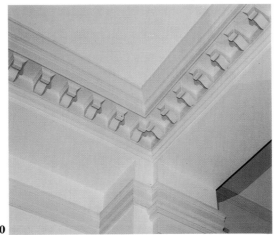

10

11

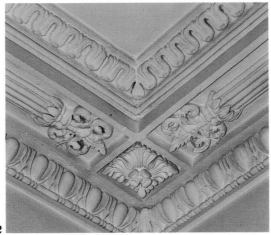

12

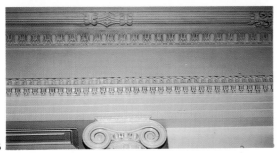

13

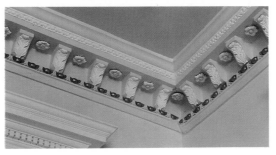

demand, often providing surprising contrasts to the rather plain exteriors of the houses. Workmen crossed the Atlantic to embellish the great houses on the eastern coast of America with the latest styles from England. They taught their techniques to local craftsmen, who imitated and developed them in both grand and modest houses.

The Adam brothers revolutionized all this with their chaste ornament in Grecian or Etruscan style for ceilings, friezes and walls. Adam decoration was spread throughout England and America by means of pattern books. Owners of humbler contemporary houses contented themselves with a straightforward cornice. The very simplest houses either continued in the floorboards-and-joists tradition or, in towns, had plain plastered ceilings and nothing more.

7,8 *Two cornices from a New York house built in 1765. The first picture shows some of the architectural wallpaper fashionable in the Federal period, used extensively in hallways in the 18th and 19thC. The second, in a bedroom, is a plain cornice in the style popular from the 18th to the 20thC.* MJ

9 *Often, plasterwork panels were inserted into beamed areas in an attempt to keep up with the new fashion.* CP

10 *Deep cornices such as this one are often found in high rooms. Owing to years of over-painting, such cornices may sometimes be left with no real detail. The most effective method of cleaning is by hand with a paint stripper. This often loosens pieces of plaster, and instant repairs may be necessary.*

11 *The fashion for white painted ceilings gave more light and started a new trend for a decorative plastered effect.* CP

12,13 *Two views of an elaborate cornice and pillar from the parlor of an early 19thC New York house. The cornice is accentuated by being painted in three tones.* OMH

14 *This early 18thC cornice would have been added during remodeling in 1728. The leaf design is of particular interest: a new mold had to be made for each leaf.* CP

15 *In this reproduction of a mid-18thC American house the cornice decoration is in carved wood.* HH

THE 19TH CENTURY

The *nouveaux riches* of the new century tended to opt for profuse decoration in their houses. Their ceilings were stuccoed and painted with landscapes and mythical scenes. Later in the century the many new houses being built also enjoyed the luxury of decoration. Cornices and friezes were cast in molds, and a sort of *papier mâché* was often used for ornaments, so that despite their elaborateness they were light enough to be screwed into place.

Compared with earlier craftwork, this molded decoration, which remained in favor into the 20th century, certainly owes more to repetition than to inspiration. Nevertheless, acanthus-leaf cornices and heavy central ceiling roses in halls and main rooms of 19th-century houses are very much part of their imitable style. They have often been made ugly by successive coatings of paint which have blurred their relief, and will be much improved with careful cleaning. There are restorers who undertake this work; however, it can done by anyone whose affection for the original is enough to inspire endless patience. A crisp relief will repay the careful work involved.

At the end of the 19th century there was on both sides of the Atlantic a new emphasis on craftsmanship and individualism. Rather than conforming to a predetermined model, each room was treated as a unique problem with its own solution with regard to the size, angle and enrichment of cornice, ceiling bands and other decoration. Flower and leaf ornament and scrolls and loops were sometimes used very expressively in domestic and public buildings. The pattern and depth of relief were scaled to suit the ceiling height. Schemes were determined by the shape of the room and the position of the windows. The acorn was a much-loved motif. Other themes included oak trees, squirrels, daisies and even fairies; sometimes these motifs were colored while the plaster was still comparatively moist.

At the same time new methods of mass-producing plasterwork were being found, using clay models to make jelly (gelatin) molds. Definition was lost in the process, so that castings from such molds were indistinct. Today, however, the jelly mold comes into its own as a way of casting replacements for damaged work to match existing ornament.

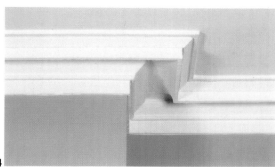

12 Cornices in bedrooms were usually simpler than those in the main rooms of the house. However, this elegant pattern would have been considered suitable for the living room in a lesser early 19thC house.   OMH

8,9,10,11 The 19thC saw a tremendous revival of interest in all things classical. In many houses columns, both Doric and Ionic, suddenly appeared as purely decorative features. They could be wooden, stone or marble.   LH, LH, CP, OMH

In the 19thC the ceiling rose became an essential adjunct of a tastefully decorated room. The size and complexity of the rose was dictated by the room's importance. There are many different types, often needing careful cleaning to show the true magnificence of the plasterwork.

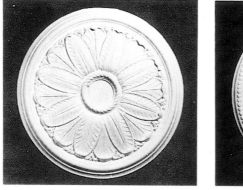

1

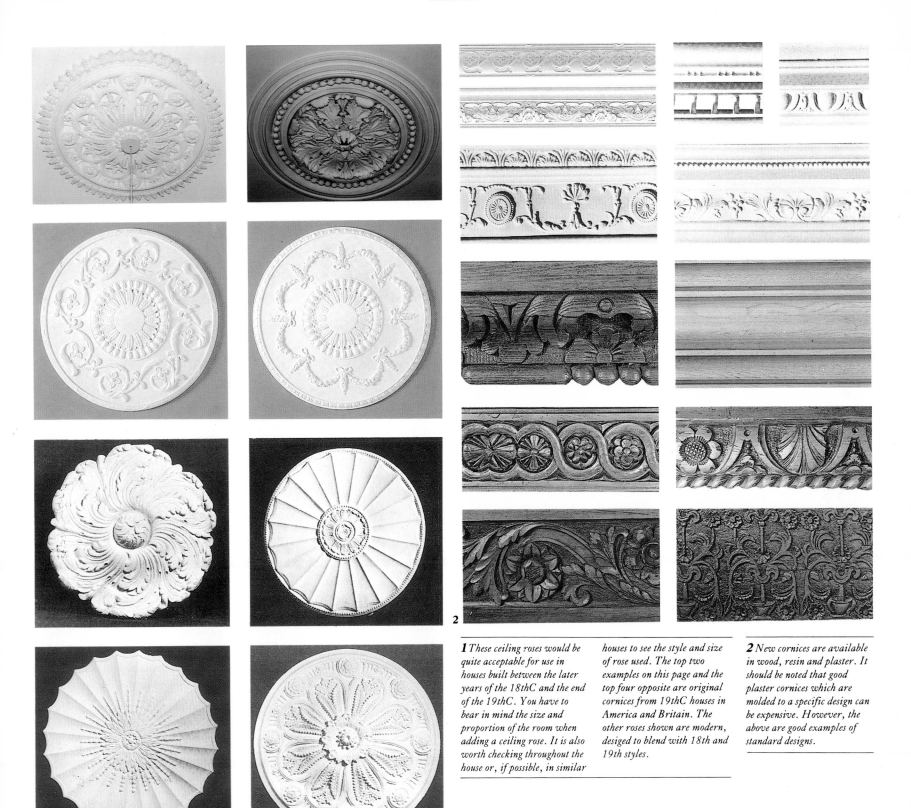

2

1 *These ceiling roses would be quite acceptable for use in houses built between the later years of the 18thC and the end of the 19thC. You have to bear in mind the size and proportion of the room when adding a ceiling rose. It is also worth checking throughout the house or, if possible, in similar houses to see the style and size of rose used. The top two examples on this page and the top four opposite are original cornices from 19thC houses in America and Britain. The other roses shown are modern, desiged to blend with 18th and 19th styles.*

2 *New cornices are available in wood, resin and plaster. It should be noted that good plaster cornices which are molded to a specific design can be expensive. However, the above are good examples of standard designs.*

Cornice cleaning

Old-fashioned tempera paints are water-soluble and can be removed with water. You can use water-soaked rags or sponges to wet the old paint, but this is a messy job and cannot easily be done without also soaking the walls and floor. A steam sprayer (which can be rented), used for stripping wallpaper, does the job with less fuss.

When tempera is thoroughly damp you can scrub it out of crevices with a bottle brush or nail brush – and sometimes you can use a small spoon to gently clean out the hollows. For intricate work, you may need to use wood-carving tools bought from an art shop.

It is not advisable to paint tempera-laden plaster relief work with oil-based paint as a stopgap until you can find time for a proper cleaning job. First, the oil-based paint cannot get a proper "purchase" on top of the flaky tempera; and secondly it will ultimately make the tempera much more difficult to remove.

These views of an early 19thC cornice show a three-stage restoration process. The first shows the uncleaned cornice, with the detail totally obscured by layers of tempera. The second shows the same cornice after hours of painstaking cleaning, using a wood-carving tool. The result is really quite dramatic. The third example was produced by expert plasterers who took a mold from a restored section. Each leaf is made up of two parts, as is each flower; the back of the cornice is produced in lengths.

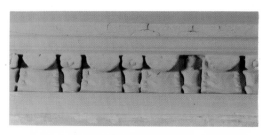

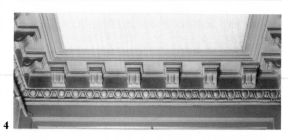

1,2 These friezes in a late 19thC house are reminiscent of earlier designs, in theme if not in execution. Period styles tend to be cyclical.   LH

3 This ceiling offers an excellent example of early embossed wallpaper. The cornice is made of a paper-like material – an early type of mass-produced period detail.   LSH

4 An authentic late Victorian look is achieved by using a period green with details in gold.   LSH

5 This "wedding cake" ceiling was introduced into a drawing room by exuberant 1880s craftsmen.   CP

6,7,8 Modern cornicing, readily available in standard lengths, can be used with reasonable success in period rooms from the end of the 18thC, especially if the rooms themselves are plain. Alternatively, if parts of the original cornice are intact, restoration is possible from a mold (picture 8).

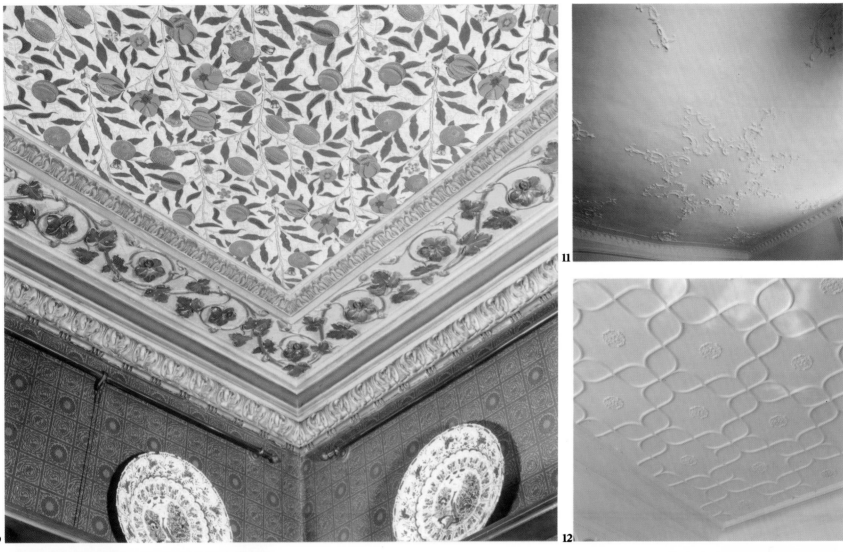

9

10

9,10 As the 19thC progressed, the style changed from light classical to the heavy late Victorian. Wallpaper was often used on the ceiling, and numerous colors and textures added to give the overall impression of exuberance. LSH

11 The late Victorians did, on occasion, emulate 18thC motifs, as in this copy of a Chinese Chippendale style. CP

12,13 By the end of the 19thC, even grand ceilings could be wallpapered to give the impression of plasterwork.

11

12

Early houses often had no stairs at all: the upper floor was reached by a ladder. Stone houses, however, were likely to have one or both of two simple stair types: a flight of stone steps ascending on the outside of the house, or a winding flight set into a wall inside. The former type persisted in regional buildings, especially in northern England and in Scotland, for over five hundred years, and appeared in America during Colonial days. Sometimes it provided access to separate quarters for servants; sometimes, especially on sloping sites, storage rooms were on the ground floor and the steps led to the living quarters above.

WOODEN STAIRS

In Europe, the upstairs rooms that became a feature of late medieval halls were reached by ladders, even when the rooms were used for living rather than storage space: they were easy to move and took up very little space. When wooden stairs first appeared, early in the 16th century, they were little more than fixed, solid ladders made of oak blocks set against the wall and cased on the open side with bare, functional paneling.

As elaborate houses began to be built for the gentry during the course of the 16th century, it was realized that stairs could be handsome features, although they remained simple compared to those of the following century. Gradually, they became

broader. They were usually of oak, in keeping with the other parts of the house. Sometimes the steps were made of solid blocks instead of the separate treads and risers now normal. Running from floor to floor in a succession of straight flights, they had stout newel posts supporting a balustrade of sturdy balusters and a broad handrail, molded like the beams. The newel posts had big carved terminals, or extended up to the ceiling and acted as structural supports for the floor above. Sometimes they were carved with elaborate designs that reflected the ornamental plasterwork of the ceiling. In less grand houses where solid, hand-carved balusters were inappropriate, craftsmen instead produced flat balusters with similar outlines but in two dimensions and often perforated to give a lighter effect.

2 When the central chimney was removed from the heart of the house, it was normally replaced by a staircase or "pair of stairs".

The dog-leg stair first appeared in the mid-17thC and has remained a firm favorite, especially in row houses, to the present day.

1 This early newel post, somewhat crudely carved, is in a style extensively used in the 17thC and early 18thC.

1

2

17th-Century Stairs

Beginning with the work at Knole House, in southeast England, in 1605, the 17th century saw even more magnificent stairways in the great houses, and scaled-down grandeur in big farmhouses. At the same time, smaller houses were moving more and more towards built-in staircases instead of ladders.

Long straight stairs with right-angled dog-leg changes in direction gave way to shorter flights punctuated by landings – an arrangement which had a dramatic visual impact. Stairs could be articulated around to form a well or could lead in separate stages to a gallery above. The balustrade and its base were painted in complex color schemes. Newel posts in the best British houses terminated in carved heraldic beasts, symbols of the owner's family. Balusters were now often rectangular but highly carved, and the stair handrails were flatter. Sometimes balusters were replaced with ornamentally carved panels, encasing the stairs to handrail level. This paneling, of painted pine or oak, would be matched by paneled wainscoting on the wall side.

The English architect Inigo Jones introduced many fine staircases in the Italian manner with marble steps and pretty iron balustrades – ironwork was often used for balustrading in the late 1600s. Jones's stairs might be curved around in a sweep instead of rising in angular straight flights, but even so they could still occupy a confined space. However, by the end of the century the tendency was for stairs to occupy key positions as they rose up the two stories of the hall, the grandest room of the house at the time.

3

3 *This secondary staircase in a 16thC English house is a good example of a simple form of stairs. It is often a mistake to use over-elaborate features in an early house.*

4,5 *Early stairs were often beautifully built, balustraded and enriched with carving. If a baluster is missing, a local carpenter should be able to make a replacement.*

6 *Although the newel post on this 17thC stairway is highly decorative, the actual balusters are flat.*

4

5

6

THE 18TH CENTURY

The concept of the magnificent entrance hall in which the stairs were the centerpiece was fully developed by Palladian architects in the houses for the wealthy built from around the 1720s in Britain and America. Marble steps were flanked by exquisitely worked iron balustrades and the ceiling above the staircase was singled out for elaborate treatment, such as *trompe l'oeil* coffering. The walls along the stairs were also treated grandly, perhaps painted with architectural subjects from classical antiquity. Many fine new town houses were built on a smaller scale, but still following the same principles, with the stairs designed to make a major impact on entrance to the house.

In houses with wooden stairs the chunky look of earlier examples would now have been out of keeping, and newel posts were much slimmed down. Balusters were made finer too, and were evenly spaced, two or three per stairs. Handrails were generally narrower, to team up with the lighter newel posts. The spiral post, which had first appeared around 1690, came into vogue for balusters and long remained fashionable, even though there were many other imaginative designs by the middle of the century. In England classically fluted and vase-shaped balusters were applied to elegant mid-18th-century stairs, and wrought iron was used in grand houses with stone stairs; however, in the United States, spiral balusters continued in popularity until the end of the century.

1,2 *This type of turning on the sticks was extremely popular in England in the 18thC and was mirrored by a similar development in America. Often one or several balusters have been broken. If this involves complicated turning, a perfect baluster may have to be removed and taken to a carpenter to be copied.*

3,4 *The paneling and decorative elements on this staircase are typical of grand houses of the mid-18thC. The use of three different patterns of turning on the balusters is common in America.*   HH

9

10

5

6

7

8

9,10 *Stair turning in the 18thC developed into a fine art form, with craftsmen producing either intricate or plain designs. Many local forms developed, which makes it difficult to replace balusters with mass-produced items. It is also worth pointing out that much decoration on stairs is hidden by layers of paint. To reveal original carving, paint must be stripped back to bare wood.*

5 *Classic 18thC wooden stairs like these can be found in town houses in both Britain and America. Many have been vandalized or replaced by plain balusters, and thus need restoring to their original condition.*　　　　*RC*

6 *This mid-18thC stairway in a New York house is a fine example of simple but elegant balusters.*　　　　*VC*

7,8 *Many 18thC houses had quite plain staircases with straight balusters and little carved decoration.*　　*MJ*

1 These cast-iron balusters were popular in the 18th and 19thC. They were frequently painted. GH

2 Stairs were often built in stone. Old stone steps which are beginning to break up are very dusty, and should be vacuumed regularly. GH

3 An interesting example of a secondary staircase added to a 17thC New York house in 1820. BH

4 A classic example of an early 19thC staircase in a row house. Note the plain balusters

5 The wooden newel post of this period had lost its 18thC flamboyance. In less grand houses in the early 19thC it was a purely functional end to the handrail.

6 In an 1830s New York house, the hole left by the bolt that holds the post into the floor joist is capped with a mother-of-pearl coat button. The story is that, when the mortgage was paid off, the button would be replaced with a silver coin.

7 An interesting solution, in a 1830s New York house, to the problem of how to make a handsome staircase without expensive turned elements. The newel post is not turned, and the simple balusters are set at an angle in the plain round banister.

8 This interestingly carved mid-19thC newel post at the top of the cellar steps actually faces the front door. BP

9,10 This excellent staircase has been well restored in a Neo-classical stone mansion built between 1837 and 1846. The cluster of balusters forming the newel post is a common 19thC device. BP

1

2

THE 19TH CENTURY

The fashion for balusters with complex shapes died out at the end of the 18th century, and square-sectioned wooden bars had become common. Paneling in place of balusters had disappeared, and so, in general, had the solid string base. In the 19th century, balusters (three per step in large houses, but two in smaller ones) almost always rested directly on the stairs themselves, and in most houses of the period they were accompanied by smooth mahogany handrails, which were characteristically oval in section.

Many 19th-century houses had a two-story rear extension, making the stairs even darker than they had been in the late 1700s: the half-landing at the first level now led to the back extension, so there was no possibility of a window. Sometimes such staircases would be lit by a skylight, with the light filtering down the well to the ground level.

3

4

5

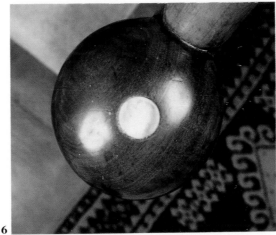

6

7

8

9

10

1

3

2

4

5

6

1 This 1830s New York staircase is a perfect example of the period.

2 A highly decorative newel post from the 1830s. The original builder of this New York house used many details from pattern books of the time. This design was probably meant to be executed in stone; but here it was made in oak instead. OMH

3 This second-floor landing newel post is much simpler than the previous first-floor example. OMH

4 By the last quarter of the 19thC, although the staircase could often be quite small, the newel post was still a major feature.

5 These cast-iron staircases, with all their intricate detail, are very much a part of the late Victorian row house. The greens and browns which predominate in this 1870s house accentuate the Victorian character. LSH

6 This is a good example of the late 19thC English Arts and Crafts grand staircase.

In the simplest Victorian houses, with front doors opening into the small front room, the staircase was a cased-in and extremely modest flight leading from the corner of the back room to a tiny landing between the two rooms on the upper floor. The large new row and semi-detached houses of the time still managed to give a flourish to the stairs, sometimes with a molded nose extending along the exposed sides of the treads as well as along the front, and often with the bottom step broader from side to side than the rest and curving around at the ends. This feature, and the handrail sweeping around above it, were fashions developed from the grander houses of the preceding century. With them went ornate cast-iron balusters or balusters turned in soft wood on a square base; the latter became standard in smaller houses by the 20th century.

In comfortable private houses of the early 20th century, the traditional wooden staircase with turned balusters and broad molded handrail enjoyed a final moment of glory before being ousted by the trend towards modernistic simplification.

7

10

11

8

9

7 *The central courtyard of this 15thC English house was filled with a staircase hall in the 1880s. Late Victorian taste demanded a spectacular stairway in a house of this importance.* CP

8,9 *This late 19thC staircase in Leighton House, London, was designed by George Aitchison. The balustrading is oak which has been stained and lacquered, the detailing in gold. The lower flight of steps (8) has a section of oak paneling on the wall side as it rises from the entrance hall.* LH

10 *By the turn of the century, balusters were being mass-produced. If you are replacing damaged balusters, always have at least one extra turned.*

11 *Many firms produce new staircases with an acceptable period feel. This example is admirable.* WB

A fireplace is one of the obvious things to install or replace when you set about restoring a period room. The right choice can bring the whole interior together; a mismatch, on the other hand, can absolutely destroy the whole carefully-wrought effect.

However, distinctions between "right" and "wrong" are not always clear-cut. There is a bewildering range of original and reproduction fireplaces available but not so much guidance on where to use them.

It is relatively easy to replace even an 18th-century fireplace correctly, as such interiors are well-documented. In this Americans are lucky because of their relatively short history. More difficult, is the question of what you put into a 15th-century house – few people really want a central hearth with a hole in the roof to let out the smoke! In such cases you have to accept a compromise, matching materials and styles that are as sympathetic as possible. Whatever type of house you are restoring, your choices will be governed by its position on the social scale and the room with which you are concerned.

In Britain, the tradition of a central open fire was still the norm in most houses until the beginning of the 16th century. In the great houses of medieval times, the fire was placed at the upper end of the large communal living hall and the burning wood was controlled by an iron fire-dog (an endiron or andiron) which also served as a spit. The basic fireplace was established when a hood was introduced to minimize smoke: this was most easily supported by a wall, so the fire was moved from a central to a lateral position. An indentation was made to accommodate the fire, and a chimney was provided, with flues that conducted smoke to holes in the wall or to a louver in the roof. However, chimney building was inhibited by a tax imposed by Rome. Until the Reformation smoke still left many houses through a hole in the roof, whether the fire was against a wall or against a plaster-covered wooden screen (usually of elm, which does not ignite easily) with a wattle-and-daub canopy and funnel.

From the 16th century a single central chimney normally heated the whole of the house. When a further room was added to the basic plan, this would be provided with its own fireplace and chimney on the end wall.

1

1 Even in the 16th and 17thC many elaborate fireplaces were imported to Britain from Italy, Spain, Portugal and France.

2 The typical 16thC inglenook fireplace which provided the family with heating and cooking facilities. It may take quite a bit of detective work to find an original fireplace, as many were filled in over the centuries. And a large original fireplace may, in any case, look out of place in a late 18thC room.

3 The walk-in fireplace or inglenook (from the Scottish Gaelic aingeal, and nook meaning corner) may well need quite extensive renovation. Old bricks should be used where possible and care must be taken in choosing an acceptable color. The main beam or mantel has sometimes been removed. It is possible to find old beams in most areas.

2   **3**

MANTELPIECES

The simplest form of mantelpiece was a hood set in the wall over the fire, supported either by piers or by a stone lintel bracket. This survived through more than three centuries, while grander or more elegant mantelpieces were being developed. In Tudor houses the deeply recessed fireplace was given a Tudor arch of stone and otherwise treated as part of the paneled wall.

4

7

5

6

4,5,6 The mantelpiece and overmantel provided the perfect surface for incorporating the decoration that was a measure of wealth and status in the 17thC. These beautifully made examples are modern reproductions. SI

7 A fine European carved marble overmantel of hybrid taste, 16thC, set over a more classically orthodox mantelpiece. Sometimes whole fireplaces were imported, but usually only the finely carved panels were set into locally made surrounds.

1

2

3

3 A wonderful example of a George II (1727-1760) Siena marble mantelpiece taken from a substantial English house in Wiltshire. These mantelpieces are extremely rare and have

frequently cost a great deal to restore. It is worth noting that such a fireplace demands a prestigious setting and would look out of place in anything but a grand room. As always, scale is crucial. COFSL.

However, the mongrel classicism of European craftsmen soon influenced the decoration. Grander houses had a carved wooden ledge above the stone arch and richly carved panels above that.

In the Elizabethan great houses the fireplace, framed with columns and an entablature topped with a highly ornamented carved wooden panel or overmantel, was the focal point of an already much decorated room. This type of mantel was elaborately applied in showy Jacobean houses too, with the owner's coat of arms carved in the panel above the fire. Inigo Jones and his pupil John Webb were later to handle this same treatment with a better understanding of classicism and Italian Renaissance models. However, their work was confined to important buildings and was not taken up generally until the 18th century.

CHANGES IN THE 17TH CENTURY

In some country districts of Britain twigs, peat, or even dung were still being burned in the middle of the room in the old manner, with the occupants seated on low stools under the smoke. In more prosperous and forested areas the fuel was wood, and fireplaces were high and wide to accommodate the logs. When coal was introduced it produced still more smoke than timber; however, coal was not in common use until the 18th century in Britain and the 19th in North America.

To reduce smoke, a chimney cloth was placed across the mantel and this soon became a decorative feature of

1 A 17thC Baroque mantelpiece in Verona marble, originally intended for a grand Italian house. Many such fireplaces were imported into England from Italy and many more were made in England by Italian craftsmen.

2 When considering the fireplace, one of the most important decisions is whether you are going to have a modern reproduction, put in a genuine period fireplace which is not original to the house or try to restore what is there. This example is authentic, but an import: a 17thC Italian mantelpiece in pale yellow Verona marble, beautiful and rare. COFSL.

the fireplace. It continued to appear in Victorian homes, even though by this time fires had supposedly been cured of smoking.

With the introduction of coal came a narrower grate placed in the wide hearth. In new buildings the fireplace itself was now set further back. This meant that in thinner-walled brick buildings the chimneystack formed a projection on the outside wall. Fireplaces in older homes tend to have been modified over the years and have often been made narrower and sometimes shallower, but if building work is being done on houses with chimneys like this, it will almost certainly reveal that the house originally had a wide fireplace.

Another feature dating back to the 17th century which may still be found in country houses, even of very modest size, is the clay or brick bread oven, an early ancestor of the kitchen range. This was a British invention, found especially in Devon and Cornwall, but exported to North America soon after the Pilgrim Fathers. And you still may find in country kitchens the built-in box in which salt was kept to dry beside the fire, and the lockable fireside spice cupboard.

7 A detail of the mantel in 6, right, showing the intricate carving and classical ornamentation that was becoming popular in both Britain and America in the late 18thC. VC

4 This example is from a mid-18thC New York house. The fireplaces in the servants' quarters or, as in this case, the children's nursery, were usually simple in style. VC

5 A simple fireplace with no mantel and surrounded by paneling – typical of mid-18thC New York. The paint is modern but in a color authentic to the period. VC

6 In the same house, a splendid fireplace of late 18thC style. It would have been added around 1780. VC

8,9 This mid-18thC fireplace is set into the paneling with Delft tiles surrounding the opening. Tiles like these have frequently been damaged either by heat or over-zealous workmen. It is interesting to discover if the tiles in such fireplaces are English or Dutch and also their date: the glaze and color can be quite different depending on origin. VC

FIREPLACE FURNITURE

Where wood was the fuel, fire dogs or andirons continued to be necessary as a means of propping up logs and keeping them in place. The early fire dogs had been permanently joined together at the base by a low bar which went across the front of the fire. By the 17th century the two dogs stood separately, one at each side of the fire.

A detachable spit was still placed between them at the front, often with a tray beneath to catch the hot fat and juices from roasting meat.

To solve the problem of damage to brickwork, a cast-iron fireback was produced with designs which range from simple to very elaborate. Stout bellows and cast-iron tongs, sometimes with a shovel for heaping up the wood ash, completed the furniture of the fireplace. Today it is possible to obtain authentic cast-iron reproductions of fire dogs and backs, bellows and tongs from specialized foundries.

THE 18TH CENTURY

In the bigger English Tudor and Jacobean houses, the fireplaces were all placed centrally, so that the smoke left the building through one chimneystack. But when classically inspired houses became the only acceptable fashion the central chimneystack was a problem in the design: it looked ungainly. One solution was to place fireplaces at the four corners of the house, and to hide the chimneytops as much as possible behind the parapet. These corner fireplaces were given very lavish treatment in early 18th-century stately homes, while simpler corner fireplaces are found in smaller houses of the time. Even when fireplaces were not set in the corners of the rooms, chimneys at the gable ends of the house became standard.

At the beginning of the century in England and America, many town houses simply had a stone or brick hearth and fireback. The hearth was often whitewashed. But with the growth of fashionable new houses, fireplaces became more sophisticated, reflecting those of the great houses. Inigo Jones's designs were at this time being circulated, along with many pattern books showing classical details. Accordingly, fireplaces were given classical frames, with columns or pilasters, and consoles supporting an entablature topped by a picture panel, the whole planned to echo the door frame of the room. In simpler houses the frames were at first of wood. Soon they were lined or made completely with marble or stone. The picture panel above the fire was widely copied in houses for the well off, while grander people preferred mirrors.

Where coal was used for fuel, the fireplace opening was made smaller. The fire basket came into being for holding the coals in the old wide hearths, while in new houses the trend was to install a cast-iron coal-burning hob grate with urn-shaped sides – this is the familiar grate of English Georgian interiors. Unlike the earlier free-standing grates and contemporary fire baskets, these grates were built-in and took up the whole width of the new narrow fireplace, in the manner which persisted into the present century.

This type of grate, its front patterned with classical motifs, its curved sides developing into the double-U shape, suits late 18th- and early 19th-century rooms perfectly. Old grates can be restored, and new or restored replacements obtained. Even if central heating is more appealing than carrying coals up and down narrow 18th-century stairs, a fireplace in the original style can be cherished for its looks. Unused chimneys need ventilation to stay dry and should never be sealed without the provision of air vents.

Because the new grates raised the height of the fire, a fender became necessary to catch any falling coals. A poker was also essential. Both fenders and pokers were made of brass, with matching tongs and shovel.

1

1 After James Gibbs published his Rules for drawing the several parts of Architecture *in 1732, his designs were copied and embellished in both England and America. In this example the picture frame has been replaced by a mirror.* CP

2 From the mid-18thC, white marble was considered the most prestigious material for the fireplace in the drawing room – not only in the grand houses but increasingly in smaller houses. This fireplace in a second-floor drawing room is in fact a 19thC copy. CP

3 An 18thC fireplace with a classical broken pediment and additional 19thC embellishments. CP

Restoring marble fireplaces

Before attempting to restore a marble fireplace, make sure that you allow yourself plenty of time. It is certainly not a job to be done in a hurry. A point to remember before you begin cleaning is not to use any acids, dyes or alcohol: marble is a porous substance, and fluids such as these will soak into it and stain, or eventually cause the marble to disintegrate.

There are three main problems to be overcome when restoring marble. First, it is likely to be broken or chipped; second, it may have been painted; and last, it may be heavily stained. If you are unlucky you may have to deal with all three!

If the fireplace has been badly damaged – large chunks have been broken off the mantel ledge, for example, or slabs have fallen off the mantel face – then you may have to break apart that part of the mantelpiece and start from scratch, gluing together sections with special marble glue. For that you will need a stone chisel and ballpeen hammer to chip away ragged edges and to pry off discarded pieces. You may have to replace parts with new marble, your local marble dealer will help to supply matching pieces. Always protect your hands with heavy-duty, leather-lined workgloves.

A marble mantelpiece usually has a marble hearth extending in front of the firebox. Replacing this is a job for a professional; marble is very heavy, and in slab form it is surprisingly fragile. It can break under its own weight if incorrectly handled.

Often a mantelpiece will only be slightly chipped, in which case it is only necessary to mix up a colored marble glue to blend with the surrounding marble. Apply this to the damaged area, allow to set and then rub down with fine wet-and-dry sandpaper until it looks like the original marble.

You can remove paint from marble by using special paint stripper formulated for stone. Work on only a few square inches at a time, using swabs of cotton wool to take off the excess stripper. Repeat this until the paint disappears. It is essential to wear rubber workgloves during this process. If you are careful, you can use a paint scraper, but remember that marble scratches easily.

Staining, due to years of neglect, is the most common problem in restoring a marble fireplace. The best way to tackle it is to use a special stain remover for marble, following the manufacturer's instructions.

When polishing marble, use a white hard polish: any coloring in the polish will stain. Rub the polish hard into the marble using a soft white cloth. (Any dye in the cloth could seep into the marble.) For a matt finish use a softer polish.

After a long and laborious restoration, it is important to look after the marble. For day-to-day upkeep use a white furniture polish to keep it clean. Remember that marble is porous, and careless placement of plantpots and glasses will cause staining.

4 This very pleasing marble fireplace has been introduced into an early 19thC house. The marble had been painted, but a professional company stripped the paint before installation. Putting in a marble fireplace is a heavy, dirty, skilled job, not to be undertaken lightly.

1 This simple French design from the 18thC was intended to be used in lesser rooms.   H

2 By the late 18thC in England, cameos of fine ceramics were often applied to mantelpieces. Such fireplaces were intended to be painted.

3 This popular mid-18thC design in the William Kent style is suitable for a grand room. Such fireplaces could be used in houses dating from the 1740s through to the turn of the century.   H

4,5 Modern reproduction fireplaces are available in marble. It is interesting to remember that, in the 18thC, fireplaces were often made in marble workshops which the 18thC architect or home owner visited to choose from the many designs available – just as he would today.   MH

6 Consideration of proportion is essential when choosing a mantelpiece. This classic 18thC design with square fluted frieze and jambs is ideal for a smaller room where a more ornate, heavily carved example would look totally out of place.   H

7 An inlaid marble fireplace decorated with Wedgwood plaques. These fireplaces became very popular in England, after 1778, when Josiah Wedgwood produced them from designs by John Flaxman. The jambs are typically in the form of architectural pilasters.   COFSL

8

9

12

10

13

ADAM-INSPIRED DEVELOPMENTS

A visually lighter mantelpiece deprived of pediments was preferred in England, and later in America, toward the end of the 18th century. Best exemplified by the Adam brothers in England, the simple albeit enriched form of pilasters and consoles supporting an entablature with a ledge or shelf continued as the model mantelpiece for most of the 19th century.

8 This carved statuary marble and Blue John (Derbyshire Spa) fireplace was made in the 1780s. The delicately carved overmantel is in the manner of Grinling Gibbons (1648-1721). CofSL.

9-14 As the 18thC advanced there were two main developments in fireplace design: first, a dominant taste for classical architecture, which was particularly encouraged by the Adam brothers in England; and secondly, fireplaces became smaller in standard town houses. These reproduction fireplaces suit houses built from the later part of the 18thC until well into the 19thC.
AB,AB,PF,PF,CofSL,AB

11

14

1-14 *The range of classically inspired fireplaces on the market from the 1760s on was enormous, with almost every conceivable classical motif applied somewhere or other. Swags, urns and foliage have never really gone out of style since. Poor modern reproductions are frequently discernible by the hesitant application of undersized motifs. 1-5 are original fireplaces in 18thC houses, and 6-14 are modern reproductions.*

GH,RC,RC,RC,HH,H,MH, H,H,MH,H,PF,MH,MH

1

2

3

4

5

6

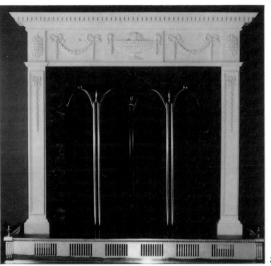

7

8

9

10

11

12

13

14

1 *A humble fireplace was a common feature of many servants' rooms in late 18thC England. This housekeeper's room in the semi-basement is typically plain but very functional.* GH

2 *This early 19thC marble mantelpiece depends for its effect on contrasting marble. Fireplaces of this style demand a grand room.* CofSL

3 *An early 19thC statuary marble mantel displaying a more exuberant classical motif. The frieze on the lintel is carved with Bacchanalian figures at play, the jambs in the form of Antonio Canova's dancing girls.* CofSL

4 *A Scottish white marble fireplace which shows more austere decoration, from the early 19thC.* CofSL

1

3

2

4

5

7

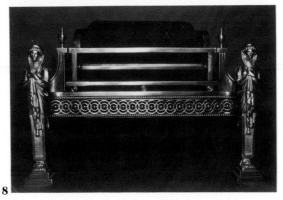

8

9

6

5 *A simple 19thC white marble fireplace imported from France. The fire screen and accessories are in keeping with the period.* MB

6 *By the mid-19thC in minor rooms cast-iron fireplaces like this were often used, often painted white.* BH

7 *This marble fireplace is actually French but would equally enhance a drawing room in America or Britain. It has the advantages of small size and simple decoration.* MH

8 *This early 18thC English fire grate was made of brass and steel. The engraved serpentine front and ball finials are typical of the period.* COFSI.

9 *This early 19thC English brass and steel dog grate could be used to good effect in fireplaces of the late 18th and early 19thC.* COFSI.

1

3

4

5

1 *A marble fireplace in a New York house illustrating early 19thC trends. The hearth raised slightly above floor-level is typically American.* MJ

2 *French influence is apparent in this fireplace in a front drawing room. White marble was universally thought to be a statement of wealth and good taste.* MJ

3 *This fireplace with its recessed hearth is made from English fossilized marble, but is original to the New York house in which it remains.* MJ

4,5 *In this 1830s New York house, the Greek Revival style is still very much in evidence but both these wooden fireplaces are restrained examples.*

6 *A wooden fireplace in a mid-1830s house. This is a reconstruction from "paint ghosts" – the traces left on the wall after a fire destroyed the fireplace completely. The more ornate mantel was used in the front parlor where guests were received.*

7 *A much plainer wooden mantel. The Franklin stove is of the period, around 1836, and would have been in the back parlor where the family spent most if its time.*

6

7

8,9 *The 19thC saw a wide diversity of styles and materials. This Greek Revival Belgian black marble fireplace dominates the room when placed in an earlier New York house in the 1860s. The grate is original. The capital on the fireplace matches the capitals on the sliding doors. In this period of nostalgia, people were very aware of proportion and symmetry.* OMH

10 *By around 1840, the American taste for intricately carved mantelpieces was waning. Marble was often used in slab form and mantels tended to be geometric – a simplification which had happened slightly earlier in Britain. This high coal grate of brass and iron is an English import. It would have been permanently blocked into the fireplace opening with masonry. It was more efficient than andirons.* BP

11 *This black marble fireplace in the same house is in the upstairs living room. The fact that the more impressive fireplaces are downstairs would tend to suggest that this upstairs room would be for the family to use, rather than for entertaining on a grand scale.* BP

12 *A classic Greek Revival white fireplace, very commonly seen in houses in New York in the 1830s.* OMH

THE END OF THE 18TH CENTURY

In Britain and America experiments towards more efficient burning eventually led to "register grates", with dampers to control the supply of air to the fire, and additional dampers in the chimney flue. These grates were cast in one piece as part of the inner frame and back of the hearth, and inserted within the mantelpiece.

Fire regulations strictly controlled chimney construction in the 19th century, and the risk of fire was further reduced by the almost exclusive use of marble or cast iron in the massive and mass-produced fireplaces of parlor floor rooms in Victorian houses and in the minor fireplaces provided in most of their other rooms. Now that plate glass was readily available, the huge ornamental mirror descended the social scale and replaced the picture or stucco panel over the fireplace. This was a forerunner of the overmantel with side mirrors and shelves around a mahogany-framed central mirror.

Gothic and Picturesque influences affected fireplace design later in the century, and the Arts and Crafts movement's nostalgic yearnings led to a taste for wide hooded hearths, with stone frames and wood mantels, in which to burn wood again. Most fireplaces, however, became smaller, with the mantel in painted pine or slate – marble was becoming too expensive. At the same time ornament became heavier from the 1860s on. Painted and glazed tiles were attached into the sides of the cast-iron insert, and tiled hoods became an integral part of the construction. At the turn of the century, Art Nouveau brought opulent curving motifs to the tiles, which until now had been patterned rather formally.

With the introduction of gas and electric fires, the outer mantelpiece became less and less imposing, simply serving as a frame for a wide area of plain colored tiles. By easy transitions this became the very modest "modern" fireplace, with free-standing grate and brick back and a surround entirely composed of tilework in mottled buff or beige. Wood-framed fireplaces remained popular in America.

Luckily, when central heating or portable electric heaters and 1950s taste conspired to banish older fireplaces, they were as frequently covered over as removed. You may be surprised how easy it is either to restore the original or put in a replacement.

Before having a new fireplace installed, have the chimney cleaned and light a fire to make sure that the chimney is sound. Before doing anything in a downstairs room check that the chimney breast has not been removed upstairs – an obvious precaution, but one which the enthusiast may overlook with distressing results!

1,2,3,4,5 By the late 19thC, there were as many fireplace designs as there were designers. In the living rooms and parlors they tended to be quite grand, while in the servants' areas they were simple and usually small. The size of the fireplace was scaled to that of the room and the degree of ornament was in strict proportion to the room's social importance. CP

6 *While the actual mantels were frequently simple, much decoration was added to the wrought-iron grates in the later 19thC.* CP

7 *Early 19thC tiles like these should be retained if at all possible. Some damage is totally acceptable and can often add to the period feel, whereas new tiles frequently detract.*

8,9 *In small rooms, cast-iron mantelpieces were common. These were frequently painted white, as were carved timber or plaster fireplaces. The Victorians would have found our love for stripped pine very amusing: it was a cheap timber which was always concealed.* CP

6

7

8

9

1 *This small fireplace in the hallway of an 1870s row house is given prominence by a gilt and mirrored overmantel. The 17thC chimney cloth reappeared at this period: it may have helped to reduce the smoke but was mainly a decorative feature.* I.SH

2 *The late Victorians used marble for their most prestigious fireplaces. While the fireplace itself could be quite understated, the brass fire accessories were quite the opposite.* I.SH

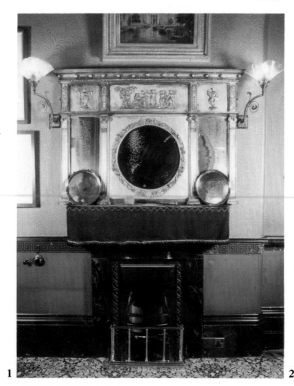

1

2

3

5

4

6

3 *The actual fireplace here is quite small but the overall impression is of a massive, extended mantelpiece.* LSH

4 *Many of these simple Victorian cast-iron grates still survive. The tiles are often older than the grate.*

5 *To recreate a Victorian fireplace you need to attend to more than merely the fabric. The colors, clutter and general confusion are all necessary parts of the Victorian mood.* LSH

6 *A detail of a small cast-iron grate with brass hood. These fireplaces were both efficient and highly decorative.* LSH

1 This type of wooden mantel with all its classical inspiration fits quite easily into the larger rooms of most substantial 19thC houses. LSH

2 A small simple stripped pine fireplace which was standard in many small homes or in secondary rooms in grander houses from the mid-19thC. The English delft tiles assist with the rustic feel, as does the original mass-produced cast-iron grate. FE

3 Late 19thC cast-iron fireplaces were frequently painted white. These functional items were also highly decorative. Note the ash drawer at the base – enhanced with a painted tile.

2

3

4 In America, as in Britain, the decorative qualities of materials such as mat black slate were fully utilized. This example had been painted white in the 20thC and had to be painstakingly stripped.

5 Toward the end of the 19thC it became increasingly popular to break up the solid mass of black slate or marble with inset panels – tiles, ceramics and marble were ideally suited.

6 This black slate fireplace in the same 1875 house has inserted Minton tiles.

7 This squat white marble fireplace is strangely positioned under a window. The situation is attributable to Lord Leighton, who placed it there as a joke. Note the mirrored shutters – is the window a mirror or not? and where does the smoke go? LH

4

6

5

7

2 *The whole feel of a Victorian fireplace must be enhanced by the surroundings as a whole, as in this evocative ensemble. Although the fireplace is classically Victorian, the real impact is derived from the collection of old glass, treen, porcelain and dried flowers.*

3 *This reproduction sand-blasted fireplace, cast from an old mold, is ideal for a house built at the end of the 19thC or the beginning of the 20thC.* AF

4 *By the end of the 19thC, mantelpieces could be marble, wood (painted and unpainted) or metal. They were sometimes simple and elegant — sometimes highly decorated and charmingly vulgar. Tiles were used to good effect. The actual grate by this period had become small, and the fire was thus more efficient. This reproduction fireplace used in a late 19thC house would add considerable character to a room.* AF

1 *The permutations of decorated cast fireplaces and multi-colored tiles are innumerable. Such features have frequently been despised and are only now receiving due attention.* MH

5,6 These mantelpieces are in an Arts and Crafts house, but have a light, classical feel. The Victorians did not feel the need to rely simply on one style. This philosophy created some interesting interiors along with some very incongruous designs.

7 The solidity of 19thC design is often mistaken for lack of taste. This grand but simple fireplace has stature and elegance.

8 This Arts and Crafts house entrance hall fireplace depends much on the Renaissance revival.

9 These solid carved wood late 19thC fireplaces have sometimes been most inappropriately sited. Their quality is undeniable but they require careful consideration of their environment to be in keeping.　　　　*LH*

5　　　　6　　　　7

8　　　　9

STOVES

Stoves in glazed earthenware or cast iron were much more common in the United States and Europe than in Britain, perhaps because the winters are more consistently extreme outside the British Isles and because wood was widely available for fuel. The completely closed European stove was adapted in Pennsylvania by Dr Benjamin Franklin, whose designs for an open-fronted box stove were imported to England. These extremely functional objects were available from the 1750s to the present day, when they have become efficient enough to function as furnaces.

1,2,3,4,5 *In the 19thC, stoves were more popular in America and Europe than in Victorian England. These reproductions can be used to good effect in any 19th or early 20thC house. They combine the decorative elegance of their Victorian and early 20thC predecessors with modern heating technology. They not only heat the room and provide a hot plate, but they also provide a focal point without the mess associated with an open fire.*

S&W,CF,CF,H&S,H&S

6

7

8

6 *Radiators can always be concealed. This screen with a marble top was a late-Victorian way of hiding the massive, ugly but useful heating contraption. The grilles could be either painted or brass.* CP

7,8 *These original 19thC cast-iron radiators look more in keeping with a period house than modern slimmer versions.*

9 *This squat radiator is unusually low and long. This type of radiator, although not authentic, does not look out of place in a large period room.*

10

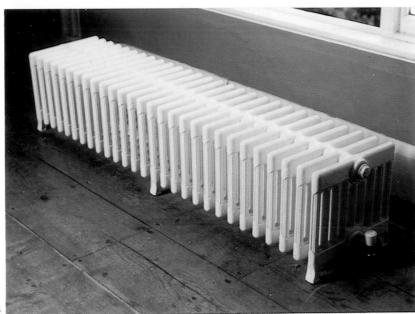

9

11

10 *This black-painted radiator is actually inset into the wall. The loss in heating efficiency is balanced by a gain in aesthetic appeal.* I.H

11 *There are manufacturers now producing efficient and modern look-alikes of the original cast-iron Victorian radiators which are fast disappearing from architectural salvage yards.* B

It was not until the 1880s that bathrooms existed as we know them. Anyone restoring an older house therefore has the choice of simple modern fixtures, which need not jar whatever the surroundings, or a , 19th- or early 20th-century style bathroom which will have a "period" look, even though the period may be different from that of the house.

Cleanliness, of course, was valued long before the 19th century. Soap was made in England from the 14th century, and the highest classes in the Middle Ages had decorated pitchers and basins in gold or silver, with brass and pewter for the slightly less well-placed. Obvious ancestors of the washstand existed as gilt and copper ornamented *lavers*, which had a surface for the metal wash bowl, a little water vessel and faucet above the bowl, a shelf for soap below, and a fixed towel rail.

Bathing in a tub was a sociable activity for nobles and their ladies. Although the tub was usually round like a barrel, longer versions more like the baths of today were also known. Medieval palaces even had precursors of the modern bathroom, with tiled floors and plumbed-in baths supplied with water from a lead tank. Queen Elizabeth I possessed vast bathing rooms lined with wainscotting and mirrors. These early models may serve as fanciful inspiration, but only the pitchers and bowls, and perhaps the *lavers*, can really be borrowed as novel but practical ideas for houses today.

1

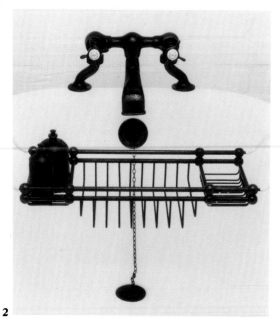

2

1 *This reproduction Victorian bathroom fixture has as its central feature a roll-top bathtub set in a mahogany panel surround. The pedestal sink, the tank on brackets and the bidet all have a Victorian or early 20thC feel. This effect is accentuated by the lighting, marbled walls and hanging antique lace.* BCS

2 *It is worth remembering that there are alternatives to brass finishes when you are considering bathroom fixtures: nickel, chrome, antique copper, antique bronze and, as here, black chrome are some of the many available. This bathtub filler and rack are based on early 20thC designs.* CS

3 *The roll-top bathtub which was so spurned in the middle years of this century has made a dramatic comeback. Its design causes a slight plumbing problem but here the brass pipework plays a decorative role.* SP

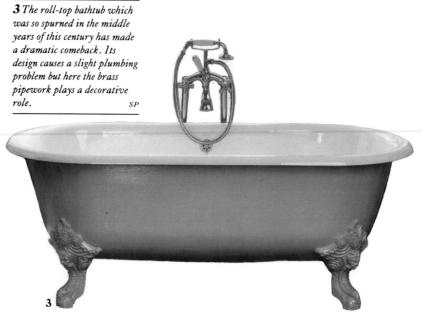

3

THE BATHTUB

By 1730 communal pumps and aqueducts supplied water to the towns, while some large country houses had their own water supply. Very occasionally, a grand house could also boast a marble-walled bathroom with a large sunken marble bathtub and piped water. Portable metal tubs were quite widely in use by this time – made of tin, flat-bottomed, roll-topped, and filled and emptied by hand. They were not unlike the simpler tin tubs, with a handle to carry and suspend them by, which were filled with hot water from the kitchen range in many houses until relatively recently.

Bathtubs as we know them could not become widespread until water tanks were installed in attics and enameling and cast-iron techniques had been developed. In France, the wealthiest few had huge "theme" bathrooms with plumbed-in bathtubs, rather like sofas in design, draped with fine cloth in a most unfunctional way. Usually, though, people bathed in portable tubs, painted outside and in.

It was from the 1850s that sheet-metal bathtubs were plumbed in and a small bedroom given over to their use. The style was decorative, with flower-sprigged wallpaper and gathered curtains. The outside of the tub would be stenciled or painted to look like wood. No attempt was made to conceal the plumbing – a blessing to anyone who wishes to recreate a bathroom of this period.

Even in the 1880s flowery wallpaper was still

4

7

5

8

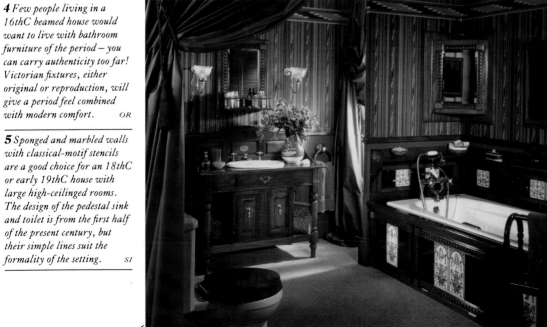

6

4 Few people living in a 16thC beamed house would want to live with bathroom furniture of the period – you can carry authenticity too far! Victorian fixtures, either original or reproduction, will give a period feel combined with modern comfort. OR

5 Sponged and marbled walls with classical-motif stencils are a good choice for an 18thC or early 19thC house with large high-ceilinged rooms. The design of the pedestal sink and toilet is from the first half of the present century, but their simple lines suit the formality of the setting. SI

6 This room successfully recreates the feeling of the late Victorian taste for opulence and elaborate decoration. The tub is enclosed in a lavish mahogany surround and is further decorated with insets of decorated tiles. The sink too is set into a washstand unit. VN

7 A Victorian-style roll-top bathtub is a much more convenient choice than the portable metal ones more usually found at the time. OB

8 The elegant proportions and painted finish of these built-in bathroom units sympathize with the proportions and style of the British Georgian house. SI

1

1,2 These are faithful reproductions of late 19thC fixtures. The roomy high-sided sink has a shape that is practical as well as decorative. Often such sinks were made in even more elaborate forms of crouching lions or dolphins. Attention to detail is reflected here in the brass and porcelain pull-flush and ornamental brackets holding the sink and tank.
TB, AS

4 Following a practice begun around the 1850s, a bedroom in this Victorian house has been turned into a bathroom. The toilet and pedestal sink are of modern design but echo the rounded line of the roll-top bathtub. As the room is spacious enough, the owners have added some original Victorian furniture – the mahogany mirror over the fireplace and the chest of drawers with its old lace cloth.
TB

3 This house built in the 1870s still has its original fixtures and decoration. Flushing toilets were well-established by this time and the embossed pedestal is typical of the period. The deep tub made from slabs of marble would have been cold-fill only: cold baths were a normal part of British life until well into the 20thC.
LSH

2

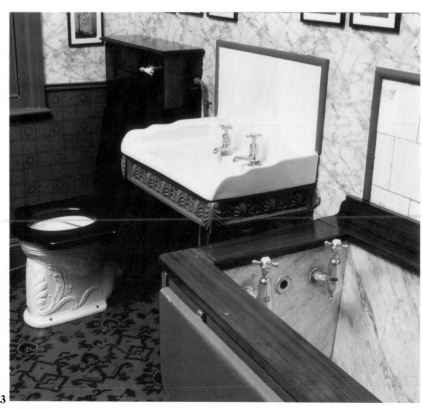

3

4

5

6

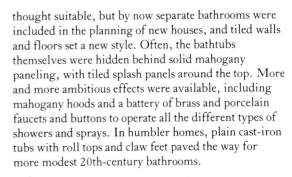

7

8

9

10

thought suitable, but by now separate bathrooms were included in the planning of new houses, and tiled walls and floors set a new style. Often, the bathtubs themselves were hidden behind solid mahogany paneling, with tiled splash panels around the top. More and more ambitious effects were available, including mahogany hoods and a battery of brass and porcelain faucets and buttons to operate all the different types of showers and sprays. In humbler homes, plain cast-iron tubs with roll tops and claw feet paved the way for more modest 20th-century bathrooms.

5,6,7 *Three bathrooms which follow the mid-19th fashion of decorating the outside of the bathtub. They also reflect the fashion then and later on in the century of adopting a bedroom style of decoration – flowery wallpaper and gathered curtains. This style of tub was produced well into this century, and works with a variety of styles of sink and toilet.* BCS, CPH, TD

8 *Classic square pedestal sinks like this were still being made thirty or so years ago, and work especially well in houses built around 1920. A black and white color scheme has a particularly good feel of the period.* OB

9 *Whether you are renovating a cottage or a 19thC townhouse, painted fixtures like these are a good choice. Their fresh blue and white coloring works well against big, bold, even geometric designs or with beams, low ceilings and plain white-painted walls.* TB

10 *The choice of tiles is important for a complete period look. The colors here – dark green with cream – are typical of the late 19thC and early 20thC. So are the border designs used at baseboard, wainscot and cornice level and the design of patterned tiles arranged in a diagonal trellis.* TB

1

4

1 *A reproduction roll-top bathtub which gives an excellent period feel without the discomfort. No attempt has been made to hide the pipework which, with the faucets and shower, is an attractive as well as authentic feature.* BCS

2 *A Spanish portable bathtub of the 18thC with carrying handles on either side. It was not until the 1850s that plumbed-in baths began to appear in any other than very grand houses. In humbler homes portable tubs were still in use until quite recently. However, this solid marble tub is quite a grand affair. A tub like this can be plumbed-in and would look splendid in a large room, perhaps with marbled walls with a stencilled Greek key border and fixtures housed in mahogany cabinets.*

3 *This roll-top tub with brass feet as well as fixtures solves the plumbing problem in an interesting way. The shower fixture and porcelain faucets are all that are visible, the pipework being hidden by paneling.* SP

4 *By contrast, this roll-top tub displays its brass fixtures as part of its decorative appeal. Note also the rack, which adds to the nostalgic feel. The marble floor and painted brick walls also add to the general mood but could make the bathroom rather cold.* CS

5 *An ordinary shower curtain would strike a jarring note in a period-style bathroom. An etched-glass screen like this one is a more appropriate choice.* BCS

2

3

5

6

7

8

9

10

WASHSTANDS AND SINKS

Tripod washstands made of wrought iron with pewter basins appeared in the 1750s. From the 1770s superior dressing-room furniture included elegant mahogany or rosewood washstands designed by Sheraton or Hepplewhite or their imitators. Set in a quarter circle, so that they could stand in a corner, they had raised, shaped backs, circular bowls and round indentations for the soap. Very soon, even washstands and gentlemen's shaving tables were disguised to look like other furniture, with tops and shelves which opened out, as if their inner workings were slightly indecent. The bidet, also for the dressing room, was introduced from France and was even more convincingly concealed in cabinetwork, while the bedroom chamber pot was hidden away in a beautifully made bedside table or cabinet.

In the 1830s washstands became larger and rectangular, with marble tops which had round openings for deep bowls, and slop pails on a low shelf. They developed into the late Victorian stands which could readily be found in junk shops until quite recently. These had patterned tiled tops and splash-

6 *Even when piped water became fairly common, sinks were still set in dark mahogany cabinets with marble tops like washstands. If you are thinking of installing a sink in the bedroom of a Victorian house, copying this idea is an authentic solution.* LSH

7 *Setting deep bowls into marble surrounds was a practice which continued into the 20thC. The classic simplicity of this one on chrome legs, dating from the 1920s or 30s, works well in a late 18thC house.* CP

8 *A fascinating example of Victorian ingenuity. This sink, still in its original marble surround, does not look particularly unusual – until you notice that it has no waste outlet. The sink is pivoted: after use you simply swing it over to empty the water into a bucket below – which is then emptied by a servant!* LSH

9 *From the late 18thC, elegant washstands were made in the shape of a quarter-circle to fit in a corner. Here is a Victorian plumbed-in extension of the same idea. Notice how well the marble splashback surround has kept its original good looks.* LSH

10 *The interior of this Neo-classical mid-19thC stone mansion is in the Greek Revival style. This pedestal sink with its pedestal in the shape of a column mirrors the overall design. The mirror frame is also classically inspired.* BP

backs with cupboards underneath. A variety of prettily decorated pitchers and bowls, perforated soap dishes and false-teeth holders went with them.

As piped water became more common, plumbed-in sinks were still given surrounds in dark mahogany. Bathrooms sported extravagantly patterned ceramic sinks which complemented the toilets and water tanks and opulent gleaming brass faucets. By the end of the century, however, plain white ceramic fixtures were beginning to take precedence over patterns, and by the time the pedestal sink was developed in the early 1900s hygenic white was universally fashionable.

1 *From the early 20thC pedestals which hid the pipework began to be fashionable. It is therefore quite allowable to use reproductions such as this.* BCS

2,3,4 *Late Victorian inventiveness produced all sorts of elaborate systems for showers and sprays, whose style is reflected in these brass and porcelain reproductions.*
TB, WA, CS

5 *Attention to small details is important when putting in a bathroom. If you can find original faucets like these, so much the better.*

6 *An unfussy traditional shape like this works well in a variety of settings from the 18thC to the 1940s* CPH

7 *A modern pine reproduction of a Victorian washstand.* TB

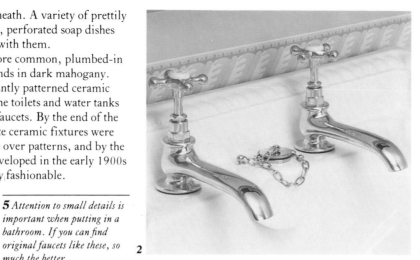

1

2

3

4

5

6

7

TOILETS

A version of the flushing toilet was invented in 1596 by Sir John Harington, and supplied to Queen Elizabeth herself. After a long and unsanitary delay, water was piped to Georgian town houses, and brick drains and public sewers were built. Outhouses were supplied in the gardens, sometimes flushing and sometimes connected to the main drain, but more often emptying into a cesspit. Real toilets, with traps and valves, were introduced in the late 1700s. In England most big houses had them by the 1840s, while in America entire cities prided themselves on modern sewer systems.

Glazed clay pipes made by Doulton were replacing the London brick sewers at the same time. Toilets too were increasingly made of various kinds of glazed earthenware, and the early types were surrounded by substantial wooden framing. The inside of the bowl was treated as an opportunity for decoration, and was florally adorned in all but the very cheapest models. The outside of the new pedestal toilet was also decorated. Doultons and Twyfords led the field, and throughout the rest of the century, in Britain and the United States, an astonishing variety of designs and decorative treatments became available.

Pedestals could take the form of crouching lions or dolphins, or were embossed with classical fluting on the outside. Both outside and inside, the bowls might be painted or printed with fruit, flower or willow-pattern designs before being glazed. Blues, reds and pinks were commonly used, and gilding was not unknown. Several reproductions of these designs, with matching basins, bidets and tanks, are now available.

Seats were usually of polished mahogany or other wood. Porcelain handles, paper-holders (often set into the back of the toilet itself) and matching porcelain tanks added to the decorative effect. Tanks were also made in cast iron, mahogany or other wood (lined with lead or copper) to match the bath paneling. Push-button flushes became available at the end of the 19th century, and surprisingly, low-level units were first made as early as 1825.

8,9,10 Three modern reproductions suitable for period bathrooms. The first shows that with a simple rounded shape plus a natural wood seat you can achieve an attractive period effect; the second has a certain turn-of-the-century feel; the third is a versatile classic shape.

CS, BCS, CPH

11 From the 1840s toilets were made of glazed earthenware and were usually set in handsome wooden framing, as in this example. Here the pull for the flush is also housed in the surround.

LSH

8

11

9

10

12,13 The Victorians had many different types of toilets, and modern reproductions are thus available in many styles. The first of these examples shows the classic high water tank supported by decorative brackets; the second is a copy of the highly ornate painted style.

BCS, BCS

12   **13**

Kitchens in old houses worked well because they had to. Perhaps the standards of ventilation, lighting and even hygiene would not satisfy us today, but, as domestic workshops, old kitchens simply had to be efficient in terms of layout and furnishings because of the almost total lack of labor-saving devices.

The ways in which old kitchens were planned, furnished and equipped are of interest for two reasons. If you are restoring a period property, a kitchen which looks as if it belongs to the appropriate era is likely to be more visually compatible with the remainder of the building than wall-to-wall plastics. Also, many people are realizing that in planning today's multi-user family kitchens there are many practical lessons to be learned from the kitchens of a century or more ago.

Consider sinks, for example. Thirty years ago everyone wanted to get rid of their deep porcelain sinks and get the latest stainless steel models instead. Today the practical advantages of the old deep sink are being appreciated anew and there is a trend towards big sinks in cast iron, plastics, stone or terrazzo, or even towards reusing old porcelain sinks in good condition, despite porcelain's vulnerability to staining and cracking.

Period kitchens, designed around a large central working table, contained a large walk-in pantry for food storage. Shelves, racks, and wall and ceiling hooks were used for items in constant use. Function dictated the form of the furniture, which was always plain and easy to keep clean.

Floors and shelves were scrubbable and walls and ceilings were generally white-washed until Victorian times, both in Europe and America.

1

2

1 It is quite practical to restore an inglenook fireplace for cooking, as this example in an Elizabethan house in Kent, in the south of England, illustrates. This "down hearth" was recreated with a mixture of antiques and reproduction ironwork hand-forged from old iron. Attention to detail is the key to success. For instance, the ropes for the spit drive were traditionally spun. ST

2 The National Trust of Scotland has completely restored this magnificent Georgian kitchen at No. 7 Charlotte Sq, Edinburgh. It contains a host of reference details which are very useful to the student of period kitchen restoration. The kitchen range is typical of models which were produced in many Scottish iron foundries at this time. They can still be found in kitchens all over Britain.

3

5

4

6

3 *In a classic English kitchen, such as this delightful Victorian example which is preserved by the National Trust at Uppark, West Sussex, everything revolved around the central work table. This was served by hutches and cooking areas, larders, still rooms, pantries and a scullery for dishwashing and wet food preparation. Note how simple and functional the furniture is and how the kitchenware creates such decoration as there is. The basic table top was of ash but pine planks were installed at a later date as it wore away. These would have been replaced from time to time.* ST

4 *When this kitchen was restored it was decided to keep as many authentic details as possible, such as the brick floor and rough plastered walls and ceiling. The table was made of English oak with a top of elm and the rack above is a copy of a Yorkshire "bacon flake". The walk-in pantry was created from a disused entrance porch. A dishwasher and microwave oven are completely hidden in cabinets when not in use.* ST

5 *The swing towards kitchens with free-standing furniture is noticeable in England generally. It started among people refurbishing kitchens for old houses. Here a "gamekeeper" sink has been pressed back into service, together with a mixture of real kitchen antiques and objets trouvés. The problem with old sinks is that they do not accept garbage disposers or basket strainer fittings but new versions which do are now available.* ST

6 *In this kitchen for a rebuilt barn in Suffolk, England, elements of traditional thinking were used to create an attractive but practical sink area. As a dishwasher is used for all dishwashing, the rack above the sink is mainly used to store and display china in regular use. The porcelain sink with brass taps is set in an oiled solid maple worktop.* ST

The fascination of old kitchens is that, compared with main living areas, no effort was made in most cases to dress them up for appearance's sake. So what you will find, unless someone has done a thorough job of "renovation", is an inbuilt record of all the ideas and changes which have come and gone since the kitchen was first built. That record can provide the clues you need to plan your restoration.

Every lump in the walls, every odd stump of iron and every piece of carpentry has a tale to tell. For example, if in the late 18th century the cook needed a new shelf, the local carpenter took the first piece of wood of about the right size that came to hand and pressed it into service: it may have been part of some old wall paneling stripped out of another part of the house a few years before. Authentic old kitchens often present a patchwork appearance of this kind.

In the few remaining period kitchens we have the purest examples of vernacular design, influenced to a far greater degree by local traditions of craftsmanship and style passed down from one generation to the next than by any awareness of passing fashion. Details of molding in old pieces of kitchen furniture, the materials used in floors and for working surfaces and the design of incidental items such as hanging racks and fireplace ironwork vary from one county or state to the next and sometimes even from town to town. Sadly, the trade in antiques and kitchenalia has displaced much valuable evidence of local traditions in the half-century or more of modernization following the advent of factory-made kitchen cabinets between the wars. In trying to reconstruct how the kitchen originally looked, a little detective work will be necessary. The original may be still there, walled up in a hidden fireplace. A

big open chimney is probably evidence of a floor-level, log-burning fireplace. Look for signs of an old chimney crane or marks to indicate where a weight-driven spit engine may have been mounted. Iron stumps in the sidewalls may indicate a later coal-burning roasting hearth.

Try to work out how the kitchen was laid out in earlier times. Clues may be offered by blocked-up doorways, changes in floor levels or materials or apparently pointless notches and breaks in beams. Consider facilities such as pantries and sculleries needed in the days before refrigerators.

It is worth checking any sheds or barns you have where old wood is stored. Old cupboards, shelves and other woodwork may have been stripped out of the backstairs areas many years before. With care such fixtures can be restored to use.

KITCHENS BEFORE THE 18TH CENTURY

The kitchen as we understand it today was born in the 18th century with the arrival of early cooking stoves in many homes. Before that, most cooking took place at various types of open fires and hearths, and water was obtained from a pump in the back yard or from a communal source.

From the 15th and 16th centuries, inglenook or walk-in fireplaces (or whatever they are called in the part of the world where you live) were being added to existing houses and incorporated in new buildings. At about the same time we begin to see early sculleries, initially little more than a roofed-over space to make access to the water pump more convenient.

Until the late 18th century, most inglenooks were entirely woodburning. They had huge chimneys which worked well enough because the fire burned continually between the end of the summer and the middle of spring. The warmth of that fireplace meant that this room was the center of all family life.

Unless you are exceptionally fortunate, no indications will now be left of how such a kitchen was originally furnished, because any furniture there was (and it did not amount to much in most cases) would

1 The kitchen is frequently the area of a house which remains virtually unaltered. This mid-18thC house was much modernized in the 19thC but the basement kitchen was fortunately left with its original features intact. MJ

2 This mid-18thC open hearth fireplace in a New York house is filled with the many kitchen implements in use during this period. VC

3 Kitchens were frequently below ground level and were often dark and gloomy places. These oak beams were whitewashed to add some light. VC

4 This 17thC open hearth in a New York house is backed by a beehive oven. This provided a multitude of cooking possibilities as well as being the main source of heat and light. BH

have been freestanding. The one essential piece was a big central table, but there might also have been a sideboard and later a dresser or hutch. People sat on benches mainly, with perhaps two "back stools" for the husband and wife.

The key to restoring such a kitchen today is simplicity. Closed cabinets are completely out of place, though for practical reasons most people will nonetheless consider them essential below the sink. A walk-in pantry solves most food storage problems, but you must disguise any modern equipment or hide it away when not in use or the effect will be spoiled.

18th- and 19th- Century Kitchens

The arrival of coal as fuel for cooking led initially to raised roasting hearths. At first, these still used spits and many of the other familiar fittings of the woodburning hearth, but later they began to evolve into enclosed cooking ranges. In the late 18th century we also begin to see sinks and indoor plumbing: it is thus quite realistic to consider restoring such a kitchen to something like its original appearance and layout.

The first built-in kitchen furniture dates from this period as the increasing range of kitchenware and utensils created a need for much more storage space. Most such furniture was very simply made from softwood using traditional carpentry. All was painted for ease of cleaning, apart from work surfaces which were regularly scrubbed or sanded and had to be replaced periodically.

The main items of furniture would still have been the center table and hutch, but tall cupboards for dried goods, preserves and the storage of reserve china and

kitchenware became commonplace. Usually such items were styled to match the wood wall paneling which gradually took over from whitewashed plastered walls. The design and construction of paneling and built-in furniture varied greatly from one part of the world to another and also at different dates. It is thus invaluable as an accurate dating guide.

In practice it is almost impossible to remove such furniture from the room in which it was made without considerable damage. That means that much of it has been destroyed during subsequent "improvements", and that much of what we are now offered as kitchen furniture of the 18th century is nothing of the sort.

A century later designers were embarking on the hunt for labor-saving devices, and the number and sophistication of the cooking ranges which came onto the market in the late 19th and early 20th centuries were remarkable. Many are still in excellent working order and can be included in a restored kitchen.

Furniture styling depended very much upon whether the kitchen was also the parlor in a small one-family house; if so, its styling became gradually more complex, although plain painted finishes were still the norm. In larger establishments, the furnishings became ever more utilitarian as the importance of ease of cleaning increased.

5 *This "tin" kitchen sink was actually made of soapstone and was part of the 1850 update of an 1830 New York house.* OMH

6 *This fireplace of c.1790 was discovered behind a Victorian wall. The fittings are in period. In the late 18thC there would have been several small fires rather than one large fire.* VNS

7 *This kitchen range would have been the height of fashion when put in place in 1850. It was made in Scotland by Abendroth Bros. in 1845 and imported to the United States. The fireplace crane was left in place.* OMH

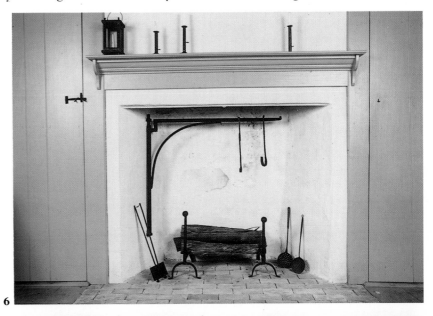

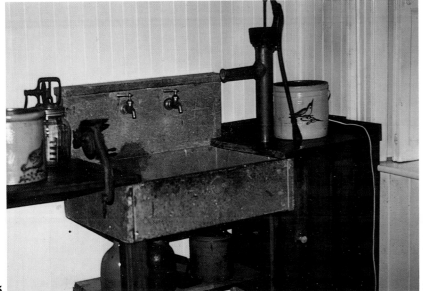

5

6

7

NEW KITCHENS IN THE TRADITIONAL IDIOM

Of course, the "traditional" kitchen furniture which is manufactured today is totally inauthentic. Generally, it is modern mass-produced furniture fitted with wood or painted fronts which ape certain elements of period style. Such ideas as "wall units" (which make things more difficult to get at, not easier) and work surfaces covered with tiles would have been laughed to scorn by any sane 19th-century cook, and the sheer impracticality of many of today's fanciful paint finishes would have been regarded in the same light. The essence of the traditional kitchen in its heyday was the practical combination of certain key elements – a big center table as the main work area; a carefully planned pantry where most food was stored; hutches and hanging racks for those items most in use; deep drawers for other kitchenware and utensils; and finally a really large sink surrounded by large scrubbable surfaces and a plate draining rack. When creating a kitchen which will be compatible with the style and atmosphere of a period house, always bear in mind that a real traditional kitchen was utterly practical and functional as well as warm, friendly and inviting.

It was the most important place in the house, even if normally used by servants. It is unrealistic to expect a modern cook to dispense with a dishwasher, food mixer, microwave and refrigerator. However, these can be hidden away in period kitchen cabinetry.

1 Interest is increasing in kitchens involving little or no built-in furniture. Some British companies are making careful copies of old items of kitchen furniture which work well in such settings. JI

2, 3 Two views of a "high Victorian" kitchen with some later practical additions in a mansion at Duns near the Scottish border with England. There are lessons to be learned from such kitchens in layout, construction, practical details and even the materials used, although modern kitchens are generally smaller. Local hardwoods have been used almost throughout for cabinets and surfaces, though the work table shown here is of pine and of an earlier date.

4 *Some of today's kitchen furniture workshops are very skilled at recapturing the spirit of past ages. This inset cabinet will be appreciated by anyone with a taste for that type of Victorian furniture which mixed design ideas from a dozen sources with such abandon.* HA

5 *The alternative to restoring a kitchen with old furniture or with reproduction woodwork styled to match the period and locality concerned is to use the traditionally-styled kitchen cabinetry which is now offered by a number of companies. This Smallbone hutch in bleached oak, for instance, would not look out of place in a kitchen dating anywhere from the 17th to the early 20thC.* S

6 *The atmosphere of a traditional British kitchen is recaptured in this apparently casual but in fact thoroughly practical hutch setting. A dishwasher lives behind one of the center doors. Much of the woodwork here has been adapted from other uses, just as most "backstairs" carpentry was a century or so ago.* ST

7 *This Continental Art Deco stove can indeed be used for decorative purposes, but is also practical and efficient for everyday use.*

CUSTOM-BUILT AND READY-MADE KITCHENS

The traditional kitchen discussed above is the purist's answer to restoration. However, many people will find the prospect of working in an original kitchen distinctly uninviting. We have become accustomed to built-in units and work surfaces. Fortunately, many firms produce kitchen furniture compatible with a period house. Many are styled after traditional patterns and some use old timber. There is a broad spectrum to choose from – innumerable colors and designs, textures and accessories. It is, however, vital to remember that country cottages demand a different style of kitchen from elegant town houses.

1 This kitchen has been carefully planned to give a modern design an old feel. The central Aga range is a convenient modern day equivalent of the Victorian cooking range. The solid pine table imitates the central table which was the hub of the period kitchen. This modern design looks apt in a period house. s

2 A modern Aga cooking range can be given a period feel with suitable accessories. AR

3 Not everyone is an advocate of unpainted solid wood kitchens, especially as many kitchens are in dark areas. This attractive painted kitchen from an English manufacturer is based on traditional hutch designs. s

1

2

3

4

6

4, 5, 6 *There are many examples of solid wood kitchens, ranging from dark solid mahogany to light honey-colored pine. Some kitchens use old wood, others are totally new although deriving from old designs. Plate racks, spice cupboards and traditional utensils give a pleasingly authentic look.*

M, S, PV

7 *An Art Deco house allows yet another design solution to kitchen planning. Note how the design on the doors is mirrored in the window glass.*

W

5

7

LIGHTING

Today we are spoiled by the convenience and design possibilities offered by electric light in the home. This is a recent luxury. Despite the introduction of gas and electricity, candles and oil or kerosene lamps were still widely used in the early 20th century, especially in rural regions.

Gas was first introduced in the 1780s. Electric light suitable for domestic purposes was not available until the late 1870s. Even oil lamps were not very useful until the invention in the 1780s of an improved reading lamp in which a current of air and a gravity feed made the wick burn ten times more brightly than before. Kerosene was not available until the middle of the 19th century. Few people restoring a period house are likely to want to return completely to the old laborious, dirty and inefficient methods, although a candlelit dinner will always hold its charms. What you can do, however, is adapt the early lamps to electricity or use them as supplementary lighting.

1

2

3

4

5

1 This free-standing iron candlestand is an accurate replica of early lighting. Candles can give out a surprising amount of heat and light.   SI

2 By 1877 this London house was illuminated by hanging gaslights (except in the dining room). The decorative ceiling rose served a useful purpose, the holes in the grille providing an outlet for noxious gas fumes.   LSH

3 This brass three-tiered chandelier would be equally at home in an 18th or 19thC environment.

4,5 Accurate reproduction Art Deco lamps help to create an instant atmosphere of the cool, contrived style of the 1930s.   EDL

EARLY CANDLES AND RUSH LIGHTS

In the great halls of medieval tradition, a big central fire was supplemented by torches thrust onto iron spikes or by light from cressets – metal baskets high up on poles, in which oil or pitch were burned. Cressets were much used in Elizabethan times. Piques (or spikes), used to impale the soft wax or tallow candles, either were small, holding a single candle, or stood four or five feet high with spikes for many candles. "Candle beams", usually of wood, with four stout bars to hold the candles (sometimes two per bar) radiating from a central bar suspended from the ceiling, were the handsome predecessors of elegant chandeliers. Brass candelabra were also used. Candles were also held aloft in staffs by servants or placed on spikes in wall sconces and on stands. Sometimes light was supplied by strips of rushes, dipped in oil and held in a simple wood-based iron stand and clip. As candles were much too expensive for ordinary cottagers, they used rush lights, sometimes dipped in mutton fat rather than less readily available oil.

The socket candlestick emerged in the 16th century, when sturdy brass candlesticks were first made. During the 17th century candleholders of all kinds became objects for display. Fashionable Britons borrowed the idea of a six- or twelve-branched brass candelabrum from the Low Countries. Candelabra were also produced in carved and gilded wood or ornamental wrought iron. Snuffers were of brass and precious metals as well as iron. In grand houses, silver sconces set against the wall helped increase the spread of light. In areas of Britain and America where fish oil was available, the poor used small oil lamps from shallow vessels with rough wicks.

6

8

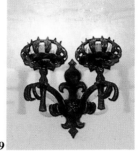

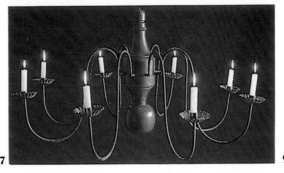

7

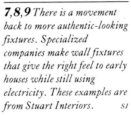

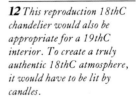

9

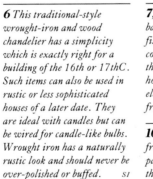

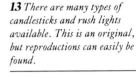

13

13 There are many types of candlesticks and rush lights available. This is an original, but reproductions can easily be found.

6 This traditional-style wrought-iron and wood chandelier has a simplicity which is exactly right for a building of the 16th or 17thC. Such items can also be used in rustic or less sophisticated houses of a later date. They are ideal with candles but can be wired for candle-like bulbs. Wrought iron has a naturally rustic look and should never be over-polished or buffed. SI

7,8,9 There is a movement back to more authentic-looking fixtures. Specialized companies make wall fixtures that give the right feel to early houses while still using electricity. These examples are from Stuart Interiors. SI

10,11 These chandeliers, also from Stuart Interiors, are particularly well-matched to their period settings. SI

12 This reproduction 18thC chandelier would also be appropriate for a 19thC interior. To create a truly authentic 18thC atmosphere, it would have to be lit by candles.

14 An original early 19thC lamp, restored and re-gilded. This would fit perfectly into any Egyptian Revival interior.

10

11

12

14

18th-Century Styles

Fine, handsome candlesticks embellished 18th-century interiors, even though each provided little light. At first, sturdy holders were still created, in a variety of metals, especially brass and bronze, to hold one or several candles. Slimmer, more elegant candlesticks were preferred by the middle of the 18th century. When more solid-looking ones later came back into fashion, they were plainer and were frequently made of sheet iron or burnished steel.

The 18th century saw more use of lanterns, which could be suspended or set against the wall (and, of course, carried). Their horn panels protected the flame from drafts. By the 1790s huge oil-burning lanterns, with a brass or iron frame housing six or eight glass panels, were hung in halls and stairways and to welcome guests at the front of the house.

Hanging light fixtures ranged from relatively modest brass ones, with a bowl-shaped body and six curved, branching candle holders, to the most exquisitely ornate chandeliers. The latter hung, huge, glittering and splendid, from the ceilings of ballrooms and drawing rooms. Some with as few as six candles nestled in a shower of sparkling cut glass hung in less grand though still substantial surroundings. On the walls of these rooms, elaborately backed sconces held yet further candles: scores would be burned in the course of an evening. In less wealthy homes tall, thin taper stands were common. These stood either on tripods, or on round or square bases, and came complete with attached scissors for snuffing the rush tapers which were burned in them.

1

5

6

1 Chandeliers occupy a lot of space and should only be used in a generously proportioned room. This example is a perfect copy of an early 19thC original.

2 *Looking-glass lights between the windows of an early 19thC house would have shed a fine, even light.* OMH

3 *A late 19thC wall light need not look incongruous in an 18thC house. As lighting developed, homeowners would instal the most modern and practical form of lighting without necessarily changing the decorative aspects.*

4 *A wrought-iron outside lantern, made in the 1930s but a perfect replica of mid-18thC style.* HH

5 *Hall lanterns give a warm and welcoming atmosphere to a hallway. This type would fit well into most late 18th and 19thC houses.* BP

6 *Gas chandeliers were a common sight in the parlor of a 19thC house. This example, typically High Victorian, has a "water-slide" system enabling the apparatus to be lowered.* OMH

7 *This 19thC hallway is devoid of the furniture and fabrics which would create the "upholstered" feel of a Victorian interior. However, 19thC lighting is enough to evoke the period.* OMH

2

3

4

7

THE 19TH CENTURY

Plain steel candlesticks continued to be fashionable during the early 19th century, when the recently discovered wax-hardening process made the candles burn more steadily and cleanly. Spermaceti candles, a product of the whaling industry, gave an even better light. Oil lamps, not much used in the 18th century, were also improved.

During the 19th century, despite readily available gas light, oil lamps were the most common source of light. When mineral oils became available in the middle of the century, they represented a huge step forward. Many Victorian kerosene lamps are still gently illuminating dinner tables and sitting rooms. Wicks can still be obtained for them, and so too can replacement chimneys and shades, should the originals get broken. Despite the limitations imposed by their working methods, Victorian oil lamps, or excellent reproductions of them, are found in an apparently endless range of designs, in glass as well as brass and other metals.

Gas was widely used in upper-middle-class homes on both sides of the Atlantic during the second part of the 19th century, until it was eclipsed by electricity. Gas light fixtures took their form from oil lamps, but could of course dispense with the reservoir. Hanging oil lamps with three or four burners fed from a central container for the oil were produced contemporaneously with suspended gas lights of similar appearance. However, gas lamps could easily be fixed to the wall as well, and piped gas lent itself perfectly to the European *fin de siècle* look, with sinuous ornamentation. **10**

12 An early 20thC rise-and-fall hanging lamp with opaline glass lampshade. The great advantage of electricity was that light was thrown downward where it was most needed. LSH

12

8 An electric bracket light in the style of a 19thC gas fitting. The glare of light bulbs can be hidden behind clear frosted, colored or engraved shades to create the mellow lighting of the era. EDL **8**

9 A good example of a reproduction 19thC hanging lamp. The original would have been fitted for gas or oil; however, adaptation to electricity does not detract from the period feel. EDL

10 This Venetian chandelier does not look out of place in a 19thC house, but really belongs to the less cluttered, classical style of the 18thC. It requires a room of high proportions. LH

11 Gas fittings often remained in place even when electricity had largely superseded gas. Their hollow pipes made them easy to convert. LSH

9

11

13

13 A typical Victorian lamp, evocative of the clutter and cosiness of the period. LSH

ELECTRICITY

From the 1880s, Edison lamps in the United States and Swan lamps in Britain brought the blessings of clean, controlable and odor-free electric light into the home. Electric light gave all possible scope to designers. Some stuck rigidly to the candle theme, and placed the light bulbs on candle-like stalks set in traditional candelabra or table-standing burners. Others exploited the bulb's relative fire-safety, devising cunning little shades to soften the bulb's glare.

Electric lights were also set in wrought-iron fittings of branches, leaves and flowers. They were equipped with shades in glass and metal, the glass fluted and shaped like bluebells and harebells, or in the form of simple globes and cones. European Art Nouveau contributed its characteristic curves and milky opaque glass in subtle colors. Perhaps most spectacular of all were the American Tiffany lamps in their glowing stained-glass shades.

These and their coolly elegant 20th-century Art Deco successors are now available in perfect reproductions from manufacturers specializing in Art Deco fixtures. Those whose purse cannot stretch to handmade reproductions will find that a search through antique and second-hand stores, or a visit to an auction sale, may still yield affordable period light fixtures. An early 20thC mottled glass bowl suspended by a brass chain or an Expressionist faceted wall light in metal housing would complete a well-contrived interior.

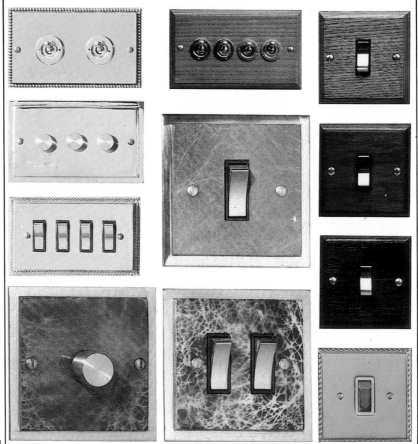

1

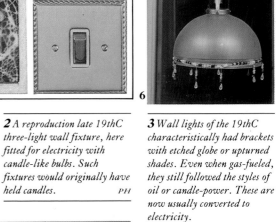

6

2

3

4

5

1 *A selection of modern reproduction lighting switches which can look preferable in a period house to white plastic. However, some people may feel that white switches are less conspicuous.*

2 *A reproduction late 19thC three-light wall fixture, here fitted for electricity with candle-like bulbs. Such fixtures would originally have held candles.* PH

3 *Wall lights of the 19thC characteristically had brackets with etched globe or upturned shades. Even when gas-fueled, they still followed the styles of oil or candle-power. These are now usually converted to electricity.*

4 *An early 19thC gilt metal hanging lantern, now wired for electricity.*

5 *Hall lanterns were still being used to light the way for guests in the late 19thC, but they had become much more ornate.* PCA

6 *Standard rise-and-fall hanging lamps of the late Victorian period and early 20thC can surprisingly still be found intact in their original settings.*

7,8,9,10 *Art Nouveau lamps have become highly desirable in recent years. Many of the best were made by the firm of Tiffany in New York, as illustrated by the examples here. These are originals. Similar lamps are to be found in auction rooms and antique shops.*

11,12,13,14,15 *Art Deco lamps can add greatly to the atmosphere of a 1920s or 30s apartment or house. These examples are reproductions but follow the lines and colors of the originals.* EDL

The visual pleasure we derive from the outsides of period houses comes partly from the architectural elements – the doors, windows and so on – and the ways in which they are treated and related to each other. Enjoyment also comes from the materials – weathered limestone, shining granite, knapped flint or bricks of every type, size and arrangement, whether Elizabethan herringbone or 19th-century polychrome, perhaps dressed up in contrasting stone on the corners (quoins), pilaster strips and window frames. The hardened oak of half-timbering, the ornamental impact of plasterwork, traditional wooden clapboarding: all have their own characteristic "feel". Additionally, the personality of a house is expressed in its immediate surroundings, the nature of the boundaries (walls, fences, railings, hedges), the materials and detailing of access points (gates, paths and steps).

1 *A stone pineapple offers a sign of welcome beside an entrance. Although such ornaments are always called pineapples, they are in fact pine cones, ancient symbols of fertility, wealth and general well-being.*

2 *These sphinxes and obelisks, proudly guarding an entrance to a fine townhouse, reflect the fascination with Ancient Egypt in the early 19thC.*

3 *This doorway combines many features from the late 18th and early 19thC. The classical pediment conflicts slightly with the decorative ironwork on the door and holding the lantern.*

4 *Exterior lead pipework was formerly treated as part of the decoration of a house.*

5 *Decorative ironwork on balconies was popular in both the 18th and 19thC.*

6 *When designing this house in New York – a perfect replica of one of 1760, built in the 1920s – the architect included some elements salvaged from old houses. However, most features here are faithful copies. The ornate carving over the entrance includes the beaver symbol of New York State.*

HH

SCROLLS, URNS AND STATUES

In post-medieval England, the Tudors elaborated doorways with terracotta panels and stucco coats-of-arms, roses and animals. Then the Jacobeans continued this tradition and developed it, sometimes covering whole facades of half-timbered houses with plaster ornament. Patterns could be simple scrolls set in large panels or, in East Anglia, swirling "parget work" decorated with clumsy but charming classical motifs such as swags.

In the late 17thC century, came the fashion for classical facades, though usually without the parapets of later classical houses. Ornament was rather in the form of bold pediments partly concealing the sloping roofs and decorated with stone swags and emblems and stone pilasters with elaborate capitals. The niches of the Palladian mansions of the 18th century were occupied by stucco figures in contemporary dress, in place of the classical statues in stone that were favored previously.

In the early 18th century, gardens of grand houses were still designed formally in the French manner, with broad avenues and *rond-points* (intersections). Main avenues were flanked with trees, but urns, vases and classical statuary along the paths also made an important contribution, and these features were continued in the facade niches, along the tops of walls and set into parapets. Stone garden urns were often encrusted with swags and cherubs.

Later in the 18th century the English passion for landscaping superseded the formal garden, but niches were still provided for classical statues, for example in clipped yew hedges, and stone lions overlooked the parkland from the balustraded terrace next to the house. **7**

Gardening and plants had become a passion at all levels of society from the middle classes upward. In an age when pattern books were disseminating details of classical design among builders, gardening manuals were also widely distributed, with advice on all subjects, including ideas for tubs and window boxes for houses without gardens.

In the 19th century many of the older features were revived. The parget work and stucco of the period have a vigor which makes them hard to distinguish them from their 17th-century models, while houses built in the same spirit as the Palladian mansions have classical statuary in the same manner, with the niches inhabited by figures such as Venus and Apollo.

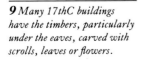

7 This 19thC house has ornamental balustrading which dominates the roof and the top of the bay window. Note also the scroll design under the balustrade. LSH

8 Classically inspired eagles are often later additions.

9 Many 17thC buildings have the timbers, particularly under the eaves, carved with scrolls, leaves or flowers.

10 It is still possible to buy garden ornaments made from old molds or based on 18th and 19thC patterns. CS

BOUNDARIES

Small country houses may be bounded with picket fences – simple wooden slats placed quite closely together and driven into the ground or fixed to supporting posts with wire, or often nailed to wooden horizontal bars themselves fixed to posts.

This style is particularly suited to American towns.

In New England, *Arbor vitæ* (thuja) makes a fine hedge, and has done for two-hundred years. Remember that such hedges need careful maintenance.

RAILINGS AND GATES

Ironwork was introduced to Britain by William and Mary when they brought the French Huguenot smith Tijou to work under their patronage in 1689. He made beautiful gates, balustrades and garden screens in sheet iron embossed into scrolls, gilded flower and acanthus leaves in a way not seen in England before. Subsequently ironwork became enormously popular, and with good reason. The gates might be set within stone posts, perhaps with niches and topped with eagles or covered urns, or fluted and bearing proud gryphons. Charming pastoral figures in lead were found on gate posts by the end of the 17th century and were in vogue during the 18th. Wrought iron might also be used for the posts themselves and for delicate arches across the top of wide gateways.

With the passage of time, upper-class styles in ironwork filtered down to the less privileged social strata. Wrought, *repoussé* (hammered) and eventually cheaper cast iron were used for plain and decorative railings, gateways and other features right up to the 20th century. In the 18th century simple, well-proportioned cast-iron work was as much favored as more elaborate wrought-iron scrolls and curves. Even simple town houses had plain cast-iron railings around

their areas (the British term for the enclosed spaces between the street and the drop to the basement) and up the steps to the front door. In the early 18th century, wrought iron flourished in England in the form of elaborate balconies, verandas and porches. Door hoods were revived, but now made in curving sheets of lead, like the veranda canopies of the same period. All such flourishes, however decorative, were still accompanied by plain boundary railings at the front of the house. Fine ironwork was also produced in America throughout this period. Much of it still survives today to beautify our streets.

Throughout the 19th century similar plain cast-iron railings continued to be provided at the front of countless new houses, and sometimes also for little balconies above the porch. By the turn of the century even the smallest houses had such railings at the front.

Towards the end of the 19th century, grand detached houses in the Queen Anne style, though so different in appearance from these row houses, also had iron-work boundary fences. In keeping with their attachment to old traditions, these were usually wrought, not cast. Fortunately the art of the smith is still flourishing today, and there are many architectural metalworkers who can restore wrought- and cast-iron work to make replacements in keeping with the style of the house.

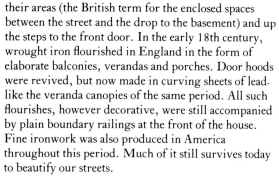

1 *Ornate wrought-iron balustrades, terminating in lantern-shaped newel posts, flank the stone steps at the entrance to this Federal-style American house.* OMH

2,3 *Two views of the fence and gate of an 1830s house in Roslyn, New York. The white painted picket fence has elaborate spear tops and the supporting posts of the gateway with their vase decoration have the importance of columns. The close-up shows the original iron hinges and shutting mechanism.*

4,5 *Wrought-iron railings are a delightful and interesting adjunct to houses of the 18th and 19thC. On smaller houses they were often quite plain but in grander houses they used many classical themes such as the pineapple or pine cone.*

6

7

8

9

10

11

12

13

15

14

6-14 *Wrought-iron, and, later, cast-iron balconies and railings were common in both grand and simple houses. It is essential to the look of our streets that rows retain a feeling of continuity. Craftsmen can reproduce perfect copies, and these do improve the overall appearance of the exteriors of period houses. Your local historical or architectural society should be able to advise on the style of balcony or railing which would have been original to the house. Otherwise, copies of neighboring styles will suffice.*

15 *On a Neo-classical stone mansion built between 1837 and 1846, the wrought ironwork sweeps down on either side of the steps to curve around the newel posts.* BP

1 *Plain railings were not always mirrored in the treatment of balconies and ironwork around windows. Houses develop piecemeal, as owners decide to introduce more up-to-date features.*

2 *The entrance porch of a late 19thC house is given greater importance with pillars, arches and a balcony above.*

3,4 *Whether in a simple terrace or grander entrance, 18thC houses often show a feeling for proportion and the continuity of classical themes.*

5 *Wrought and plain ironwork provide a useful security device for this basement of an early 19thC house.*

STEPS AND STAIRS

The great Palladian houses had magnificent double staircases curving or angling up to a terrace along the house. On a smaller scale, the front doors of town houses (however close to the street) were from the late 17th century almost universally approached by stone steps the breadth of the door frame. No fine house, however handsome, would be quite so imposing without the steps leading up to its front door.

When the entrance was at a sufficiently high level, the flight of steps could be longer. However, until well into the 19th century often as few as two or three treads were needed. The builder's or architect's skill in judging proportions came fully into play: it is surprising how harmonious two steps can be. The lower step in 18th-century houses may rise only slightly above the street; sometimes it is wider than the step above and curved at the sides; and often a molded nose finishes the edge of each step.

Railings around the basement area usually continued up the sides of the steps to the porch or front door. In more elegant houses, the railings included lamp holders and conical link extinguishers, which may still survive, as may iron shoe scrapers of various designs.

Houses of the 19th century may have lacked the finely judged proportions of their predecessors but their broader entranceways, set higher up from street level and farther back, enabled them to have impressive flights of stone steps. These might have simply molded noses, continuing round the rounded-off corners, or be flanked by wide stone flat-topped or solidly balustraded ramps, in keeping with the solid, comfortable houses. Later Victorian houses with semi-basements and set close to the road have ended up with an awkwardly steep flight of inelegant steps, compensated for, perhaps, by the lofty rooms inside. In the early 20th century, the main rooms were once again at ground level, and have remained there ever since.

6

8

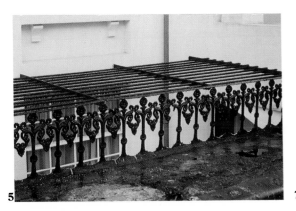

5

7

6 *A long flight of steps leads up to the side door of a 1748 Bronx mansion. The lattice work under the steps is to facilitate a good flow of air.* VC

7 *A Victorian house in London where cast-iron railings and gate are matched by low rails in front of the bay windows. The areas too have simple railings cutting them off from the approach to the house. The front door is reached by a flight of stone steps, flanked by flat-topped balustraded ramps terminating in pillars and flower urns.* LSH

8 *Steps to the front door were standard even in the simple terrace. These steps are tiled. Note also the highly decorative ironwork on the upper floor.*

We generally think of the conservatory as a Victorian invention, and indeed it had its heyday in the 19th century. However, it was first popular in the 18th, in the form of the elegant orangery. The advantages of a conservatory, not only as a place for plants but also as a living and dining area with a summery atmosphere, remain undiminished today.

The orangery was a gracious extra room in the elegant 18th-century mansion in both England and America. It satisfied the 18th-century passion for the pastoral – a terrace would often run along the outside, adjoining the garden – and as the name implies it was a place where exotic fruits could be grown. These would be raised in tubs so that they could be set out or even planted in the summer. Orangeries were designed and built in the same manner as the rest of the house. Although the walls consisted of glazed windows on three sides (the fourth often being joined to the house), the parapets usually concealed a conventional slate or tiled roof. After cast iron began to be used in the 1770s, the orangery retained its noble, restrained form. It was at this period a carefully proportioned, unobtrusive building, very different from its showy Victorian relative, which bristled with cast-iron ornament and flaunted huge sheets of polished glass.

By the end of the 18th century the metamorphosis had begun. Robert Adam designed orangeries with slighter glazing bars and coved ceilings. Some wooden-framed glass roofs were also to be found at this time.

However, it was Joseph Paxton and his contemporaries in the 1830s who completed the

1

2   3

1,2 These two large conservatories are essentially glasshouses in the tradition of the 19thC. It is a modern convention to paint conservatories white: Victorian examples would more often have been green. Green canvas awnings give excellent shade while retaining a period feel. ML

3 A conservatory that joins two sections of a house in the form of a corridor with roof and frontage aligned. ML

4

5

6

8

7

4 *In townhouses where there is no space to put a conservatory in the garden, one answer is to add one at second floor level over a protruding downstairs room.*   ML

5 *An original Victorian "window-box" type of conservatory. These are close relations to the "Wardian cases" in which travelers transported ferns and other exotic plants from foreign places.*   LSH

6,7 *A Victorian-style conservatory that completely fills the space between an L-shaped house and an adjacent outbuilding. Notice how the transitional feel between indoors and out is accentuated by using the same tiling on the conservatory floor and the terrace: if you do this, make sure the tiles will stand up to the weather.*   ML

8 *A conservatory must harmonize with the building to which it is attached. Here, the stone and brick base blend with the main dwelling.*   MJ

transformation. Paxton's passion was as much for plants as it was for the new technology of glass and iron. The vogue for collecting and displaying new exotic varieties spread rapidly. In 1851, the year of the Great Exhibition in London, window tax in Britain was finally abolished; the duty on glass, which had made heavier glass prohibitively expensive, was removed in 1857. The Crystal Palace, built by Paxton for the Exhibition, started a craze for glasshouses and conservatories. The demand was quickly met by prefabricated glass-and-iron structures, some with underfloor heating for tropical trees, or glazed extensions to the sitting room in which to cultivate ferns. Americans enthusiastically followed the fashion.

The new ornamented conservatories, perfect for mid-19th-century houses whose design was free from classical constraints, remained in fashion until the First World War. In larger row houses they sometimes provided all the garden there was, and in the smallest they were little more than exotic lean-tos. Early 20th-century examples were less ornate, and might well be preferable if you are adding onto a small house.

Although they can make the rooms from which they extend darker, conservatories are wonderfully light in themselves and remove the need for double glazing. However, they do need their own heating and shading systems to avoid extremes of climate hostile to sensitive plants. In the northern hemisphere, a south-west wall is the safest choice of situation.

If you are adding a conservatory to a pre-19th-century house, a building modeled on the orangery would be more authentic, with large windows in the same style as the house rather than a prominent all-glass room which would strike an anachronistic note. For Victorian and later houses, glass and metal styles are perfectly acceptable.

Very satisfactory reproduction period conservatories are available today. They are expensive but they add a whole new living area, and provided that they are carefully integrated in style and scale they give a special atmosphere of elegance and exoticism to both house and garden.

ANDIRON (OR ENDIRON): *a metal bar, supported on feet, to hold burning logs above hearth level (also called FIREDOG).*

ARCADING: *a series of arches on columns or PIERS which can be freestanding or attached to a wall.*

ARCHITRAVE: *the molded frame around a window or door; or, more properly, the lowest portion of an ENTABLATURE.*

BACON FLAKE: *traditional north of England name for a wood rack hung from the kitchen ceiling on extended iron hooks. It was used to store cured hams and smoked bacon sides during the winter. "Bread flakes", to a somewhat different design, were used in a similar way to store loaves and the large cookies which were traditionally cooked on iron plates over open fires.*

BALUSTER: *a banister, typically turned and undulating in form (which is why the term baluster is given to coffee pots, glass stems etc. of this shape).*

BALUSTRADE: *a series of BALUSTERS supporting a handrail or coping.*

BAROQUE: *rather heavy, flamboyant style which originated in Italy in the early 17th century and appeared in England and North America late in the same century.*

BATTEN DOOR: *a door made from rows of vertical planks, nailed or pegged to supporting horizontal planks.*

BOSS: *an ornamental knob at the intersection of ribs in a ceiling or a vault.*

BULL'S EYE: *see CROWN GLASS.*

BUTLER SINK: *a large, oblong proprietary English sink of all-white or white and beige porcelain on fireclay. In England the name is now commonly used for all sinks of this type, though most are later and much deeper laboratory sinks. The true Butler sinks were rarely more than 6in deep.*

CAMES: *the strip of metal used for leaded lights.*

CAPITAL: *the crowning feature of a column.*

CASEMENT WINDOW: *a window with the sash hung vertically and which opens inward or outward by means of a hinge.*

CHAMFER: *to cut or grind off bevel-wise the edge of a piece of wood or stone originally right-angled.*

CONSOLE BRACKET: *ornamental bracket, often of S-form and usually having more height than projection.*

CORNICE: *a decorative projecting molding around the top of a wall or arch (in an interior it usually disguises the join between walls and ceilings); the projecting top section of an ENTABLATURE.*

CROWN GLASS: *a sheet of glass made by blowing a bubble and spinning it rapidly on the rod; a BULL'S EYE is formed where the rod is attached.*

DEPRESSED ARCH: *a shallow slightly pointed arch.*

DOGLEG STAIRCASE: *two parallel flights of stairs with a half-landing between them.*

DOORFRAME: *the ARCHITRAVE enclosing a door.*

DOWN HEARTH: *Southern English name for an open fireplace in which a log fire was formed directly on the floor of the INGLENOOK. Often used for cooking as well, using turnspits, pots and griddle plates hung over the fire from bars or cranes and three-legged gunmetal pots pushed into the edge of the fire.*

ENTABLATURE: *in classical architecture, the top part of a column made up of ARCHITRAVE, FRIEZE and CORNICE; a decoration made up in this way popular from the mid-18th century.*

FANLIGHT: *a window over a door, often semi-circular with radiating glazing bars.*

FENDER: *a low metal screen which prevents burning coals or logs from rolling into the room.*

FENESTRAL: *a lattice frame across which oiled or waxed paper or linen was stretched to keep out drafts while letting in the light.*

FIELDED PANEL: *panel with the center raised in profile.*

FIREBACK: *a thick cast-iron panel put at the back of a hearth to protect the wall and to reflect heat into the room.*

FIREDOG: *see ANDIRON.*

FLAG: *stone slab used for flooring.*

FREESTONE: *stone that cuts well in any direction, notably fine-grained sandstone or limestone.*

FRIEZE: *the middle section of an ENTABLATURE: the upper part of a wall directly below the cornice.*

GRATE: *a framework of bars to hold a fire.*

INGLENOOK: *a recess for a seat beside a fireplace, often covered by the chimney breast.*

KNAPPED FLINT: *flints split and laid so that the smooth black split surfaces form the facing of the wall.*

LIGHT: *vertical opening between MULLIONS of a window.*

LIMEWASH: *in England a mixture of slaked lime and water used for painting walls.*

LINK: *a torch.*

LINENFOLD: *a paneling decorated with designs representing vertical folds of linen.*

LINTEL: *a horizontal beam or stone across an opening.*

MANTELPIECE: *the frame around a fireplace which may be made from brick, stone, marble or wood. In Europe, sometimes called a chimneypiece.*

MULLION: *upright dividing a window into two or more LIGHTS.*

NEWEL POST: *the upright post at the end, or at the corner, of the handrail of a staircase; on a circular staircase, the column around which the stairs wind.*

OVERMANTEL: *an ornamental structure placed over a MANTELPIECE.*

PALLADIAN: *a style of architecture taken from the designs of the 16th-century Italian architect Palladio. Inigo Jones took the style to England in the 17th century but the great revival of Palladianism was brought about by Lord Burlington and Colen Campbell in the first quarter of the 18th century.*

PANELED DOOR: *a door constructed of panels set within a frame.*

PANTILE: *a roofing tile with a curved S-shaped section.*

PARGET WORK: *a style of molded plaster decoration particularly associated with the eastern counties of England.*

PARLOR FLOOR: *see PIANO NOBILE.*

PARQUETAGE: *thin hardwood laid in patterns on a wood sub-floor.*

PAVIORS: *thin "bricks" used for flooring.*

PEDIMENT: *a low-pitched gable above a portico, door or window which may be either straight-sided or curbed; a broken pediment is one which is open at the top.*

PIANO NOBILE: *the principal story of a house — more lofty than the others — containing the reception rooms; there is a basement or ground floor below and shallower floors above. In North America, often referred to as the parlor floor.*

PIER: *a solid vertical masonry support or post; the solid section of wall between openings — windows, doors etc — in a building.*

PILASTER: *a shallow column or PIER set against a wall and projecting only slightly from it.*

PITCH FLOORS: *floors made from small pieces of stone laid like cobblestones and arranged in patterns.*

PLATE GLASS: *glass used for mirrors and windows, originally made by pouring molten glass onto an iron plate.*

QUARRY (OR QUARREL): *a small pane of glass, most often diamond-shaped, used for medieval leaded windows.*

RABBET (OR REBATE): *a rectangular recess along an edge of a piece of wood or stone to receive a tongue of another piece.*

REEDED: *decorated with parallel convex moldings which touch one another.*

REREDOS: *a screen. The term is more commonly used for the decorative wall or screen behind an altar.*

RESTORATION: *the time of the reinstatement of the monarchy in England in 1660.*

REVEAL: *the side surface of a recess or of the opening for a door or window between the frame and the outer surface of the wall. If the reveal is cut diagonally it is called a splay (or splayed) reveal.*

ROASTING HEARTH: *Late 18th-century cooking hearth in which coal was burned in a grate of variable width raised well above the floor of an inglenook on horizontal bars. These hearths were the predecessors of early cooking ranges.*

ROCOCO: *the delicate and elegant style which followed the BAROQUE, characterized by S-curves, naturalistic motifs and a tendency towards asymmetry.*

SASH WINDOW: *a window composed of sliding glazed frames (sashes) running in vertical grooves.*

STENCIL: *originally "to spangle", from the Old French estinceller: now describes a method of decoration where paint is brushed over a cut-out design usually in varnished manilla paper.*

STILES: *the vertical parts of a door, window, or other frame.*

STRAPWORK: *decoration consisting of interlaced bands and shapes like fretwork.*

STRINGS: *the sloping sides of a staircase which hold the treads and risers.*

STUCCO: *smooth or modeled plasterwork.*

STUDS: *secondary vertical wall timbers.*

TABERNACLE FRAME: *a style of door surround composed of columns or pilasters surmounted by an ENTABLATURE.*

TESSELATED FLOOR: *a floor composed of small cubes of marble, stone or glass embedded in cement.*

TRANSOM: *a bar dividing a window opening horizontally.*

TROMPE L'OEIL: *something which gives the appearance of reality by means of paint, architecture etc; literally "something that deceives the eye".*

TUDOR ARCH: *a very flattened arch coming to a definite point.*

WAINSCOT: *wood paneling on an internal wall.*

WATTLE AND DAUB: *a type of wall construction whereby laths are plastered over with mud.*

Books about old houses abound in general and specialized bookshops. Most of them focus either on exterior architecture or on one particular period style. Many restored historic houses have shops which carry an assortment of books about the period they represent. Museums, too, often have excellent bookshops. The Metropolitan Museum of Art in New York, the Boston Museum of Fine Arts, and the National Gallery in Washington, DC, all have very large stocks of design books. Another specialized bookshop is:

Urban Center Books
The Villard Houses
457 Madison Avenue (at 51st Street)
New York
NY 10022
(212) 935-3595
Which carries a splendid array of books and magazines in all languages on architecture and design, and will give information by mail or phone.

University bookshops are another good source for these books. It is impossible to choose a definitive booklist for home restoration, because new books are published constantly, and much depends on the period of the house being restored. However, two very expensive books on interior design are invaluable. They are _Interior Decoration_ by Mario Praz and _Authentic Decor_ by Peter Thornton. If buying them is not possible they are worth seeking out in a library. Although both focus on furnishings, the many illustrations give an incomparable survey of the proportions and details of period rooms.

The Fine Tool Journal
PO Box 4001
Pittsford
VT 05763
(802) 483-2111
(800) 248-8114
A newsletter on tools for collectors and craftsmen. This splendidly personal publication includes news, classified ads, letters and an absentee auction for those interested in old hammers, saws, planes, etc. Annual subscription available.

Old-House Journal magazine publishes a frequently updated _Catalog_, available from bookshops or direct from the magazine:

The Old-House Journal
2 Main Street
Gloucester
MA 01930
(508) 283-3200
This is a very extensive list of product sources useful to house restorers.

To identify house styles, one of the most useful and complete books is _A Field Guide to American Houses_ by Virginia and Lee McAlester. It deals with exterior architecture, but many of the fine line drawings of window and door details pertain also to interior style.
Magazine articles and advertisements are probably the best up-to-date sources for ideas and products. _The Old-House Journal_ and _Victorian Homes_ are extremely useful magazines, as is _Historic Preservation_, available only to members of:

The National Trust for Historic Preservation
1785 Massachusetts Avenue
Washington
DC 20036
(202) 673-4000
For a modest annual membership fee, National Trust members receive the organizations monthly newspaper, _Preservation News_.
National and regional "shelter" magazines often feature articles about historic houses. Some of the best-known are _House and Garden, Architectural Digest, House Beautiful, Colonial Homes, Decorating Remodeling, Southern Living, Texas Homes,_ and _Sunset_. There are many more, and a visit to a good magazine shop which specializes in design will produce lots of ideas.

There are many organizations devoted to the preservation of old houses, whether historically significant or simply family homes of past eras. They include the following:

The National Trust for Historic Preservation
1785 Massachusetts Avenue
Washington
DC 20036
(202) 673-4000
The Trust publishes Historic Preservation, _a bi-monthly magazine,_ Preservation News _a monthly newspaper and administers many of the country's finest historic houses and gardens. Modest annual membership fee._

The Center for Historic Houses
The National Trust for Historic Preservation
1785 Massachusetts Avenue
Washington
DC 20036
(202) 673-4000
This section of the National Trust is geared particularly to the needs of homeowners. It organizes lectures and workshops all over the country, and will refer owners of old houses to the appropriate preservation organizations.

Lower Hudson Conference Historical Agencies and Museums
2199 Saw Mill River Road
Elmsford
NY 10523
(914) 592-6726
Serves Dutchess Putnam, Rockland and Westchester counties. Holds workshops, provides onsite technical assistance, publishes the directory of Historical Agencies, Museums and Local Historians _for its area and has a lending library of technical books and video tapes._

The New York Landmarks Conservancy
141 Fifth Avenue
New York
NY 10010
(212) 995-5260
Publishes The Restoration Directory, _a listing of services in the New York City area, from archaeologists and architects to roofers and stone masons. The book is annually updated, and can be ordered from the Landmarks Conservancy._

Preservation Associates, Inc.
117 S. Potomac Street
Hagerstown
MD 21740
(301) 791-7880
A nationally oriented firm providing a broad range of specialized preservation consulting and rehabilitation services. They are experienced with State and Federal laws and regulations as well as having technical expertise in rehabilitation projects. Will guide projects through government regulations, technical and design phases and the actual rehabilitation work.

Antiquarian Traders
4851 South Alameda Street
Los Angeles
CA 900588
(213) 627-2144
Specializing in American Renaissance, Revivial Victorian, American Oak, Country French, Art Nouveau, Art Deco, English and Architectural antiques.

Great Gatsby's
5070 Peachtree Industrial Boulevard
Atlanta
GA 30341
(800) 962-5229
Auctioneers of fine antiques and architectural appointments from all over the world. Paneled rooms, marquetry, ornately hand-molded furniture. Marble and brass statuary, bronze entryways, chandeliers, fountains, saloon decor, stained glass windows, paintings and collectibles.

Below is a brief sample of the thousands of specialized and localized services available to house restorers.

ARCHITECTURAL SALVAGE YARDS

These concerns which save and sell original components from old buildings due to be demolished are ideal sources for authentic restoration material. Sometimes you can find exactly matching windows or doors from a house built at the same time as the one you are restoring; more often the finds are similar but not identical. Research is important before plunging into the world of architectural salvage – it is easy to be dazzled by the many wonderful objects, and to buy things of the wrong period or style. Measure carefully. Although many yards will modify and even help instal what they sell, it is not really in the spirit of restoration to cut up old paneling or doors more than absolutely necessary. When restoring old buildings, become your own expert; if you see houses of a similar period to yours being torn

down, approach the demolition contractor and ask them if you can purchase components on the spot. Salvage yards tend to come and go according to the available supply of materials. Watch local newspapers for notices of auctions and new sources for old materials.

Irreplaceable Artifacts
14 Second Avenue at Houston Street
New York
NY 10013
(212) 777-2900
Large range of architectural components. These yards always seem to have a particularly interesting supply of statuary and garden ornaments. Write with requirements.

Joe Ley Antiques, Inc.
615 East Market Street
Louisville
KY 40202
(502) 583-4014
Two acres of architectural antiques, from plumbing and hardware to carousel horses and antique toys. Also a wide selection of lighting and paneling, as well as doors and windows and fireplaces. Brochure available but as the stock is constantly changing, it's advisable to write with requirements.

Materials Unlimited
2 West Michigan Avenue
Ypsilanti
MI 48197
(313) 483-6980
Vast selection of everything to build or restore period and period-style houses. A salvage yard with the usual fine antiques saved from demolished buildings. Also a great many lines of reproduction hardware, metalwork, doors, moldings, etc. Catalogs of reproduction lines available, and custom work done, especially of leaded and beveled glass panels. Inquiries welcome.

Nostalgia Architectural Antiques
307 Stiles Avenue
Savannah
GA 31401
(912) 232-2324

Besides their architectural salvage operation, which specializes in artifacts from fine old Georgia houses, this company manufactures replicas of these items. Some are made with old parts, while others are reproduced from their own originals. A large line of plumbing fixtures, ironwork, doors and windows and capitals. Custom work undertaken. Illustrated catalog available.

United House Wrecking
535 Hope Street
Stamford
CT 06906
(203) 348-5371
Acres of architectural antiques salvaged from Connecticut houses. Famous for French doors, both antique and reproduction, they also carry other sorts of doors and windows, porch parts, fireplaces and all the elements you would use to restore an old house. Write with requirements.

Walker's
PO Box 309
Tallmadge
OH 44278
(216) 633-1081
Historic building materials from Ohio barns, from beams and siding to entire structures. They also have dismantled houses in many styles including Greek Revival and old log cabins ready for reconstruction. Plans as well as assistance in reconstruction available. Free brochure.

The Wrecking Bar of Atlanta, Inc.
292 Moreland Avenue NE
Atlanta
GA 30307
(404) 525-0468
This firm, which displays its stock in a historic house, preserves and restores everything from old houses except the floors and ceilings. They will custom design and fabricate from antique materials, and send photographs and measurements in response to requests for specific items. Free brochure.

The Renovator's Supply
6439 Renovator's Old Mill
Millers Falls
MA 01349
(413) 659 2241

Antique Baths & Kitchens (S. Chris Rheinschild)
2220 Carlton Way
Santa Barbara
CA 93109
(805) 962-8598
The company produces a small line of bathroom and kitchen fixtures designed for Victorian houses. High and low tank toilets, with oak tanks. A range of sinks include a marble vanity, a fluted pedestal, copper and brass basins, as well as a handmade copy of a very old copper kitchen sink. Custom shapes and sizes may be ordered. Brochure available.

The Antique Hardware Store
43 Bridge Street Dept PD
Frenchtown
NJ 08825
(908) 996-4040
Pedestal sinks and their hardware, as well as other sorts of hardware, lighting and weathervanes. Their motto: "If they still make it, we can get it!" Full-color catalog available.

Ferguson Enterprises
1502 Slocum Street
Dallas
TX 75207
(214) 761-9333
Suppliers of toilets, basins, faucets, tiles, marbles and wallcoverings. Classical, Art Deco and high-tech styles. Catalog available.

Renovation Concepts
9611 Humboldt Avenue
South Bloomington
MI 55431
(612) 884-4288
An enormous supplier of everything for renovation, they stock all sorts of old-style plumbing fixtures, hardware, lighting and molding. Looseleaf trade catalog and free brochure available.

Vintage Plumbing Bathroom Antiques
9645 Sylvia Avenue
Northridge
Granada Hills
CA 91324
(818) 772-1721

Suppliers of turn-of-the-century American mansion quality bathroom fixtures. Will answer technical questions, and restore customers' pieces. Reference library of manufacturers' catalogs from 1880s to 1915. Free brochure.

Kohler Co.
Dept AL8
Kohler
WI 53044
(414) 457-4441

COLUMNS

Chadsworth Columns
Chadsworth Inc.
POBox 53268
Dept 1
Atlanta
GA 30355
(404) 876-5410

Authentic replications of Greek and Roman columns. Architectural wood columns, wooden pedestals and table bases. Catalog available.

Classic Architectural Specialities
3223 Canton Street
Dallas
TX 75226
(214) 748-1668

Wooden architectural columns in a variety of sizes and styles. The shafts may be plain or fluted with a choice of three base styles and nine capital styles. Custom designs executed. This company makes a variety of porch posts as well as a range of molding and Victorian gingerbread.

Design Toscano
15 E. Campbell Street
Arlington Heights
IL 60005
(800) 525-0733

Nation's largest collection of handcast classical columns, table bases, architectural elements, brackets and friezes.

Robinson Iron
Robinson Road
Alexander City
AL 35010
(205) 329-8486

Manufacturers of cast-iron columns in many different patterns which can be combined in different ways for a variety of effects. This company casts lamp posts, as well as fences, statuary and fountains. Brochure available.

A. F. Schwerd Manufacturing Company
3215 McClure Avenue
Pittsburgh
PA 15212
(412) 766-6322

Wooden columns in several architecturally correct styles. Bases may be ordered in aluminum, ornamental capitals in a durable composition material. Custom work is a large part of their business. They also make copper lanterns and several designs of wooden posts.

Worthington Group Ltd
PO Box 53101
Atlanta
GA 30355
(404) 872-1608
(800) 872-1608

Columns, mantels, balustrading. Catalog available.

CONSERVATORIES

Conservatories that blend in style with older houses have become a rarity in America. It has been the habit to attach modern metal-framed greenhouses to period houses, because they are inexpensive and generally quite energy-efficient. Custom-built "period" structures can be commissioned from some American companies, but they are expensive and have mostly been used in Botanical Gardens. The situation is improving because of the expansion into the USA of the English companies below – more competition, both imported and domestic, is sure to follow.

To keep up with developments, watch the journals of the Botanical Gardens as well as *Horticulture* and *Garden Design* magazines, where greenhouse companies advertise regularly. A comprehensive recent book on the subject is *Living Under Glass* (Clarkson Potter).

Conservatory Center
160 Friendship Road
Cranbury
NJ 08512
(908) 329-0999

Wood-framed conservatories, either free-standing or attached. They are built according to a modular system, so the sizes can be modified within quite a wide range without incurring extra cost. The styles are very elegant: windows can be adapted to differing architectures by the addition of wooden arches or small panes; rooflines can be embellished with a variety of ornaments depending on the effect desired. The conservatories are either primed or painted at the factory as instructed. Ventilation and double-glazing systems are designed with the building. Custom projects undertaken and conservatories made to individual designs. Free brochure.

Everlite Greenhouses, Inc.
9515 Gerwig Lane Suite 115
Colombia
MD 21046
(301) 381-3881

Janco Greenhouses
9390 Davis Avenue
Laurel
MD 20707-1993
(301) 488-5700
(800) 645-9527

Machin Conservatories
951 North Park Avenue
Ext Redding
CT 06896
(203) 268-6648

Manufacturers of extremely stylish wood-framed conservatories and garden buildings which are fabricated to order. The company offers a supervisory service for instalation nationwide. Roofs can be of a simple shed shape, but usually are curved in the ogee form characteristic of this company. Roof glazing is done in unbreakable polycarbonate clear plastic. A line of wooden garden trellis is also available, to complete the outdoor environment. Detailed brochure available.

Sturdi-built Greenhouse Manufacturing Co.
11304 SW Boones Ferry Road
Portland
OR 97218
(503) 244-4100
(800) 722-4115

Sunbilt Solar Products
109-10 180th Street
Jamaica
NY 11433
(718) 297-6040

Very large manufacturing company of all types of glass and framed enclosures. Including skylights, overhead glazing, solar greenhouses, solar rooms and sunrooms.

DOORS AND WINDOWS

Beech River Mill Company
Old Route 16 Center
Ossipee
NH 03814
(603) 539-2636

A small family-owned business which has changed hands only once since its founding in 1856. They use original Victorian-era machinery to produce paneled and louvered doors and shutters, both interior and exterior. Their products are ordinarily made in pine, but they will work in a variety of fine woods.

Blaine Window Hardware, Inc.
17319 Blaine Drive
Hagerstown
MD 21740
(301) 797-6500

This company maintains an inventory of over 20,000 parts to replace any broken component of a door or window. They have a library of parts designs, old prints and plans, from which they make their products. Screens and weatherstripping replaced. It is hard to imagine an old door for which they cannot find or make perfect replacement hardware. Catalog available.

Cain-Powers, Inc.
Route 1
Box AAA
Bremo Bluff,
VA 23022
(804) 842-3984

A studio specializing in beveled glass for doors and windows. All their work is produced in their shop on turn-of-the-century equipment.

Ferguson's Cut Glass Works
4292 Pearl Road
Cleveland
OH 44109
(216) 459-2929

Cary Ferguson is an artist and designer in glass, specializing in beveled glass windows. He will reproduce the large intricately cut door panels common in late 19thC buildings and will also execute original designs according to individual customer requirements. Designs can be carved into glass and a variety of doors in a range of woods produced. Free brochure.

Golden Age Glassworks
339 Bellvale Road
Warwick
NY 10990
(914) 986-1487

Barbara Arrindell is a stained-glass artist who restores old glass and also designs and manufactures windows and lights to old original specifications according to individual customer requirements. These are mainly custom work, but she has prepared a portfolio of slides of executed designs which is a useful reference. She also imports English 19thC stained and etched glass panels, providing authentic materials for her work.

Historic Windows
PO Box 1172
Harrisonburg
VA 22801
(703) 434-5855

This company specializes in the production of interior shutters, all of which are made in solid hardwoods. They offer eight different patterns of paneling, including recessed panels, which are more often found in European houses than American ones. Brochure and sample available.

Hope's Architectural Products, Inc.
84 Hopkins Avenue
Jamestown
NY 14701
(716) 665-5124

Steel, aluminum and PVC windows and doors. For refurbishment of period buildings, steel windows in traditional styles with hinged or pivoted opening casements supplied with the glazing bars sub-dividing the lights as required, including the classical "Georgian" proportion of panes. Curved, raked and shaped frames provided. Catalog available.

Kenmore Industries
1 Thompson Square
PO Box 34
Boston
MA 02129
(617) 242-1711

This company's specialty is fine wooden carved doorways in Federal, Adam and Georgian styles. There are 15 different doorways, all produced in solid mahogany. The doors are fairly elaborate in style but relatively simple to instal, as they are shipped in about six sections. Kenmore makes carved overdoors in several designs such as Gothic half-round and a historic dolphin carving. Some doors can be adapted for use as windows. Custom work for large quantities only. Free brochure and catalog available.

Marvin Windows
Box 100
Warroad
MN 56763
(218) 386-1430
(800) 346-5044

A large manufacturer of wooden windows which are distributed nationwide. The many basic shapes can be combined to fit most styles of architecture. The line includes patio and terrace doors, casement and double-hung windows, bays and bows. There are arched, triangular, hexagonal and trapezoidal windows, and all can be double or triple glazed with or without authentic divided lights. A Gothic light pattern is now available. Some custom sizing may be available. Free catalog.

Materials Unlimited
2 West Michigan Avenue
Ypsilanti
MI 48197
(313) 483-6980

A comprehensive renovation supply company which has a large stock of antique house components, and also carries reproduction wooden doors and beveled and leaded glass panels. Custom glasswork a specialty. A wide range of catalogs and photos of antique material supplied in response to written requests with specifications.

Maurer & Shepherd Joyners, Inc.
122 Naubuc Avenue
Glastonbury
CT 06033
(203) 633-2383

A small firm which does fine custom work only. They can make any sort of door or window appropriate to 17th and 18thC buildings. Free brochure.

Mendocino Millwork
Hallelujah Redwood Products
Box 669
Mendocino
CA 95460
(707) 937-4410

"With the proper selection of components from our catalog, any style of Victorian home can be reproduced" is their claim. If it isn't in the catalog, which is quite small, they will custom-make it. All products are made from Northern California redwood, but the company will make special orders in other woods. Catalog available.

Sheppard Millwork
21020 70th Avenue
West Edmonds
WA 98020
(206) 771-4645

This company manufactures paneled doors and stocks a variety of styles. They also make moldings and fireplace mantels, and will match existing elements. Custom work.

Silverton Victorian Mill Works
PO Box 2987
Durango
CO 81302
(303) 387-5716

Period window styles, suitable for both Victorian and Colonial houses. A large selection of exterior and interior details in stock. Several styles of paneled doors and their frames. Replacement sash, storm and thermal window kits. Large selection of molding and paneling. Custom work. Color catalog available.

Walker's
PO Box 309
Tallmadge
OH 44278
(216) 633-1081

Historic building materials including a range of old doors and windows. They stock dismantled buildings including barns, houses and log cabins. Contact Dennis C. Walker with exact requirements. Free brochure.

The Woodstone Company

PO Box 223
Patch Road
Westminster
VT 05185
(802) 722-4784 or 722-9217

A custom architectural millwork company with its primary focus in the manufacturing of high quality windows and doors. They use the finest grades of lumber available and take great pride in their pegged mortise and tenon joinery. Many glazing options including insulated glass and Low-E glass. Custom work only. Brochure available.

FABRICS AND WALLPAPERS

Finding and buying fabric for house restoration in the USA is complicated by the "to-the-trade-only" custom of many of the finest fabric houses. You may find the perfect material photographed in one of the leading magazines such as *Architectural Digest* or *House and Garden*, but will need the help of a decorator or architect in order to buy it. There is really no way around this restriction except to look in the decorating departments of large department stores which often carry samples of designer lines. Local upholsterers in many communities may also have sample books and some showrooms allow clients to enter with their decorators. The retail shops listed below have extensive lines of traditional fabrics, and might be the first place to look when trying to find the perfect drape and upholstery material.

Laura Ashley

6 St James Avenue
Boston
MA 02116
(617) 457-6000

This company, originally English but widely distributed throughout North America, has three differently distributed fabric lines, which are all suitable for use in older houses.

The Laura Ashley shops sell a wide range of chintzes and other cotton and linen materials suitable for drapes and upholstery, sorted into coordinated color schemes, as well as lace, made up into curtains and by the yard.

Brunschwig et Fils

979 Third Avenue
New York
NY 10022
(212) 838-7878

Trade only. Brunschwig et Fils produces its own designs and works with museums and restoration projects. The scope of the collection is wide, including hundreds of floral prints and other patterns suitable for residential use.

Lee Jofa

979 Third Avenue
New York
NY 10022
(212) 688-0444

Trade only. An extensive collection of lines of fabrics, including some reproduced from documents at the American Museum of the China Trade. Crewel, chintzes and tartans also available.

Osborne & Little

65 Commerce Road
Stamford
CT 06902
(203) 359-1500
Showroom: Suite 1503N
D & D Building
979 Third Avenue
New York
NY 10022
(212) 751-3333

Designers and manufacturers of furnishing fabrics, wallpapers and borders, many in period styles.

Raintree Designs, Inc.

979 Third Avenue
New York
NY 10022
(212) 477-8590

Manufacturers of the Victoria Morland line of fabrics and wallpapers in English Country and French Provincial styles available from paint and wallpaper stores across the country. They also print the similarly distributed Laura Ashley fabrics and wallpapers. Catalog available.

Scalamandre

37-24 24th Street
Long Island City
NY 11101
(212) 980-3888

Trade only. Well known for its fine reproduction work, Scalamandre is often the source to which architects and designers turn for custom fabrics, wallcoverings, trimmings and carpets. To date, Scalamandre has reproduced or produced materials for over 1,000 restoration projects, including Gracie Mansion, New York; the Mark Twain House, Hartford CT; the Golani Palace, Honolulu; and Blenheim Palace in England. Catalog available.

F. Schumacher & Co.

939 Third Avenue
New York
NY 10022
(212) 415-3900

Schumacher and its subsidiary, Waverly Fabrics, produce a large number of historical fabric lines such as Colonial Williamsburg and Sturbridge Village, widely available at department and fabric stores. Schumacher also has a to-the-trade-only showroom at the above address, with many fine damasks and other fabrics suitable for home restoration. Catalog available.

FIREPLACES AND STOVES

Antique Stove Heaven

5414 South Western Avenue
Los Angeles
CA 90062
(213) 298-5581

Axon Products

171 Eugenia Drive
Ventura
CA 93003
(800) 457-3343

Danny Alessandro, Ltd.

Edwin Jackson, Inc.
307 East 60th Street
New York
NY 10022
(212) 421-1928 or (212) 759-8210

and: 8409 Santa Monica Boulevard
Los Angeles
CA 90069
(213) 654-6189

This combined company has been America's largest fireplace specialists since 1879 and their stock offers very wide scope. Their specializations feature antique and reproduction mantels and fireplace surrounds made in every available material and with large varieties of finishes, which will complement all kinds of interior decor from contemporary to traditional. Custom work is a speciality. Brochure available.

Barnstable Stove Shop

Route 149
PO Box 472
West Barnstable
MA 02668
(508) 362-9913

This Cape Cod company restores and rebuilds old stoves. A few woodburning stoves from the earliest days 1820-1870, and a wide selection of coal and/or woodburning ones from 1880-1920 are available.

Bryant Stove Works

Box 2048
Thorndike
ME 04986
(207) 568-3665

This is a family concern selling antique stoves only. All have been reconditioned and are in perfect working order. The speciality here is cookstoves, wood, coal, and gas-burning. They have about 150 stoves in stock at all times, and will search for special items on request. They will restore customers' own stoves, and carry parlor stoves and parts for many makes of antique stove.

Driwood Molding Company

PO Box 1729
Florence
SC 29503-1729
(803) 669-2478

This company's very extensive inventory of molding styles can be combined in innumerable ways to make up mantels in virtually any style or size desired. Custom work.

Elmira Stove Works
5 Hoffman Street
Kitchner
Ontario
Canada N2M 3M5
(519) 669-5103
The Oval Cookstove has been in use since 1906, burning coal and/or wood. The styling is the same, but the stove has been updated to electricity recently, and there is a combination electric/gas/ wood model. These stoves also heat water if desired. The same company makes free-standing heating stoves and fireplace inserts for efficient wood heating. Free brochures.

G. G. Girolami & Company
944-946 N. Spaulding Avenue
Chicago
IL 60651
(312) 227-1959
A company which makes plaster castings of all sorts of stone decorative details, including fountains, ceilings and fireplaces. They then finish the pieces in a very wide variety of finishes and colors. Custom work.

Henkel Inc.
PO Box 1322
Hammond
LA 70404
(504) 345-1016
Convection cooker woodstoves.

The House of Webster
Box CL9004
Rogers
AK 72757
(501) 636-4640
Cast-iron, authentic reproduction country ranges fully converted to electricity.

Marshall Galleries Inc.
8420 Melrose Ave
Los Angeles
CA 90069
(213) 852-1964
Specializing in European fireplaces.

Nostalgia Architectural Antiques
130 Huston Street
Savannah
GA 31401
(912) 232-2324
This architectural antique showroom makes reproductions of some of the most popular styles of fireplaces and ironwork which are, in many cases, becoming scarce. One of the few sources in the USA for cast-iron old and reproduction fireplaces, many with their ornate summer covers intact. Wood, art stone and plaster mantels also stocked. Custom work. Catalog available.

Old World Molding and Finishing, Inc.
115 Allen Boulevard
Farmingdale
NY 11735
(516) 293-1789
Moldings, brackets and carved ornaments can be combined to make mantels in any style. Catalog available.

Sunshine Architectural Woodwork
2169 Sunshine Drive
Fayetteville
AR 72701
(501) 521-4329
(800) 628-8004
Magnificent Colonial-style wooden mantels, many with paneled overmantels. These are ordinarily manufactured in paint- or stain-grade wood, but can also be made in fine woods and in special sizes. Catalog available.

Vermont Structural Slate Company, Inc.
Box 98 Fair Haven
VT 05743
(802) 265-4933/34
(800) 343-1900
Fireplaces and hearths, as well as slate products: roof shingles and paving, floors and stairs, countertops and fountains. Fabricated material only. Free brochure.

Virginia Metalcrafters
1010 East Main Street
PO Box 1068
Waynesboro VA 22980
(703) 949-9400
Several designs of andirons, mostly brass, but some iron, including hessian soldiers. They have cast-iron firebacks and fire tools with many styles of finials. Coal grates, fenders, screens and jamb hooks are also available.

FLOORS

Aged Woods
2331 East Market Street
York
PA 17402
(717) 840-0330
(800) 233-9307
Old wood boards, either distressed as they came from old buildings, or milled from old wood. White and yellow pine, oak, American chestnut, cypress and other woods stocked. The boards can be used for floors or may be milled into paneling, doors, mantels, etc. Field stone, roofing slate, old beams and barn siding also stocked. They will send samples with a refundable deposit. Free color brochure.

Broad-Axe Beam Co.
RD 2 Box 417
Brattleboro
VT 05301
(802) 257-0064
Hand-hewn beams. Wide pine and hardwood flooring. Illustrated brochure available.

Carlisle Restoration Lumber
HCR 32 Box 679
Route 123
Stoddard
NH 03464-9712
(603) 446-3937
A source of select wide-board pine or oak in widths and thicknesses that will match the boards in many old buildings. Free brochure.

Expanko Cork Co., Inc.
Box 384
West Chester
PA 19380
(215) 436-8300
Suppliers of a wide range of cork-based materials to the specialist flooring trade, working with interior designers and other specifiers.

Harris-Tarkett, Inc.
PO Box 300
2225 Eddie Williams Road
Johnson City
TN 37605-0300
(615) 928-3122

Widely distributed flooring, both solid hardwood and laminated, in unfinished or pre-finished plank and parquet styles. Free brochures.

The Joinery Co.
PO Box 518
Dept L-30
Tarboro
NC 27886
(919) 823-3306
Stockists of 200-year-old durable heart pine. In-house milling and handbuilding by craftsmen. Full color brochure available.

Kentucky Wood Floors
PO Box 33276
Louisville
KY 40232
(502) 451-6024
Plank and parquet floors in a dizzying variety of woods from oak and walnut to padauk and zebrawood. Free catalog with many suggested styles and colors, including the floor they made for the Oval Office of the White House. Any style or combination of woods made to order. A large network of distributors around America and abroad. Brochure available.

Old South Co.
POBox 7096
Dept CL 390
Tarboro
NC 27886
(919) 823 8100
Rare and unique flooring, antique flooring, select hardwoods, tongue and groove, extra-wide widths, quarter-sawn cuts.

Robinson Lumber Company, Inc.
4000 Tchoupitou Street
New Orleans
LA 70115
(504) 895-6377
Collects Longleaf Pine from old buildings and saws it into floorboards. Hardwoods and mahogany also stocked. Free price list.

Shep Brown Associates
24 Cummings Park
Wodurn
MA 01801
(617) 935-8080

US distributor for Dennis Ruabon Ltd. UK manufacturers of unglazed floor quarry tiles, for refurbishment and renovation.

The Structural Slate Co.
222 East Main Street
PO Box 187
Pen Argyl PA 18072
(215) 863-4141
Gray Pennsylvania slate for all uses, particularly floors and roofing. Complete and informative free brochure.

Tiresias, Inc.
PO Box 1864
Orangeburg
SC 29116-1864
(803) 534-8478 or 534-3445
A mill that recycles old heart pine timbers into floorboards which have the grain and color of those in old houses. They can also make available floorboards from new heart pine and other fine woods, such as walnut, mahogany, black cypress and wormy chestnut. Free brochure.

Vermont Structural Slate Company, Inc.
Box 98
Fair Haven VT 05743
(802) 265-4933/34
(800) 343-1900
Gray, green, purple Vermont slate for all sorts of uses such as flooring, paving, stairs and even walls. They make slate roofing material and interitor details such as counter tops and fireplaces. Free brochure.

HARDWARE

Anglo-American Brass Co.
PO Box 9487
San Jose CA 95157
(408) 246-0203

Manufacturers of a very extensive line of brass hardware in a large variety of antique styles. They make hooks to hang pictures from Victorian-style picture molding. Brass screws and cabinet hardware also available. Custom casting made to order. Showroom and extensive catalog.

The Antique Hardware Store
43 Bridge Street
Dept PD
Frenchtown
NJ 08825
(908) 996-4040
Wide variety of old-style hardware, weathervanes and lighting. Their motto, "If they still make it, we can get it!" Full-color catalog available.

Ball and Ball
463 West Lincoln Highway
Exton
PA 19341
(215) 363-7330
A manufacturer of fine and authentic hardware for doors, shutters and furniture of all historic American periods, brass and iron hinges, knobs, etc. They stock a very large selection, but will also do custom work to match existing hardware or new designs. Their showroom and hardware museum near Philadelphia display their full line of hardware, lighting and accessories such as andirons and trivets. Catalog available.

B & B Sales and Imports, Inc.
3699 Industry Avenue
Lakewood
CA 90712
(310) 595 8824
US Agent for Brass Tack Hardware Ltd, a UK company which manufactures and distributes decorative brass door hardware and accessories. Their range includes locks, hinges and furniture, electrical accessories and bathroom fixtures. Decorative grills for covering radiators.

Gainsborough Hardware Industries, Inc.
3640 Windsor Park Drive
NE Suit 100
Suwanee
GA 31074
(404) 945-9989
Manufacture door hardware, much of it suitable for old houses. Many styles in porcelain, glass and brass. Also stoneware and wooden knobs. Free brochure.

Historic Housefitters Co.
Farm to Market Road
Brewster
NY 10509
(914) 278-2427
Iron and solid brass door hardware for old or traditional-style houses. Custom ironwork is undertaken. Hand-forged iron thumblatches, strap hinges, H hinges and fireplace tools made. Also available are leaded crystal, porcelain, solid brass door and cabinet hardware. Copper and brass light fixtures. Catalog available.

Horton Brasses
Nooks Hill Road
POBox 120 CL
Cromwell
CT 06416
(203) 635-4400
Antique and reproduction furniture hardware. Catalog available.

Kayne & Son Custom Forged Hardware
76 Daniel Ridge Road
Candler
NC 28715
(704) 667-8868
These blacksmiths work in forged and cast metal. All the forged pieces are made to order, and they also carry a good selection of cast pieces in brass, bronze, copper, tin and steel. They will do custom work, repair and restorations. Two catalogs, one for forged and one for cast work, available.

Brian F. Leo
7532 Columbus Avenue South
Richfield
MN 55423
(612) 861-1473
A custom-fabricator of hardware and architectural ornaments with some items in stock. Questions from architects and house restorers welcome. Catalog of door and window hardware available.

Mel-Nor
303 CL Gulf Bank
Houston
TX 77037
(713) 445-3485
Factory sale of benches, lights, mailboxes and much more. Catalog available.

Moultrie Manufacturing Co.
Dept MH 100
Drawer 1179
Moultrie
GA 31776-1179
(800) 841-8674
Cast-iron mailboxes and other pieces for home and garden.

Omnia Industries, Inc.
PO Box 330
Cedar Grove
NJ 07009
A large commercial manufacturer of solid brass door hardware. Many of their styles, which are very widely distributed, are suitable for old houses. Of special interest are narrow backset locks which might be used on a non-standard old door. Brochures available to architects and distributors.

Pacific Trader
210 Third Avenue South
Seattle
WA 98104
(800) 877-1663
Variety of period household furniture and effects.

Plexa Craft Products, Inc.
5406 San Fernando Road
Glendale
CA 91203
(818) 246-8201
A group of hardware companies under one roof. Plexa Craft makes door hardware using Plexiglas. Crafts Metal produces solid brass cabinet, bathroom, door and furniture hardware in traditional styles. SECO makes hand-crafted hardware, much of it in authentic antique styles. Custom work. Catalogs available for all three companies.

PRG
PO Box 1768
Rockville
MD 20849-1768
(301) 309-2222
A mail order company selling instruments for building diagnostics, such as moisture meters and survey tools. They also have hard-to-find and foreign books on these subjects. Book lists and product flyers sent on request.

The Country Store
28 St James Street
Geneva
IL 60134
(708) 879-0098
Brass light and switch hardware. Catalog available.

The Renovator's Supply
Miller's Falls
MA 01349
(413) 747-0173
Brass and iron hardware for Colonial and Victorian houses available at reasonable prices. They stock door and cabinet knobs, bath hardware and lighting plus some fireplace accessories. Brass railings and components for bars or stairs are stocked, as well as weathervanes and a cupola on which to mount them. Catalog available.

The Smithy
RD1
Wolcott
VT 05680
(802) 472-6508
Robert Bourdon runs a one-man business producing iron hardware and just about everything else from chandeliers to frying pans, from trunk handles to sculpture. Reproduction and original custom work. Free brochure.

Tremont Nail Company
PO Box 111
8 Elm Street
Wareham
MA 02571
(508) 295-0038
Their specialty is hardened cut steel nails in many shapes appropriate to restoration work. They will ship quantities from one pound to a truckload. They also operate the Company Store at Elm Street and Rte 28 in Wareham, where they stock brass stencils, iron and brass hardware and unfinished wooden objects as well as the nails.

Williamsburg Blacksmiths, Inc.
PO Box 1776
Goshen Road, Route 9
Williamsburg
MA 01096
(413) 268-7341
Hand-forged iron hardware for interior and exterior doors and cabinets, as well as bootscrapers, nails and tin sconces. Showroom on Rte 9 in Williamsburg.

The Woodbury Blacksmith and Forge Co.
161 Main Street
PO Box 268
Woodbury
CT 06798
(203) 263-5737

Hand-forged iron hardware, faithfully copied from good originals. They also make fireplace equipment and lighting fixtures. Custom work from artefacts or drawings.

KITCHENS

Americans are inveterate kitchen remodelers. One reason that no genuine Colonial kitchens remain is that improvements in equipment as well as new fashions in furnishing were embraced with alacrity by homeowners, even in the earliest times. Nowadays, a new kitchen is frequently the first priority when an American family moves into a new house – which they do with great frequency. In contrast, the British have tended always to stay for long periods in the same house. Many houses in Britain have been inhabited by the same family for generations. Until very recently, household help was both easier to find and much less expensive in Britain than in America. For these reasons, American kitchens were seldom updated, and have not been seen as a center for family activities until the last few years.

Every American town has both kitchen suppliers, who either make or distribute cabinets as well as appliances in many cases, and kitchen designers who will devise custom layouts and cabinetry at moderate cost. Wood-fronted cabinets in traditional designs have always been popular in America, and are available in all price ranges to suit any budget through these localized sources. In contrast, a very recently-perceived desire for more interesting kitchen arrangements has encouraged the growth of nationally active kitchen design companies in Britain. They can provide the home-owner with a complete design scheme that is suitable for an older house, taking into account the obvious needs of a modern family, and will supervise instalation by workmen who are often unfamiliar with modern kitchen cabinets and appliances. The growing need for these services explains the popularity of the "brand-name" kitchen (such as Smallbone) in England as opposed to the more individualistic approach of the American kitchen.

Allmilmo Corporation
70 Clinton Road
Fairfield
NJ 07006
(201) 227-2502
Traditional and modern kitchen styles.

Cooper Pacific Kitchens
8687 Melrose Avenue
Suite G 776
Los Angeles
CA 90069
(310) 659-6147
Kitchen interiors ranging from the ultra-modern to the more traditional styles of Baroque, Flemish and solid oak.

Poggenpohl US Inc.
8010 Woodland Center
Boulevard Suite 400
Tampa FL 33614
(813) 888- 9292
Manufacturers of quality kitchen furniture.

Smallbone
(Distributed by Siematic Corp.)
886 Town Center Drive
Langhorn
PA 19047
(215) 750-1928
Hand-crafted kitchens in old pine and English oak.

St Charles
1401 Greenbrier Parkway
Suite 200H
Chesapeake
VA 23320
(804) 424-3900
Designers and manufacturers of kitchens specializing in custom cabinetry. Catalog available.

Wood-Mode
Dept 77
Kreamer
PA 17833
(800) 635-7500
Custom-built kitchen cabinetry.

They make several brass and glass hanging fixtures and sconces, as well as tin and copper lanterns and sconces suitable for older houses. All can be electrified or fitted for candles. Catalog available.

The Brass Lion
5935 South Broadway
Tyler
TX 75703
(903) 561-1111
Manufacturers of 17th to 19thC style brass lighting fixtures: chandeliers and sconces as well as brass and glass hanging bell lights with hand-blown glass parts.

City Lights
2226 Massachusetts Avenue
Cambridge
MA 02140
(617) 547-1490
Restored and reconditioned lighting from 1850-1920. All the fixtures have antique glass parts, though they do also carry reproduction shades. Catalog and photos available.

Classic Lamp Posts
3645 N.W. 67th Street
Miami, FL 33147
(305) 696-1901
(800) 654-5852

LIGHTING

Authentic Details
The Mill Road
West Rupert
VT 05776
(802) 394-7713
This company, located in an old mill in the hills of Vermont, makes reproductions of Colonial and early American lighting fixtures. Materials are maple and brass, but a pewter or gunmetal finish can be applied. They will stain wooden sections of their chandeliers and sconces, or will paint fixtures according to customers' needs. Custom work. Catalog and free brochure available.

B & P Lamp Supply, Inc.
843 Old Morrison Highway
McMinnville
TN 37110
(615) 473-3016
A tremendous supply of Victorian-style lamps and supplies with an array of hand-painted glass shades, and a selection of standing and hanging lamps. In stock are parts for old lights, including Aladdin lamps, on sale to the decorating and construction trades only. Catalog available to trade customers only.

Ball & Ball
463 W. Lincoln Highway
Exton
PA 19341
(215) 363-7330
Manufacturers of reproduction 18thC lighting fixtures, including the magnificent Independence Hall chandelier.

post styles and five luminaire shapes to make outdoor lampposts suitable to virtually any style of house. Fairly easy to instal, as the posts are made of Polysteel", a type of reinforced plastic laminate that does not need painting. Free color brochure.

A. J. P. Coppersmith & Co.
20 Industrial Parkway
Woburn
MA 01801
(617) 245-1223
Manufacturers of antique-style indoor and outdoor lighting in a variety of finishes including: copper, brass, pewter-color and verdigris. All are sold electrified, but may be ordered partly or completely candle-lit. Lampposts, mirrored sconces and brass candlesticks are also stocked. Catalog available.

Hurley Patentee Manor
Box 464
Route 209
Hurley
NY 12443
(914) 331-5414
Approximately 200 authentic lighting devices: chandeliers, lamps, sconces, lanterns, bettys, etc. All are made on the premises and may be fitted for electricity or candles. They carry waxed candle sleeves. Catalog available.

King's Chandelier Company
PO Box 667
Highway 14
Eden
NC 27288
(919) 623-6188
A manufacturer of crystal chandeliers, mostly of the "ballroom" sort. They do have some brass and brass-and-glass lights suitable for Colonial houses, and many designs have a Victorian flavor. They may be able to make some adjustments in designs, but do not undertake custom work "from scratch." Catalog available on request.

The London Venturers Company
2 Dock Square
Rockport
MA 01966
(508) 546-7161
A gallery of refurbished 19th and early 20thC glass and brass fixtures. They will supply antique shades and search for specific fixtures. Catalog available.

Gates Moore
River Road
Silvermine
Norwalk
CT 06850
(203) 847-3231
Colonial-style handmade fixtures in tin, copper, pewter and painted wood. Manufacturers of chandeliers, sconces and lamps to be used on posts. Many designs have been developed for and used in historic houses. Custom work.

Paxton Hardware Ltd.
7818 Bradshaw Road
Upper Falls
MD 21156
(301) 592-8505
Primarily a manufacturer of furniture and cabinet hardware, this company carries a very extensive line of lamp parts, many of which could be used in repairing Victorian lighting. They also carry a selection of glass shades, from hurricane shades to beautiful hand-blown and hand-decorated flowered shades. Color catalog available.

Progress Lighting
Erie Avenue and G Street
Philadelphia
PA 19134
(215) 289-1200
The largest manufacturer of residential lighting fixtures in the USA, this company's products are extremely widely distributed. They have a small line of authentically detailed Victorian reproductions, and several Colonial-styled chandeliers. Catalog available.

Rejuvenation House Parts
901 N. Skidmore
Portland
OR 97217
(503) 249-0774
Manufacturers, with a large retail store in Portland, of authentic reproductions of Victorian and Mission style lighting fixtures in solid brass as well as stockists of glass shades in many colors such as apricot etched and shiny pal. Custom work. Catalog available.

Renovation Concepts
9611 Humboldt Avenue South
Bloomington
MN 55431
(612) 884-4288
An extremely large and complete source for a wide range of renovation building materials. Inquiries welcome.

Roy Electric Co., Inc.
1054 Coney Island Avenue
Brooklyn
NY 11230
(718) 434-7002
Reproductions of Victorian chandeliers and sconces, using authentic fixtures as models. Fixtures are solid brass. Store carries large selection of glass shades. Catalog available.

The Saltbox
3004 Columbia Avenue
Lancaster
PA 17603
(717) 392-5649
A collection of over 250 chandeliers in brass and tin. Copies of very early lights and later, more elegant styles.

St. Louis Antique Lighting Co.
801 N. Skinker
St. Louis
MO 63130
(314) 863-1414
This company restores old lighting and manufactures its own designs, both original and reproduction. They carry a wide range of glass shades suitable for old lighting.

Shaker Workshops
PO Box 1028
Concord
MA 01742
(617) 646-8985
A small selection of beautiful and plain lights to complement their Shaker furniture. Lights are crafted in antiqued tin. Catalog available.

Stair & Co. Ltd
942 Madison Avenue
New York
NY 10021
(212) 517- 4400
A range of antique glass chandeliers, restoration work also undertaken.

Sturbridge Yankee Workshop
Blueberry Road
Portland
ME 04102
(207) 774-9045
(800) 343-1144
These Early American stores carry a selection of lighting suitable for old houses, as well as furniture, rugs and a wide range of other house furnishings. Free catalog available.

Victorian Lighting Works
PO Box 469
251 S. Pennsylvania Avenue
Center Hall
PA 16828
(814) 364-9577
Manufacturers of Victorian-style lamps and chandeliers in solid brass. They stock a selection of glass shades. Catalog available.

Virginia Metalcrafters
PO Box 1068
1010 E. Main Street
Waynesboro
VA 22980
(703) 949-9400
Manufacturers of decorative reproductions of lights in brass, wood, copper, tin and other materials. They make Colonial Williamsburg, Historic Newport, Old Salem, Old Sturbridge Village and Mystic Seaport designs. Many of the chandeliers can be ordered wired or unwired. Candlesticks and candelabra are also available and come in brass or iron. Custom work. Color catalog available.

METALWORK AND FENCING

Architectural Iron Company
PO Box 126
Schocopee Road
Milford
PA 18337
(717) 296-7722
(212) 243-2664
Commercial, residential, and also institutional custom iron work undertaken. They have reproduced fences and gates for Gramercy Park and other historic sites in New York City and the Eastern USA. They have some stock items such as fencing, balusters and grills. Send postage for catalog.

Cassidy Bros. Forge, Inc.
US Route 1
Rowley
MA 01969
(508) 948-7303

Custom architectural ironwork for houses and public buildings. They work extensively on restoration projects and will provide detailed drawings and, if necessary, a representative to supervise installation. Color brochure.

Materials Unlimited
2 West Michigan Avenue
Ypsilanti
MI 48197
(313) 483-6980
A selection of cast-iron fences, gates and posts can be ordered from this architectural-supply firm. Custom work. Brochure on request.

Moultrie Manufacturing Company
PO Drawer 1179
Moultrie
GA 31776
(912) 985-1312
(800) 841-8674
Many styles of fences, gates and exterior ironwork in aluminum. They offer a Planning and Design Kit from which designs may be selected. They will also do custom work and make detailed drawings. The company also makes outdoor furniture, fountains and a wide spectrum of garden ornaments, as well as exterior columns. Most of the designs are related to Old South traditions, but many would be equally suitable in old-house settings elsewhere. Catalog available.

Nostalgia Architectural Antiques
130 Huston Street
Savannah
GA 31401
(912) 232-2324
Many ornate Southern-style patterns of cast-iron fencing, all of which are made according to individual customer requirements. Brackets, gates and grills also available.

Old and new components for house restoration in stock. Further cast-iron items include stair rail and statuary. Catalog available.

Robinson Iron
Robinson Road
Alexander City
AL 35010
(205) 329-8486
Cast-iron fountains, sculpture and fencing for new projects and restorations. Many pieces are cast from pre-Civil War patterns by traditional methods. They offer beautiful urns and vases which would add the finishing touch to a formal garden or terrace, and hitching posts for the horsey set. Custom work, from duplication of fences to brass hinges. Brochure available.

Vintage Wood Works
513 South Adams
Fredericksburg
TX 78624
(512) 997-9513
Victorian and Country gingerbread designs for porches, brackets, gables and spandrels. Catalog available.

Walpole Woodworkers
767 East Street
Walpole
MA 02081
(508) 668-2800
This company makes a variety of styles of wooden fencing in white cedar. Board and palisade styles provide privacy, while all sorts of lattices and pickets can be used to enhance any sort of old house. Styles may be combined, and there are many different posts and gates to provide finishing touches. A fence using stock elements will probably suit most requirements, but custom work can be done. Several showrooms in the Northeast for fences, buildings and furniture. Catalog available.

MOLDING AND PANELING

A & M Wood Specialty, Inc.
358 Eagle Street North
PO Box 3204
Cambridge, Ontario
Canada N3H 5M2
(519) 653-9322
A company dealing in fine woods for furniture inlay – even musical instruments. Suppliers of flooring, paneling and molding strictly on a custom basis in quantities over 200 linear feet. Free brochure.

Chadsworth Inc.
Box 53268
Atlanta
GA 30355
(404) 876-5410
Authentic and replica architectural elements, wooden pedestals, columns and table bases. Catalog available.

Classic Architectural Specialities
3223 Canton
Dallas TX 75226
(214) 748-1668
Suppliers of a range of products for renovation, especially Victorian gingerbread, doors, porches, fireplaces and gargoyles. They make a very wide assortment of corbels, gables, brackets, railings etc. Catalog available.

Cumberland Woodcraft Co., Inc.
PO Drawer 609
Carlisle
PA 17013
(717) 243-0063
An extremely extensive line of Victorian-style millwork in hardwoods. For exterior decoration, they have many patterns of corbels, brackets, etc., as well as all sorts of decorative elements, moldings, staircase parts and paneling for interiors. They also make a variety of gazebo kits, oak bars (custom-built) and cafe tables and chairs. Their oak lattice can be custom-framed for interior screens or garden dividers. Custom-work.

Driwood Molding Company
PO Box 1729
Florence
SC 29503-1729
(803) 669-2478
A large selection of moldings, generally stocked in popular wood but which can be manufactured to order in walnut, oak, mahogany and a variety of other woods. Exterior moldings and doors are also stocked. Custom work is carried out to their own or customer's designs. Catalog available.

C. G. Girolami & Company
944-946 N. Spaulding Avenue
Chicago
IL 60651
(312) 227-1959
A very large selection of moldings produced in various period styles, which are fabricated in hard plaster. They make capitals and ceiling ornaments such as ceiling medallions and cornices, as well as entire plaster ornamented ceilings. These can be shipped in their white state or alternatively finished in an infinite variety of colors, wood-grained and metallic finishes, and can also be colored to the customer's requirements. Catalog available.

Gold Leaf Conservation Studios, Inc.
PO Box 50156
Washington
DC 20091
(202) 638-4660
William Adair, one of the country's leading gilders, has worked on projects at the White House and San Simeon. Most of the firm's work is with restoration of picture frames and furniture, but they will undertake architectural gilding projects for private clients. Brochure available.

Haas Wood Working Co., Inc.
64 Clementina
San Francisco
CA 94105
(415) 421-8273
This company offers hand-turning products as well as semi-automatic production. They will make any wood molding product from drawer knobs to 12-foot porch columns, panels and stair rail systems. Some patterns of molding are in stock, or they will work with designers and architects to supply specific patterns for customers' requirements, and will even supply furniture made to order. Free brochure.

Hosek Architectural Studios
2101 Market Street
Denver
CO 80205
(303) 296-8327
This family firm makes all sorts of ornamental plasterwork from old molds which may for example have been in the family for generations. They make ceiling medallions, cornices and any kind of ceiling ornamentation, as well as entire ceilings cast from English Stately Home originals. Cast fireplaces are made in fiberglass-reinforced gypsum which can be sealed to look like marble. The same material is used to make exterior columns. Custom work. Catalog available.

Mark A. Knudsen
1100 East County Line Road
Des Moines
IA 50320
(515) 285-6112
Basically this is a one-man shop where Mark Knudsen turns wood either by hand or on a special German machine. All work is tailored to customers' individual requirements and products range from sized from spindles and stair components to columns. Free brochure available.

Mad River Woodworks
PO Box 1067
Blue Lake
CA 95525
(707) 668-5671
Victorian millwork to standard designs: spandrels, corbels, moldings and ornate screen doors in stock. This company also manufactures several patterns of ornamental redwood shingles and decorative siding. Custom work. Catalogue available.

Maurer & Shepherd Joyners, Inc.
122 Naubuc Avenue
Glastonbury
CT 06033
(203) 633-2383
A small firm which does only custom work recreating the warmth and texture of authentic "Colonial joinery." Free brochure.

Mendocino Millwork
Hallelujah Redwood Products
Box 669
Mendocino
CA 95460
(707) 937-4410
This company manufactures all sorts of decorative period features to restore a Victorian house, such as moldings, brackets, corbels, porch railings and appliques. Stocked items are in redwood, but custom work can be done in a variety of woods. The catalog includes many different styles of exterior shingles and interior moldings are available.

W. F. Norman Corporation
PO Box 323
214-32 N. Cedar Street
Nevada
MO 64772
(417) 667-5552
(800) 641-4038
A very old company which has been making pressed metal ceilings since the turn of the century and still continues to manufacture them to their old designs. They also stock metal cornices and molding. Their recent purchase of the metal stamping division of Kenneth Lynch & Sons of Wilton, CT has greatly enlarged their repertory of moldings, swags, ornaments, capitals, weathervanes and other decorative details appropriate to period interior design. Ceiling and ornament catalog available.

Nostalgia Architectural Antiques

130 Huston Street
Savannah
GA 31401
(912) 232-2324
A very complete source for renovation supplies. This company carries a line of plaster ornamental moldings imported from England. The line includes cornice moldings, ceiling medallions and a niche. Full catalog as well as molding catalog available.

The Old Wagon Factory

POBox 1427
Dept CL60
Clarksville
VA 23927
(703) 374-5717
A large selection of hand-crafted wooden doors in Victorian and Chippendale styles in all sizes. Catalog available.

Old World Molding & Finishing, Inc.

115 Allen Boulevard
Farmingdale, NY 11735
(516) 293-1789
A large selection of moldings and mantelpieces suitable for old houses. A patented modular paneling system allows them to produce whole paneled rooms pre-fitted at the factory. Custom work. Catalog available.

The Renovator's Supply Factory

Renovator's Old Mill
Miller's Falls
MA 01349
(412) 659-2441
Hardware for Colonial and Victorian houses at reasonable prices. Catalog available.

San Francisco Victoriana

2070 Newcombe Avenue
San Francisco, CA 94124
(415) 648-0313

Manufacturers of wood molding and plaster ornament in styles particularly geared to the Victorian houses in which San Francisco is so rich. The plaster ornaments include ceiling medallions, cornices, swags and capitals. Custom work in both materials. They also stock the Crown Anaglypta embossed wallcovering from England and have a stock of antique embossed wallpaper borders made in Germany between 1892-1914. Catalog and sample packets of wallcoverings and borders available.

Sheppard Millwork

21020 70th Avenue West
Edmonds
WA 98026
(206) 771-4645
A custom shop which stocks some patterns of molding and makes several designs particularly for Victorian houses. Mantelpieces, doors and stair parts made to order, and existing millwork matched. Free brochure.

Silverton Victorian Mill Works

PO Box 2987
Durango
CO 81302
(303) 387-5716
Stockists of a full line of moldings, door and window casings and paneling, as well as plate rails which can be combined with other moldings. They carry several patterns of decorative siding and wood brackets. Custom work to order on special doors and windows, vergeboards, beading and fluting, and sawn ornamentation.

W. P. Stephens Lumber Co.

22 Polk Street
Marietta
GA 30064
(404) 428-1531
This lumber yard carries the usual range of stock moldings, but their specialty is custom architectural millwork. They will match existing elements, and make entire paneled rooms, cabinets, spiral staircases, as well as doors. Both hardwoods and paint-grade lumber used. Catalog available.

Sunshine Architectural Woodworks

2169 Sunshine Drive
Fayetteville
AR 72701
(501) 521-4329
A full line of paneling and molding in hardwood. The standard wood is poplar, but many other fine woods are also available. All paneling is made to order, and the moldings can be combined to make stacked cornices. Catalog available.

Tiresias, Inc.

PO Box 1864
Orangeburg
SC 29116-1864
(803) 534-8478 or 534-3445
Heart pine boards for flooring and paneling. They mill the timbers, and make beams and mantels as well as floorboards. Most of the timbers are old, but some new pine and other fine woods are also milled. Custom work is undertaken. Free brochure

Vintage Wood Works

PO Box R
Highway 34 South
Quinlan
TX 75474
(903) 356-2158
Authentic Victorian gingerbread and other interior and exterior pine details for Victorian houses which are shipped unfinished. This manufacturer also makes all the components for constructing gazebos and porches. The gazebo is shipped as a kit for do-it-yourself assembly. Shingles suitable for walls and roofs are also available. Custom work. Catalog available.

Walker's

PO Box 309
Tallmadge
OH 44278
(216) 633-1081

A large concern which specializes in the supply of historic building materials and features salvaged from dismantled buildings. The company also stocks barn siding in a variety of woods. Various woods are also supplied for the purposes of replacement paneling as well as for use in larger-scale reconstruction projects. There is also a wide selection of architectural antiques, period features and fixtures as well as hardware and plumbing fixtures. Write with individual requirements. Free brochure available.

J. P. Weaver Company

2301 West Victory Boulevard
Burbank
CA 91506
(818) 841-5700
A company started in 1914 by the fourth generation of the Weaver family in the composition ornament trade. Today the company produces close to 8,000 varieties, and has the capability to make any ornament which cannot be found in their repertoire from individual customer designs or requirements. They are also prepared to make cast stone ornaments for external use. The firm produced ornaments for many elaborate projects from William Randolph Heart's San Simeon to Walt Disney's Epcot Center. Design sheets are available on request, as well as a costly two-volume set of beautifully produced books on the history of Architectural Decoration, illustrated with the complete range of Weaver designs.

Worthington Group Ltd

PO Box 53101
Atlanta
GA 30355
(404) 872-1608
(800) 872-1608
Good variety of stone and plaster moldings, mantels, balustrading. Catalog available.

PAINTS AND STAINS

Laura Ashley, Inc.
6 St James Avenue
Boston MA 02116
(617) 457-6000
A line of soft colors coordinated with this designer's wide range of fabrics and wallpapers. The interior and exterior paints are available in the many Laura Ashley shops, or by mail order from the above address. Subscription to catalogs available.

Evergreen Painting Studios, Inc.
635 West 23rd Street
4th Floor
New York
NY 10011
(212) 727-9500
Jeffrey Greene and his studio are reputed to be the leading muralists in America today. They painted the trompe l'oeil monument to Cincinnatus in Cincinnati and a mural in the new Equitable Building in New York City. Faux finishes, gold leafing and every sort of decorative painting indoors and out undertaken on commission.

Gold Leaf Conservation Studios, Inc.
PO Box 50156
Washington
DC 20091
(202) 638-4660
One of the country's leading firms in the business of replacing or repairing gold leaf. The bulk of their work is for museums and public buildings, but private commissions are also undertaken. William Adair, the head of the firm, warns that gold-leafing is not a craft for the amateur, and that gold paint is not a satisfactory substitute on objects of value. Projects should be discussed directly with William Adair.

Martin Senour Company
1500 Midland
101 Prospect Avenue NW
Cleveland
OH 44115
(216) 566-2316
Colonial Williamsburg colors for exterior and interior use. Many distributors around the country.

Benjamin Moore & Co.
Chestnut Ridge Road
Montvale
NJ 07645
(201) 573-9600
Two brochures, "An Interior Historical Color Collection," and "An Exterior Historical Color Collection" are published by this paint company and available at their many outlets throughout the country. If none of these colors seems quite right, there are more than 1,000 others to choose from.

Janovic Plaza
(Main Office)
30/35 Thomson Avenue
Long Island City
NY 11101
(718) 392-3999
Everything for the would-be painter including a computerized paint-mixing system. They will match any sample of paint, wallpaper, fabric or whatever. They also carry a range of supplies for painting such as special brushes for stippling, dragging and marbling, as well as shellac, gold leaf etc.

The Old Fashioned Milk Paint Company
Box 222
Groton
MA 01450
(508) 448-6336

A furniture company which branched out to supply itself with the paint and wood it needed. The milk paint, sold in eight authentic colors, comes as a powder, measured and ready for mixing. Wide pine floorboards are also sold through the firm's own Craftsman Lumber Company. Paint and floorboard brochures are available.

Pratt & Lambert
75 Tonawanda
Buffalo
NY 14207
(716) 873-6000
This large and widely distributed paint company makes a special line of paints for restored houses which it developed for the Henry Ford Museum and Greenfield Village. The paints are available for both interior and exterior use in oil or latex finishes.

UK SUPPLIERS

The following companies are of special interest to house restorers in the USA. Many of these are able to supply and help ship to the American market and some also have their own US agents and outlets whose addresses will be given on request.

BATHROOM FIXTURES

A & H Brass
See DOORS AND WINDOWS

Architectural Components Ltd
See DOORS AND WINDOWS

Czech & Speake Ltd
39c Jermyn Street
London SW1Y 6DN
(071) 439-0216

also: 244 Cambridge Heath Road
London E2 9DA
(081) 980-4567
Manufacturers of bathroom fixtures. Edwardian range including sink mixers and accessories, in solid brass with porcelain fixtures, available in polished brass, lacquered brass, nickel and chrome. Complementary range of accessories. Catalog available.

Eleanor Greeves
12 Newton Grove
Bedford Park
London W4 1LB
(081) 994-6523
Design and hand-printing of ceramic wall tiles, specializing in repeating foliage patterns, supplied direct from workshop in any of ten alternative colors. Special designs and other colors can be produced to order. Catalogs available.

Peter Chapman Antiques Ltd
See GENERAL SUPPLIERS

CONSERVATORIES

Marston & Langinger Ltd
Showroom and design studio:
192 Ebury Street
London SW1W 8UP
(071) 824-8818
Suppliers of both standard designs and one-offs, including conservatories enclosing pools as well as conservatory furniture, ornamental garden urns, etc.

Amdega
Faverdale
Darlington
Co Durham DL3 OPW
Manufacturers and designers of period-style conservatories. Custom made.

DOORS AND WINDOWS

ADN Associates
Langham House
302-308 Regent Street
London W1 5AL
(071) 255-2043
Export agency for G & H Products Ltd. Manufacturers and suppliers of electrical fixtures in three ranges: Georgian, Regency and Victorian, all complemented by a full range of door and cabinet hardware.

A & H Brass Ltd.
201-203 Edgware Road
London W2 1ES
(071) 402-1854/3981
Suppliers of brass door and window fixtures, electrical accessories, chandeliers, lights and bathroom fixtures.

Architectural Components Ltd.
(Locks and Handles)
4-8 Exhibition Road
London SW7 2HF
(071) 581-2401 and 584-6800
From three showrooms near the South Kensington Museums and Underground station, they supply a large range of period features used in the renovation and furnishing of property. Over 6,000 different items in stock – door and cabinet fixtures, bathroom accessories, all types of locks, window fixtures, hinges, drape hardware, door closers, grills and vents, fireplace furniture.

Beardmore Architectural Ironmongery
3-5 Percy Street
London W1P 0EJ
(071) 637-7041
Ornamental period-style brassware, from electrical accessories to door furniture.

Comyn Ching Ltd.
296 Penistone Road
Sheffield S6 2FT
(0742) 852200

Showroom in London. Specialists in door furniture, locks, hinges, door closers, sliding door gear, wholesale and export. A large range of black antique ironmongery.

T. Crowther & Sons Ltd.
See GENERAL SUPPLIERS

Charles Harden
14 Chiltern Street
London W1
(071) 935-2032
Specialists in brass, glass and china door furniture, bathroom fixtures in brass, chrome and gold-plated finishes. The firm has been in existence for 58 years.

Cotswood Door Specialists Ltd
63A Park Road
Kingston-upon-Thames
Surrey KT2 6DE
(081) 546-3621
Suppliers of high-quality hardwood joinery, with an emphasis on doors and entrances, with associated moldings, architraves, baseboards etc.

Hartley Wood & Co. Ltd.
Portobello Lane
Monkwearmouth
Sunderland
Wearside SR6 0DN
(091) 567-2506
UK manufacturers of stained glass both hand-blown antique and rolled glass. Products sold in the USA and Canada through the following distributors: Hollander Glass in Los Angeles, New York, Toronto and Chicago; S.A. Bendheim Co., Inc. in New York; Architectural Emphasis Inc. in Oakland, Houston and New York.

Knobs & Knockers
Unit 2
Glory Farm House
Murdoch Road
Oxon OX6 7BP
(0869) 321771

Leading retailers of architectural ironmongery with over 50 branches throughout the UK, also providing a full scheduling and estimating service.

Peco of Hampton
72 Station Road
Hampton
Middlesex
(081) 979-8310
Original period doors, over 2,000 in stock in all types, including stained glass and sandblasted glass front doors. They also repair stained and sandblasted glass.

Peter Chapman Antiques Ltd.
See GENERAL SUPPLIERS

Posterity Architectural Effects
Baldwins Farm
Dymock Road
Newent
Gloucestershire
Stockists of architectural salvage items, doors, windows, staircases, fireplaces and more.

Stuart Interiors
See GENERAL SUPPLIERS

Tomkinson Stained Glass
87 Portobello Road
London W11 2QB
(071) 267-1669
Specialists in the restoration of stained-glass windows and manufacturers of stained-glass windows and Georgian leaded lights. Stockists of antique windows and doors and architectural items. Catalog available on request.

A Touch of Brass Ltd.
210 Fulham Road
London SW10 9PJ
(071) 351-2255
Suppliers of quality brass goods, including fixtures on doors, walls and furniture, with many different ranges to suit every period of architecture from the 16thC. Over 2,000 items in stock.

Verdigris Art Metalwork Restorers
Arch 290
Crown Street
London SE5 0UR
Repairs, fine patinas, French gilding, metal coloring and lacquering expertly carried out.

Whiteway & Waldron Ltd.
305 Munster Road
London SW6 1BT
(071) 381-3195
Stained-glass and architectural fixtures, including doors and fireplace surrounds.

Winther Browne & Co., Ltd.
Nobel Road
Eley Estate
Edmonton
London N18 3DX
(081) 803-3434
Suppliers and manufacturers of period home products including authentic-styled beams, available in dark oak, light oak, gray or unstained finishes. Doors, staircases, windows and moldings also available.

FABRICS AND WALLPAPERS

Bentley & Spens
Studio 25
90 Lots Road
London SW10 0QD
(071) 352-5685
Specialists in batik and hand-painted fabrics for fashion and interiors with a good choice of silks and cotton. A wide range of designs or artwork can be commissioned to individual requirements and advice given on suitable fabrics. Customers are able to visit the studio, by appointment.

Christian Fischbacher (London) Ltd.
Springbell Terrace
London W14 0AE
(071) 602-7250

Suppliers of the fine cottons and voiles of Switzerland and famous for their printed cotton furnishing fabrics produced in Britain and USA. In Switzerland there are 16 designers and colorists at work, while the British collections are designed by invited designers. Catalog available.

Colefax & Fowler
39 Brook Street
London W1Y 2JE
(071) 493-2231
The two showrooms in Belgravia and Mayfair offer a range of typical English chintzes and wallpapers. Several designs still produced by hand block printing. Catalog available.

Elizabeth Eaton
30 Elizabeth Street
London SW1W 9RB
(071) 589-0118/9
The company offers a full decorator service of advice on interior use of period houses, services of a qualified architect renowned for work on period property, joinery and cabinet making to drawings, advice on painting and decorating, preferably executed by their own team of workmen under their supervision. They are also the sole UK agents for the following US companies specializing in period wallpapers and fabrics: Schumacher, The Williamsburg Collection; Clarence House, French Collection; Waterhouse, Boston; Katzenbach & Warren. Catalog available.

Hamilton West Wallpapers
18 St Marys Grove
Richmond
Surrey
TW9 1UY
(081) 940-4850

Specialists in documentary reproductions of 18th to early 19thC wallpapers. Designs are taken from recently discovered fragments found in London houses. Printing to order in special colors.

Lyn Le Grice Stencil Design Ltd.
The Stencilled House
58 Chapel Street
Penzance
Cornwall TR18 4AF
(0736) 64193
Stenciling and designing fabrics and wallpapers.

Mary Fox Linton Ltd.
Hewlett House
Unit 45
Havelock Terrace
London SW8 4AS
(071) 627-4844
Wallpaper and floorcovering suppliers.

John S. Oliver Ltd.
33 Pembridge Road
London W11 3HG
(071) 727-3735
Wallpapers reproduced from a pattern of the client's own sample or design in colors of their choice. Pattern books available.

The Original Choice
56 The Tything
Worcester WR1 1JT
also: Castle Farm
Gaydon
Warwickshire CV35 0HE
Specialists in expertly restored antique fireplaces. 100 fireplaces on display, mostly originals in marble, pine,

mahogany, oak and cast-iron. Complete design and installation service, mantelpieces made to measure, stained glass sold, restored and made. Mirrors, doors, overmantels, lamps, tiles, fenders, firestools and more.

H. A. Percheron Ltd.
99 Cleveland Street
London W1P 5PN
(071) 580-1192/5156
Exclusive furnishing fabrics and trimmings. A fine range of traditional damasks, brocades, velours and plain fabrics available; fabrics can be made to order for special requirements. Trimmings of all kinds from a comprehensive stock collection and made to order in any coloring.

Stuart Interiors
See GENERAL SUPPLIERS

Watts & Co., Ltd.
7 Tufton Street
London SW1P 3QE
(071)222 7169/2893/1978
A collection of genuine Victorian wallcoverings and damasks. The papers, to be seen in the Houses of Parliament and the National Portrait Gallery, can be hand-blocked or screen printed and all orders are colored as individually desired. Catalog available.

Zoffany Ltd.
63 South Audley Street
London W1Y 5BF
(071) 629-9262
Manufacturers of document wallpapers, including the hand-printed Temple Newsam Collection. Reproductions of original papers can be hand-printed to commission order on inquiry. "The Red Book of Paperhangings" and "The Temple Newsam Collection" available in the USA through Schumacher.

FIREPLACES AND STOVES

Acquisitions (Fireplaces) Ltd.
4-6 Jamestown Road
London NW1 7BY
(071) 485-4955
Reproduction fireplaces using traditional materials. Wood and cast-iron mantels, cast-iron inserts, some incorporating hand-painted tiles from a wide range of designs.

Antique Fireplace Warehouse
194-196 Battersea Park Road
London SW11 4ND
(071) 627-1410
Specialists in cast-iron fireplaces, pine surrounds and marble chimneypieces. Restoration and installation service.

T. F. Buckle (London) Ltd.
427 Kings Road
London SW10 0LR
(071) 352-0952
Specialists in antique mantelpieces in pine, marble and stone; reproduction mantelpieces in old and new pine; reproduction Victorian spiral staircases in cast-iron. Reproduction grates. World-wide shipping arranged.

James Gray & Son Ltd.
89 George Street
Edinburgh EH2 3EZ
(031) 225-7381
Specialists in the design and supply of period fireplaces, Georgian, Regency and Victorian reproduction and original fireplace mantelpieces, cast-iron Victorian fireplace interiors with hand-painted ceramic tile inserts, reproductions and originals.

Hallidays
The Old College
High Street
Dorchester-on-Thames
Oxfordshire OX10 7HL
(0865) 340068
Specialists in Georgian paneling and fireplaces, particularly carved pine mantelpieces. Catalog available.

House of Steel Antiques
400 Caledonian Road
London N1 1DN
(071) 607-5889
Stockists of antique architectural and ornamental metalwork, 300-400 Victorian and Edwardian cast-iron fireplaces, original garden furniture, urns and statuary, spiral staircases, railings, balconies and gates. Restoration and polishing of metalware and fireplaces. Sand-blasting. Castings in iron, brass and aluminum.

Petit Roque Ltd.
5a New Road
Croxley Green
Herts WD3 3EJ
(0923) 779291/720968
Designers and instalers of individual fireplaces. Also producing period Adam-style fireplaces, countertops, marble flooring, marble wall tiles, gas, log/coal fires and all fireplace accessories.

M. A. Pope (Fireplaces)Ltd.
14 Western Parade
Barnet
Hertfordshire
Manufacturers of marble fireplaces.

H. W. Poulter & Son
279 Fulham Road
London SW10 9PZ
(071) 352-7268
Specialists in English and French antique marble chimneypieces, grates, fenders, fire irons, etc.

Stuart Interiors
See GENERAL SUPPLIERS

Townsends (Hallmore Trading Ltd)
81 Abbey Road
London NW8 0AE
Specialists in the supply, salvage, restoration and instalation of antique fireplaces. Suppliers of gas/coal effect fires to fit any fire basket. Over 100 antique fireplaces in stock. Marble and slate hearths made to order. Design service available.

Walcot Reclamation
108 Walcot Street
Bath
Avon BA1 5BG
(0225) 444404
Architectural antiques with a wide range of fireplaces and accessories from all periods, also stained glass, paneled doors, flooring, roofing, beams, architectural joinery and bathrooms stocked.

Mr Wandle's Workshop
200-202 Garratt Lane
Wandsworth
London SW18 4ED
(081) 870-5873
Suppliers and restorers of authentic Victorian cast-iron fireplaces, grates and other accessories. Also stocks Victorian kitchen ranges and stoves.

Whiteway & Waldron Ltd.
See DOORS AND WINDOWS

Wing & Staples
The Forge
Motcombe
Nr Shaftesbury
Dorset SP7 9PE
(0747) 53104
Period pieces reproduced from drawings or from photographs. Restoration, traditional or contemporary ironwork undertaken. A choice of finishes available, antique appearance, armor bright, matte or glass paints. Contracts with the Department of the Environment Historic Monuments, and the National Trust. Brochure available.

FLOORS

Capital Tile Supplies
PO Box 80
Eagle House
Eagle Street
Coventry CV1 2RJ
(0203) 633336
Suppliers of a wide range of wall and floor tiles, including specialized service for designers, architects and specifiers. Catalog available.

Castelnau Tiles
175 Church Road
Barnes
London SW13 9HR
(081) 741-4159
Suppliers of marble, terra cotta and Mexican floor tiles. Wide choice of Italian and French tiles for walls and floors.

Ceramic Consultants Ltd.
The Old Brewery
Wish Ward
Rye
Sussex TN31 7DH
(0797) 223038
Hand-decorated wall and floor tiles made to order. Export orders welcome. Contract and hotel work as well as for decorators and private customers.

Criterion Tiles Ltd.
196 Wandsworth Bridge Road
London SW6 2UF
(071) 736-9610
and:
2A England's Lane
Hampstead
London NW3 4TG
(071) 482-2608
A range of English and Continental ceramic tiles with a variety of effects, including hand-applied transfer and stenciling, relief molding and in-glaze hand-painting, screen-printing in special colors for floors, fine terra cotta, slate and large quarries, both glazed and unglazed. Creative advice given. Catalog available.

Domus Tiles Ltd.
33 Parkgate Road
London SW11 4NP
(071) 223-5555
Suppliers of glazed and unglazed floor and wall ceramic tiles, plain and patterned, refined porcelain stoneware

frostproof heavy-duty tiles, including relief finishes, polished finishes, anti-slips, step treads and baseboards, natural rustic terra cotta tiles, patterned resin-bonded marble tiles.

Fired Earth
102 Portland Road
London W11 4LX
(071) 221-4825
Designers and manufacturers of ceramic tiles, made and fired by craftsmen using centuries-old methods and techniques. Over 35 different types of terra cotta tiles in stock. Suitable for kitchens, dining rooms, halls conservatories, patios, etc. Also reproduction early English delft tiles and other glazed tiles. Catalog available.

Paris Ceramics
583 Kings Road
Chelsea
London SW6 2EH
(071) 371-7778
Specialists in ranges of floor and wall tiles, including old French tiles retrieved from period houses and restored; hand-crafted delft tiles made to traditional 17thC designs, and others. Viewing by appointment only.

H. & E. Smith Ltd.
Britannic Works
Broom Street
Hanley
Stoke-on-Trent
Staffs ST1 2ER
(0782) 281617
Restore and instal Victorian and Edwardian tiles and Art Nouveau tiles, for walls and floors, internal and external fixing. Also hand-painted and embossed Victorian tiles for fireplaces. Catalog available.

Stone Age
40 St John's Hill Grove
Battersea
London SW11 2RG
(071) 738-2554
Real stone floor tiles. Perfect for conservatories, halls, kitchens and bathrooms.

GENERAL SUPPLIERS

Bailey's Architectural Antiques

The Engine Shed
Ashburton Industrial Estate
Ross-on-Wye
Herefordshire HE9 7BW

Large stock of traditional fixtures and fittings, including their own range of recycled lead planters and fountains, brass and aluminum brackets and blacksmith-made door knockers.

Charles Hammond Design Services Ltd.

Pepys Court
84/86 The Chase
London SW4 ONG
(071) 627-5000

Interior decorators and designers supplying interior furnishings, cornices and ceiling medallions.

Chilstone Garden Ornaments

Sprivers Estate
Horsmonden
Kent TN12 8DR
(0892) 723553

Specialists in reproducing antique ornaments and architectural items including Doric and Ionic columns, architraves, cornicing, balustrades, mullions, temples, and a range of over 250 classical garden ornaments.

Conservation Building Products Ltd.

Forge Works
Forge Lane
Cradley Heath
Warley
West Midlands B64 5AL
(0384) 64219

Stockists of a large selection of period roofing tiles, fixtures, finials, bricks, oak beams, joists, quarry floor tiles, paving, pine doors, paneling and architectural ironwork.

T. Crowther & Son Ltd.

282 North End Road
London
SW6 1NH
(071) 385-1375/6/7

A world-renowned, family-run antique business, established over one hundred years ago, which operates from a very large late Georgian period building. It specializes in, among other things, Georgian architectural features, such as oak and pinewood paneling, carved wood and marble chimneypieces and metalware accoutrements, i.e. grates, fenders and fire-irons. The stocks of antique garden ornaments and statuary are probably the largest in the UK, and include sundials, fountains, classical statues and animals figures, temples, urns and vases, seats and benches, wrought-iron gates, columns and doorways. Inside the large galleries are 18thC English wall lights and chandeliers, and interior doorways. For room paneling, a complete service is offered from design advice and drawings through manufacture and adaption, to fixing on site, if required.

Crowther of Syon Lodge Ltd.

Busch Corner
London Road
Isleworth
Middlesex TW7 5BH
(071) 560-7978

Britain's largest and best-established firm of architectural antiques and period garden ornament dealers, buying and selling period paneled rooms, antique chimney pieces, wrought-iron entrance gates, classical statuary and a wide range of period garden ornaments, including temples, vases, seats and fountains. Extensive business with overseas clients. Catalog available.

Eaton-Gaze Ltd.

86 Teesdale Street
London E2 6PU
(071) 739-7272

Ornate plasterwork including cornices, ceiling centers, friezes, panel molding, dados, columns, pilasters, niches, trusses, arches and moldings, mantelpieces, plaster, wood and fiberglass fireplaces, brass fireplace accessories, marble trims, fire-backs and canopies.

Gillespie UK Ltd.

Alma House
38 Crimea Road
Aldershot GU11 1UD
(0252) 23311

Specialists in suspended and decorative ceilings, screens and space-dividers, sculptures, murals, crests and emblems, domes, Islamic decoration, architectural features and textured cladding. Catalog available.

Haddonstone Ltd.

The Forge House
East Haddon
Northampton NN6 8DB
(0604) 770711

Design and supply reconstructed stoneware for garden, interior and architectural decoration, including balustrades, temples and pavilions, porticos, columns and pilasters, pier caps and finials as well as an extensive range of garden urns and ornaments. Services include contract work, interiors, restoration and special commissions. Catalog available.

The London Architectural Salvage & Supply Co.

St Michael's Church
Mark Street
London EC2A 4ER
(071) 739-0448

A vast range of architectural details, including ornamental features and stained glass, as well as doors, fireplace surrounds and grates, statuary and stone garden seats. Catalog available.

Pageant Antiques

122 Dawes Road
London SW6
(071) 385-7739

Dealers in 18th and 19thC garden furniture and ornament as well as fine chimneypieces, in marble and wood. Catalog available..

Peter Chapman Antiques Ltd.

10 Theberton Street
133 Upper Street
London N1 (071) 226-5565

Specialists in architectural antiques such as fireplace surrounds in wood, cast iron and marble, cast-iron tiled fire inserts, fireplace accessories, tiles, doors in pine, oak and mahogany, with stained-glass or cut and etched panels, leaded lights, railings, gates, wrought-iron work, statuary, bathroom fixtures and plasterwork. Restoration and repair service available.

Renaissance

262 Hansworth Road
Hansworth
Sheffield S13 9BS
(0742) 446622

Manufacturers of period entranceways, interior and exterior moldings including fascias, door frames, pilasters, porticos, bow window units and columns.

Stuart Interiors

Barrington Court
Barrington
Ilminster
Somerset TA19 0NQ
(0460) 40349

One of the UK's leading specialist designers with particular expertise in recreating 16th and 17thC English decor. A complete design and furnishing service including paneling, doors, staircases, stonework, furniture and a vast range of accessories is available. An exclusive range of "early" fabrics has been launched in conjunction with Tissunique. Stuart Interiors, with its comprehensive range of furnishing accessories — from rare and expensive antiques to copies of early painted and hand-made pottery on display – aims to create a national center for all aspects of early English interior design in both a commercial and an academic context. They also sponsor regular lectures and exhibitions relating to the social history, domestic life, architecture and house interiors of the period. Color brochure available.

Walcot Reclamation

108 Walcot Street
Bath
Avon BA1 5BG

Architectural antiques with a wide range of fireplaces and accessories from all periods; also stained glass, paneled doors, flooring, roofing, beams, architectural joinery and bathrooms in stock.

Winther Browne &Co Ltd

Eley's Industrial Estate
Nobel Road
Edmonton
London N18 3DX

Suppliers and manufacturers of period home products including authentic styled barns, available in dark oak, light oak, gray or sustained finish. Doors, staircases, windows and moldings also available. Catalog available.

KITCHENS

Alno (UK) Ltd.
Unit 10, Hampton Farm Industrial Estate
Hampton Road West
Hanworth
Middlesex TW13 6DB
(081) 898-4781
Manufacturers of built-in kitchens, including traditional rustic, period and classical styles in red-brown oak with solid oak fronts, natural oak, light oak and brown oak; also in gray-white pigmented effect with pewter knobs.

Chalon Originals
Chalon UK Ltd.
Hambridge
Somerset TA10 0BP
(0458) 252374
Handmade kitchens in traditional and period styles of 18th and 19thC. Antique pine hand-painted to create the effects of ageing, painted in any twelve period colors.

John Mead Country Kitchens
Roadside Farm
Pewsey, Wilts SM9 5NB
(0672) 62365
Manufacturers of solid wood kitchens in sawn English oak, old pine, ash, cherry or lacquered hardwood. Also individual items such as charcoal grills, wooden cornices and bookshelves. Catalog available.

Sutton Kitchens
30 Beacon Grove
High Street
Carshalton
Surrey SM5 3BA
(081) 669-5281

Family business who design and refurbish kitchens in period houses dating back to the 16thC. Doors are hand-crafted in 200- or 400-year old reclaimed oak or reclaimed pine.

Woodstock Furniture Ltd.
23 Pakenham Street
London WC1X 0LB
(071) 837-1818/3220
Design custom-built kitchens in solid hardwood, e.g. maple and cherry. Catalog available.

LIGHTING

A & H Brass
See DOORS AND WINDOWS

Christopher Wray's Lighting Emporium
600 Kings Road
London SW6 2DX
(071) 736-8434
Lighting specialists. Catalog available.

Mrs M. E. Crick Ltd.
166 Kensington Church Street
London W8 4BN
(071) 229-1338
Specialists in 18th-20thC lighting.

T. Crowther & Son Ltd.
See GENERAL SUPPLIERS

Delomosne & Son Ltd.
Court Close North
Wraxall, Chippenham
Wilts SN14 7AD
(0225) 891505

Antique dealers specializing in a wide range of 18th and 19thC English glass chandeliers and candelabra.

Hooper & Purchase
303 Kings Road
London SW3 5EP
(071) 351-3985
Selling 18th and early 19thC English and Continental antique chandeliers and wall lights.

John Cullen Lighting
216 Fulham Palace Road
London W6 9NT
(071) 381-8944

Jones Antique Lighting
194 Westbourne Grove
London W11
(071) 229-6866
The largest selection of individual original lighting in Europe c. 1860-1960.

M. W. United Ltd.
3 Willow Business Park
Willow Way
London SE26 4QP
(081) 699-9003
Specialists in a wide range of traditional chandeliers.

Planet Shades Ltd.
PO Box 118
Lampard Grove
London N16 6XB
(081) 806-1013
Manufacturers of silk and fabric lampshades, hand-polished and antique brass, chandeliers and wall brackets, glass shades and single pendants.

W. Sitch & Co. , Ltd.
48 Berwick Street
London W1 4JD
(071) 437-3776
Dealers in 19thC chandeliers, wall brackets, floor standards and other lighting fixtures.

METALWORK AND FENCING

Britannia Architectural Metalwork & Restoration
5 Normandy Street
Alton
Hampshire GU34 1DD
(0420) 84427
Stockists of standard traditional railings, balusters, brackets, gratings, etc., including Victorian and Georgian patterns. Restoration and repair work, pattern making and design services. Will deliver abroad. Catalog available.

Clark Hunt Albion Ltd.
318-326 Southbury Road
Enfield
Middlesex EN1 1TT
(081) 804-5324
Manufacturers of cast-iron spiral and straight staircases. Catalog available.

House of Steel Antiques
See FIREPLACES AND STOVES

Safety Stairways Ltd.
Unit 45, Owen Road Industrial Estate Willenhall
West Midlands WV13 2PX
(0251) 263133
Cast-iron reproduction staircases, including Tudor, Georgian, Regency and Victorian styles.

Southwell Stockwell Ltd.
26A Rye Lane
London SE15 3AX
(071) 635-0950
Street railings, balustrades, balconies etc.

Spiral Staircase System

The Mill, Glynde
Sussex BN7 8SS
(0273) 858341
Manufacturers of spiral staircases. Design service available.

Stuart Interiors

See GENERAL SUPPLIERS

Wandsdown Joinery Works Ltd.

327 Lillie Road
Fulham
London SW6 7NR
Specialists in period staircases, paneled rooms in old pine, lined oak, mahogany and all types of special joinery. Catalog available.

Weller Patents Development

1/8 Grand Parade Mews
Rear of 926-110 Upper Richmond Road
London SW15 2SP
(081) 788-6684
Specialist fabricators of internal and external architectural metalwork, including balustrading, gates, balconies and staircases, to client's requirements – either original designs or copies of existing designs, highlighting/matching period details.

PAINTS, STAINS AND STENCILS

Andrew Bradley

1 St Saviour's Terrace
Larkhall, Bath
Avon BA1 6RL
(0225) 317025
Decorative finishes, marbling, stippling, rag-rolling, dragging, design and cutting of stencils for specific interior finishes. Designs and paints murals to individual requirements.

Davies Keeling Trowbridge Ltd.

3 Charterhouse Works
Eltringham Street
Petergate
London SW18 1TD
(081) 874-3565
Specialist decoration including marbling, stippling, graining, stone blocking, plaster effects, trompe l'oeil, murals and stenciling.

Eleanor Allit

Thickthorn Cottage
108 Leamington Road
Kenilworth
Warwickshire
CV8 2AA
(0926) 52395
Stencil designers offering a range of standard designs to choose from or alternatively specially designed to customer's individual requirements. A variety of textural grounds are provided, such as sponging and color-washing. Stenciling can be used on almost any surface: walls, ceilings, floors, furniture etc. Catalog available.

T. J. Plant

7 Bramham Gardens
London SW5
(071) 370-2945
Mural painter working in private homes and gardens, and commercial premises. Commissions undertaken.

PANELING

David Ackroyd Ltd

Henley Farm
Henley Common
Church Stretton
Shropshire SY6 6RS
Repairs and replacements of existing woodwork. Also turning, inlaying, carving and a range of paint finishes.

Eaton-Gaze Ltd.

See GENERAL SUPPLIERS

The Architectural Heritage of Cheltenham

Architectural Heritage Ltd.
Taddington Manor
Taddington, Near Cutsdean
Cheltenham
Gloucester GL54 5RY
(0386) 73414
Manufacturers and suppliers of period paneling, marble, wood and stone fireplaces, antique and garden statuary.

Wansdown Joinery Works (Southern) Ltd.

327 & 339 Lillie Road
London SW6 7NR
(071) 385-0351
Specialists in period staircases, paneled rooms in old pine, limed oak, mahogany and all types of period carpentry.

USEFUL UK ADDRESSES

The following organizations will be of particular interest to those who want to gain a deeper understanding of period styles.

Acanthus Associated Architectural Practices Ltd.

Voysey House
Barley Mow Passage
London W4 4PN
(081) 995-1232
Specialist knowledge in the following disciplines: specialist consultancy on listed buildings and conservation areas; historic building surveys and analysis; feasibility studies on uses for old buildings; garden and landscape design.

Art Workers Guild

6 Queen Square
London
WC1N 3AR
(071) 837-3474
Guild of artists, architects, craftsmen.

C. B. Brooking

Woodhay
White Lane
Guildford
Surrey GU4 8PU
(0483) 504555
The Brooking Collection preserves an astonishing range of architectural elements rescued from demolition. It comprises up to 20,000 building components and provides a unique record of the development of architectural details, with particular reference to features such as windows, doors, fireplaces, decorative ironwork, etc. Information service available.

Building Conservation Trust

Apartment 39
Hampton Court Palace
East Molesey
Surrey KT8 9BS
(081) 943-2277
An independent educational charity established to promote the better care of buildings of all types and ages.

The Guild of Master Craftsmen

166 High Street
Lewes
East Sussex BN7 1XU
(0273) 477374
A trade association who will help to put you in touch with experienced craftsmen able to carry out restoration work. The Guild also publishes a "Guide to Restoration Experts."

Royal Institute of British Architects (RIBA)

66 Portland Place
London
W1N 4AD
(071) 580-5533
Leading national architectural body.

The Victorian Society

1 Priory Gardens
Bedford Park
London W4 1TT
The national amenity society responsible for preserving Victorian architecture.

Acknowledgments

Martin Miller, Geoff Dann, John Helfrick and Caroline Brown were specially commissioned to take photographs for this book. Thanks are also due to the *The World of Interiors* for Clive Frost's photograph on page 69, no. 9, and to David C. Golby for the photographs on page 73, nos. 10 and 11.

The following people allowed photography in specific houses in Britain or gave generously of their time or expertise: Jacqui and Colin Small, Alan and Smokey Parsons, Jeremy and Annie Parker, Christopher and Frances Everill, Ian and Jill Pooley, Doug and Pam Stewart, Paul and Angie Marsh, Gaby Tubbs, Liz and John Denning.

The kindness of the people who gave their time and expertise to help complete the American material in this book cannot be overstated. Constraints of time made it impossible to include more than a tiny fraction of the historic riches available in the United States, but the people listed below opened the authors' eyes to the incredible variety and quality of period details in the New York area alone. The lesson they taught us all was to look closely at what is available within a very confined area. All over the country, there are examples of grand and vernacular architecture, either restored or waiting discovery by someone who can recognize their true worth.

Among those who have shared their wisdom with us are: Jane Sullivan Crowley at the Metropolitan Historic Structures Association, whose kindness opened so many doors for us; Caroline Brown, whose knowledge of historic architecture is exceeded only by her photographic skill and who allowed us access to the resources of the National Society of Colonial Dames in the State of New York; John Helfrick, whose interest went far beyond the normal duties of a photographer as he introduced us to the Roslyn Landmark Society on Long Island; Dr and Mrs Roger Gerry, the leading lights at Roslyn, who spent so many hours helping us to understand the fine points of the houses they have helped to save; and Dr Stanley Fischer, who opened his lovely house to us.

In the houses associated with MHSA, we are grateful for the help of the following people:
Joe and Carolyn Roberto at the Old Merchant's House, to which they have devoted their lives and energies for a decade; Mrs Jean Bartlett of the International Garden Club, who arranged access to the Bartow-Pell House; Patrick Broome at the Morris-Jumel House; and Audrey Braver at the Bowne House.

We have been fortunate indeed to work with all of these people.

For individual photographs and access to interiors we are also grateful to the sources named in the credits list below. The code letters are those used in picture captions throughout the book.

A Amdega, Faverdale, Darlington, County Durham.

AB A. Bell, Kingsthorpe Road, Kingsthorpe, Northampton.

AF Acquisitions (Fireplaces) Ltd, 269 Camden High Street, London NW1.

AH Architectural Heritage, Boddington Manor, Boddington, Nr Cheltenham, Gloucestershire.

AR Aga-Rayburn (Coalbrookdale) Glynwed Consumer & Building Products Ltd, PO Box 30, Ketley, Telford, Shropshire TF1 1BR

AS Armitage Shanks, Armitage, Rugeley, Staffordshire.

AS&S Architectural Salvage and Supply Co., St Michael's Church, Mark St off Paul St, London EC2

B Bisque, The Radiator Shop, 244 Belsize Rd, London NW6.

Be Beardmore Ltd, 3-5 Percy St, London W1P 0EJ.

BCS B.C. Sanitan, 12 Nimrod Way, Reading, Berks.

BH Bowne House, 37-01 Bowne Street, Flushing, New York, NY 11354.

BP Bartow Pell Mansion, Shore Road, Pelham Bay Park, Bronx, NY 10464.

Br Brass Art Craft (Brassart) 76 Atwood St, Lye, Stourbridge, West Midlands.

C Crown Decorative Products Ltd, PO Box 22, Queen's Mill, Hollins Rd, Darwen, Lancashire BB3 0BD.

CB Christopher Boulter, 43 Goodrich Rd, London SE22.

CF Classic Furniture Group, Audley Avenue, Newport, Shropshire.

C&F Colefax and Fowler, 39 Brook St, London W1.

CG County Group, 102 High St, Tenterden, Kent CN30 6HU.

CP Chilston Park, Sandway, Nr Maidstone, Kent.

CPH C.P. Hart, Newham Terrace, Hercules Road, London SE1.

CS Czech and Speake, 39c Jermyn Street, London SW1.

C of SL Crowther of Syon Lodge, London Road, Isleworth, Middlesex.

EDL End of Day Lighting, 44 Parkway, London NW1.

EW Erme Wood Forge, Woodlands, Ivybridge, Devon PL21 9HF.

FE Fired Earth Country Floors, Middle Aston, Oxfordshire.

G&G Goddard & Gibbs Studios, 41-49 Kingsland Road, London E2.

GH The Georgian House, 7 Great George Street, Bristol, Avon.

GJ G. Jackson & Sons Ltd, Rathbone Works, Rainville Road, London W6.

H Hallidays, 28 Beauchamp Place, Knightsbridge, London SW3.

Ha Hathaway Country Kitchens, Clifford Mill, Clifford Chambers, Stratford-upon-Avon.

HH Headquarters House, 215 East 71st Street, NYC 10021

H&H Herschel House, 19 New King's Street, Bath.

HJ Hodkin & Jones (Sheffield) Ltd, 515 Queen's Road, Sheffield S2 4DS.

HPS Hand Painted Stencils, 6 Polstead Rd, Oxford OX2 6TW.

HW Hamilton-Weston Wallpapers, 11 Townsend Rd, Richmond, Surrey TW9 1YH.

H&S Hunter & Son (Mells) Ltd, Frome, Somerset BA11 3PA.

JBF The James Buchanan Foundation for the Preservation of Wheatland, 1120 Marietta Ave, Lancaster, Pennsylvania 17603.

JL John Lewis of Hungerford, 13 High Street, Hungerford, Berkshire.

JO John S. Oliver Ltd, 33 Pembridge Rd, London W11 3HG.

LAS London Architectural Salvage and Supply Co. Ltd, Mark Street, London EC2 4ER.

LG Lyn Le Grice, Alsia Mill Street, Buryon, Cornwall TR19 6HG.

LH Leighton House, 12 Holland Park Road, London W14.

LSH Linley Sambourne House, 18 Stafford Terrace, London W8.

MA Marthe Armitage, 1 Strand-on-the-Green, Chiswick, London W4 3PQ.

M Moben Kitchens Ltd, 100 Washway Road, Sale, Cheshire M33 1RE.

MH Marble Hill Fireplaces Ltd, 72 Richmond Road, Twickenham, Middlesex.

MJ Morris Jumel Mansion, West 160th and Edgecombe Avenue, New York, NY 10032.

ML Marston and Langinger, Hall Staithe, Fakenham, Norfolk.

MR Maria Rosenthal, Kingsgate Workshops, 110-116 Kingsgate Road, London NW6 2J6.

OB Original Bathrooms, 143-145 Kew Road, Richmond, Surrey TW9 2PN.

O&L Osborne & Little, 304 King's Road, London SW3.

OMH Old Merchants House, 29 East 4th Street, New York, NY 10003.

PC Paris Ceramics, 543 Battersea Park Road, London SW11.

PCA Peter Chapman Antiques, 10 Theberton Street, Islington, London, N1.

PF Patrick Fireplaces, Guildford Road, Farnham, Surrey GU9 9QA.

PH Phillip Henderson Co., 27 John Adam Street, London WC2.

PV Pine Village, 42-43 Peascod Street, Windsor, Berks.

RC No. 1 Royal Crescent, Bath, Avon.

S Smallbone of Devizes, Unit 10-11, Nimrod Way, Elgar Road, Reading, Berks.

SG Sekon Glassworks Ltd, Essian Street, London E1 4QE.

SI Stuart Interiors, Barrington Court, Barrington, Nr Ilminster, Somerset TA19 0NQ.

S of D Shaws of Darwen, Waterside, Darwen, Lancashire BB3 3NX.

S&P Strutt & Parker 13 Hill St, London SW1.

SP S. Polliack, Norton Industrial Estate, Norton, Malton, North Yorkshire YO17 9HQ.

SR Sylvia Robinson, Clarence House, Winchester Hill, Romsey, Hampshire SO51 7NJ.

ST Studio Two, 3d Town Street, Thaxted, Essex CM6 2LD.

S&W Smith & Wellstood Esse (1984) Ltd, Bonnybridge, Stirlingshire FK4 2AP.

SWH Sands Willet House, The Cow Neck Peninsula Historical Society, 336 Port Washington Boulevard, Port Washington, New York, NY 11050.

T Tissunique, 10 Princes St, Hanover Sq, London W1.

TB Traditional Bathrooms, 105 Regents Park Road, London NW1 8UR.

TP Tim Plant, 7 Bramham Gardens, London SW5.

TC Toynbee-Clarke Interiors Ltd., 95 Mount Street, London W1.

V Verdigris, Clerkenwell, Unit B.18, 31 Clerkenwell Close, London EC1.

VB Victoriana Bathrooms Ltd, 439 Leethorpe Road, Grimsby DN31 3BU.

VC Van Cortlandt Mansion, W.242nd Street and Broadway, Bronx, NY 10471.

VNS Van Nostrand Strakins House, 221 Main Street, Roslyn, New York.

W Woodstock Furniture, Pakenham Street, Mount Pleasant, London WC1.

Wa Watts & Co, 7 Tufton Street, Westminster, London SW1.

WA W. Adams & Sons Ltd, Westfield Works, Spon Lane, West Bromwich, West Midlands B70 6RH.

WB Winther Brown & Co. Ltd, Nobel Road, Eley's Estate, Edmonton, London N18 3DX.

WW Warren Wilkey, 741 Main St, Roslyn, New York.

W&W Whiteway & Waldron Ltd, 305 Munster Road, London SW6.

Z Zoffany Ltd, 27a Motcomb St, London SW1.